Content Distribution for Mobile Internet:
A Cloud-based Approach

Zhenhua Li · Yafei Dai · Guihai Chen
Yunhao Liu

Content Distribution
for Mobile Internet:
A Cloud-based Approach

 Springer

Zhenhua Li
Tsinghua University
Beijing
China

Guihai Chen
Shanghai Jiao Tong University
Shanghai
China

Yafei Dai
Peking University
Beijing
China

Yunhao Liu
Tsinghua University
Beijing
China

ISBN 978-981-10-9360-9   ISBN 978-981-10-1463-5   (eBook)
DOI 10.1007/978-981-10-1463-5

Printed on acid-free paper

This Springer imprint is published by Springer Nature
The registered company is Springer Science+Business Media Singapore Pte Ltd.

Preface

Content distribution (also known as *content delivery*) is the most fundamental function of the Internet, i.e., distributing *digital content* from one *node* to another node or multiple nodes. Here digital content includes webpage, image, software, audio, video, and so on; a node can be a large server cluster, a personal computer, a smartphone, a tiny sensor, *etc.* Typical content distribution systems include Akamai, BitTorrent, eMule, Skype, Xunlei, QQXuanfeng, and so forth. Since Amazon's launch of Elastic Compute Cloud (EC2) in 2006 and Apple's release of iPhone in 2007, Internet content distribution has illustrated a strong trend of *polarization.* On one hand, great fortune has been invested in building heavyweight and integrated data centers, in order to achieve the economies of scale and the cost efficiency for content distribution. On the other hand, end user devices have been growing more lightweight, mobile, and heterogeneous, thus posing rigorous requirements on the traffic usage, energy consumption, speed, and latency of content distribution.

Through comprehensive real-world measurements, we observe that existing content distribution techniques often exhibit poor performance under the settings of cloud computing and mobile Internet. To address the issue, this book investigates content distribution for mobile Internet with a cloud-based approach, by designing novel traffic-saving, energy-efficient, high-speed, and delay-tolerant content distribution techniques and frameworks that automatically adapt to mobile scenarios.

The major content of this book is organized in six parts, which are further elaborated into ten chapters. Specifically, we start with the background and overview in Part I. Then, since cellular traffic is the most expensive among all Internet traffic, its cloud-based optimization is first explored in Part II. Next, video content dominates the majority of Internet traffic, whose delivery deserves deep investigation in Part III. Moreover, P2P content distribution incurs little infrastructure cost and can scale well with the user base; however, its working efficacy can be poor and unpredictable without the assistance of cloud platforms, which is carefully addressed in Part IV. In addition, as an advanced paradigm of content distribution, cloud storage services like Dropbox and Google Drive have quickly gained enormous popularity in recent years, which are widely studied in Part V. At last, we summarize the major research contributions and discuss the future work in Part VI.

To be more specific, we summarize the main body of the book as follows:

Part II *Cloud-based Cellular Traffic Optimization.* As the penetration of 3G/4G/5G data networks, cellular traffic optimization has been a common desire of both cellular users and carriers. Together with the Baidu PhoneGuard team, we design and deploy TrafficGuard, a third-party mobile traffic proxy widely used by over 10 million Android devices (Chap. 2). TrafficGuard effectively reduces cellular traffic using a network-layer virtual private network (VPN) that connects a client-side proxy to a centralized traffic processing cloud. Most importantly, it works transparently across heterogeneous apps, so it is not constrained to any specific app.

Part III *Cloud-based Mobile Video Distribution.* Driven by the special requirements of mobile devices on video content distribution, we measure and analyze the industrial "cloud downloading" (Chap. 3), "cloud transcoding" (Chap. 4), and "offline downloading" (Chap. 5) services based on the Tencent Xuanfeng system and popular smart home routers. In particular, we diagnose their respective performance bottlenecks and propose the corresponding optimization schemes.

Part IV *Cloud-assisted P2P Content Distribution.* Through large-scale measurements and analysis of industrial cloud-assisted peer-to-peer (P2P) systems like QQXuanfeng and Xunlei, we extract the basic model of "cloud tracking" content distribution in Chap. 6. Further, we design the "cloud bandwidth scheduling" algorithm to maximize the cloud bandwidth multiplier effect in Chap. 7.

Part V *Cloud Storage-oriented Content Distribution.* We are the first to discover the "traffic overuse problem" that pervasively exists in today's cloud storage services. Also, we propose and implement a variety of algorithms to address the problem, such as BDS—batched data sync, IDS—incremental data sync, ASD—adaptive sync defer (Chap. 8), and UDS—update-batched delayed sync (Chap. 9).

In this book, we provide a series of useful takeaways and easy-to-follow experiences to the researchers and developers working on mobile Internet and cloud computing/storage. Additionally, we have built an educational and experimental cloud computing platform (http://www.thucloud.com) to benefit the readers. On top of this platform, the readers can monitor (virtual) cloud servers, accelerate web content distribution, explore the potentials of offline downloading, acquire free cloud storage space, and so forth. Should you have any questions or suggestions, please contact the four authors via *lizhenhua1983@gmail.com*, *dyf@pku.edu.cn*, *gchen@cs.sjtu.edu.cn*, and *yunhaoliu@gmail.com*.

Beijing, China   Zhenhua Li
May 2016   Yafei Dai
                                                                                        Guihai Chen
                                                                                        Yunhao Liu

Acknowledgments

First of all, we deeply appreciate the Chinese Association for Artificial Intelligence (CAAI) for the precious CAAI Ph.D. Thesis Award. In 2015, only eight Ph.D. theses across China received this award. To my knowledge, it was this award that drew the initial attention of Springer on my academic research results. After that, the editors Xiaolan Yao, Jane Li, and Celine Chang have kept in contact with me and provided plenty of useful information and materials for my preparing the book. Specifically, I wish to thank the following people for their contributions to this book:

- Prof. Christo Wilson (@ Northeastern University) guided me closely in my four best researches published in NSDI'16, IMC'15, IMC'14, and Middleware'13. I have learnt so much from him regarding how to properly tell a story, organize a manuscript, present a viewpoint, draw a figure, list a table, and so forth.
- Dr. Tianyin Xu (@ UCSD) helped me closely in conducting the researches published in NSDI'16, IMC'15, and IMC'14. I sincerely appreciate his devotion, honesty, patience, and selflessness during our collaboration.
- Zhefu Jiang (@ Cornell University and Google) helped develop the Linux kernel extension to our proposed UDS (update-batched delayed synchronization) middleware for cloud storage services. In addition, he provided valuable suggestions on the design and implementation of TrafficGuard.
- Weiwei Wang, Changqing Han, Junyi Shao, Xuefeng Luo, Min Guo, Cheng Peng, and Tianwei Wen (@ Baidu Mobile Security) helped develop the TrafficGuard system. Meanwhile, Xin Zhong, Yuxuan Yan, and Jian Chen (@ Tsinghua University) helped evaluate the client-side latency penalty and battery consumption of TrafficGuard.
- Yan Huang, Gang Liu, and Fuchen Wang (@ Tencent Research) helped develop the Xuanfeng system. Meanwhile, Yinlong Wang and Zhen Lu (@ Tsinghua University) helped evaluate the performance of multiple offline downloading systems including smart home routers.

- Prof. Yao Liu (@ SUNY Binghamton) helped evaluate the performance of Dropbox and WeChat in the US. I have learnt a great deal from her concerning measurement-driven research.
- Prof. Ben Y. Zhao (@ UCSB) guided me in conducting the researches published in NSDI'16 and Middleware'13. Also, I used to be a teaching assistant for his summer holiday course at Peking University.
- Prof. Zhi-Li Zhang (@ University of Minnesota) offered me freedom, trust, and valuable guidance during my 1-year visiting life at the University of Minnesota. Also, Dr. Cheng Jin (@ University of Minnesota) helped evaluate the performance of multiple cloud storage services in the US.
- Bob and Joanne Kraftson, as well as Mark and Jaycelyn Colestock, helped me a lot when I was visiting the University of Minnesota. They brought me warm, happy, and unforgettable memories.
- Prof. Xiang-Yang Li (@ University of Science and Technology China and Illinois Institute of Technology) provided useful suggestions on my research published in NSDI'16. I'm impressed by his hard working and diligence.
- Prof. Roger Zimmermann (@ National University of Singapore) helped me with the research published in JCST'15. I am impressed by his patience and elegance.
- Dr. Tieying Zhang (@ Chinese Academy of Sciences) helped me with the research published in IWQoS'12. Also, we collaborated on a number of other researches.
- Dr. Ennan Zhai (@ Yale University) kept in touch with me on a number of topics. Recently, our collaboration produced the first INFOCOM paper in my career.
- Dr. Yiyang Zhao, Dr. Jian Li, Zihui Zhang, Zhinan Ma, Lin Cui, Shuang Xin, Kun Duan, Songyang Wang, and Yong Yi (@ Tsinghua University) helped me a great deal in dealing with numerous affairs and issues in both my work and life.

This work is supported in part by the High-Tech Research and Development Program of China ("863—China Cloud" Major Program) under grant 2015AA01A201, the National Basic Research ("973") Program of China under grants 2014CB340303 and 2012CB316201, the National Natural Science Foundation of China (NSFC) under grants 61432002 (State Key Program), 61471217, 61232004, 61472252 and 61133006, and the CCF-Tencent Open Fund under grant IAGR20150101.

Beijing, China   Zhenhua Li
May 2016

Contents

Acronyms

AP	Access point, or WiFi home router
ASD	Adaptive synchronization defer
BDS	Batched data synchronization
BT	BitTorrent
C/S	Client/Server content distribution
CCN	Content centric networking
CDN	Content distribution (delivery) network
CloudP2P	Hybrid cloud and P2P content distribution
DASH	Dynamic adaptive streaming over HTTP
EC2	Elastic compute cloud
HLS	HTTP live streaming
IDS	Incremental data synchronization
NDN	Named data networking
P2P	Peer-to-Peer content distribution
P2SP	Peer-to-Server&Peer content distribution
PUE	Power usage effectiveness
QoS	Quality of service
RFID	Radio frequency identification device
S3	Simple storage service
SDN	Software-defined networking
TUE	Traffic usage efficiency
UDS	Update-batched delayed synchronization
VBWC	Value-based web cache
VoD	Video on demand
VPN	Virtual private network
WWW	World Wide Web, or "World Wide Wait"

Chapter 1
Background and Overview

Abstract This chapter presents the background and overview of the book. First, we introduce the basic concept and history of Internet content distribution. Next, we illustrate the "heavy-cloud versus light-end" polarization of Internet content distribution under the novel settings of cloud computing and mobile Internet. Afterward, we review various frontier techniques that attempt to address current issues of Internet content distribution. At the end, we outline the entire book structure.

1.1 Internet Content Distribution

Content distribution (also known as *content delivery*) is the most fundamental function of the Internet, i.e., distributing *digital content* from one *node* to another node or multiple nodes. Here digital content includes webpage, image, document, email, software, instant message, audio, video, and so forth. A node can be a giant data center, a large server cluster, a home router, a personal computer, a tablet or smartphone, a tiny sensor or RFID (radio frequency identification device), *etc*. From a historical perspective, existing techniques for Internet content distribution can be generally classified into the following four categories:

1. *Client/Server (C/S)*. The tidal wave of the Internet first rose at the Silicon Valley of the US in 1990s, represented by several pioneering companies like Yahoo! and Netscape. At that time, digital content distributed over the Internet is mainly composed of webpages, images, documents, and emails. Because these content is limited in terms of type, quantity, and capacity (size), using the simplest client/server technique (as shown in Fig. 1.1) to directly deliver content through TCP/IP connections can usually meet the requirements of Internet users.
   C/S content distribution was first embodied by the classical UNIX/BSD Socket implementation (IETF RFC-33) in 1970s. Notably, one author of the UNIX/BSD Socket is Vinton Cerf, known as the "Father of the Internet," the ACM Turing Award winner in 2004, and the president of ACM during 2012–2014.
2. *Content Distribution Network (CDN)*. As the Internet became more ubiquitous and popular, its delivered digital content began to include large-size multimedia content, particularly videos. Meanwhile, the quantity of content underwent

Fig. 1.1 Client/server
content distribution.
(Reprinted with permission
from [12].)

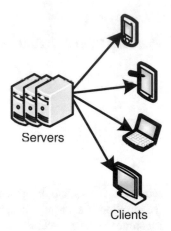

Servers

Clients

an exponential growth. Both issues led to severe congestions on the Internet
when most content was distributed in the C/S manner. As a consequence, "World
Wide Web" (WWW) gradually deteriorated into "World Wide Wait". In 1995,
Tim Berners-Lee, the inventor of WWW, posed a challenging problem to his
colleagues at the Massachusetts Institute of Technology: "Can we invent a fun-
damentally new and better way to deliver Internet content?"

Interestingly, the man who gave the first solution to this problem was just his
office neighbor, Prof. Tom Leighton. Leighton's research team proposed the idea
of CDN, namely content distribution network or content delivery network, and
founded the first CDN company called Akamai in 1998. CDN optimizes the performance of Internet content distribution by strategically deploying *edge servers*
at multiple locations (often over multiple ISP networks) [9]. These edge servers
cooperate with each other by replicating or migrating content according to content
popularity and server load. An end user usually obtains a copy of content from
a nearby edge server, so that the content delivery speed is greatly enhanced and
the load on the original data source is effectively reduced.

To date, CDN has been the most widely used technique for accelerating Internet content distribution. Besides Akamai, representative CDN service providers
include Limelight (founded in 2001), Level3 (founded in 1998), ChinaCache
(founded in 1998), ChinaNetCenter (founded in 2000), and so on.

3. *Peer-to-Peer (P2P)*. Although CDN is widely used across the Internet, it is subject to both economical and technical limitations. First, CDN is a charged facility
that only serves the content providers who have paid (typically popular websites
like YouTube and Netflix), rather than a public utility of the Internet. Moreover,
even for those content providers who have paid, CDN is not able to accelerate the
distribution of all their content, since the bandwidth, storage, and coverage of a
CDN are constrained. Then the question is: can we simply leverage the resources
of content receivers to accelerate Internet content distribution? More specifically,
now that every end-user device possesses a certain amount of bandwidth, storage,

Fig. 1.2 Peer-to-peer
content distribution.
(Reprinted with permission
from [12].)

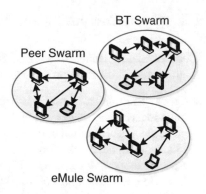

and coverage, can we organize the numerous end-user devices into peer-to-peer data swarms in which shared content is directly delivered among interested peers (as demonstrated in Fig. 1.2)?

In 1999, the Napster music sharing system offered a solid and splendid answer to the above question—50 million users joined Napster in 6 months. Although Napster was then shut down soon for copyright reasons, it started the prosperity of P2P content distribution. Following the step of Napster, a series of well-known P2P systems quickly appeared, such as BitTorrent (abbreviated as BT), eDon-key/eMule, KaZaa, Skype, and PPLive [4]. These systems confirmed the huge power of content distribution concealed in Internet end users.

P2P content distribution also bears its intrinsic limitations. First, end-user devices do not work stably (i.e., highly dynamic). Second, end-user devices are diverse in bandwidth and storage capabilities (i.e., highly heterogeneous). Third, the users and content in peer swarms are short of reputation and quality authentication (i.e., highly unreliable). These limitations make it difficult to predict and control the performance of P2P content distribution, and thus the quality-of-service (QoS) perceived by users can hardly be guaranteed.

4. *Hybrid content distribution.* To address the potential limitations and meanwhile inherit the advantages of C/S, CDN and P2P, hybrid content distribution techniques came into being. They aim to integrate the stability and reliability of C/S and CDN, as well as the economy and scalability of P2P. Inevitably, their designs, implementations, and deployments are often quite complicated. As a matter of fact, most popular P2P systems (e.g., Skype, PPLive, PPStream, and UUSee) have transformed their network architectures to a hybrid mode. On the other side, many C/S and CDN-based systems (e.g., Youku, Tudou, and LiveSky [30]) have integrated P2P techniques.

1.2   Cloud Computing and Mobile Internet

Since Amazon's launch of EC2 in 2006 and Apple's release of iPhone in 2007, Internet content distribution has demonstrated a strong trend of *polarization*:

- On one hand, great fortune has been invested in building heavyweight and integrated data centers ("heavy-cloud") all over the world. Recent years have witnessed great successes of cloud computing [3] (e.g., Amazon EC2, Google App Engine, Microsoft Azure, Apple iCloud, Aliyun, and OpenStack), big data processing (e.g., Apache Hadoop, Cassandra, and Spark), cloud storage (e.g., Amazon S3, Dropbox, Box, Google Drive, and Microsoft OneDrive), virtualization (e.g., VMware, VirtualBox, Xen, and Docker), and so forth. Based on these cloud platforms, today's content distribution systems can reliably host a huge amount of content, purchase any amount of ISP and CDN bandwidth on demand, and adaptively migrate content and schedule bandwidth, in order to achieve the economies of scale and the cost efficiency [2].
- On the other hand, end user devices have been growing more lightweight and mobile ("light-end"), as well as highly heterogeneous in terms of hardware, software, and network environments. The release of iPhone and iPad, together with the flourishing of Android Open Handset Alliance, have substantially extended the functions of mobile devices from traditional voice calls and text messages to almost all kinds of Internet applications. Besides, growth in mobile devices greatly outpaces that of personal computers. Nevertheless, most existing content distribution techniques are still geared for personal computers at the moment. When applied to mobile scenarios, they often exhibit unsatisfactory or even poor performance. Mobile devices have diverse sizes and resolutions of screens, support different formats of content and applications [23], and are quite limited in traffic quotas (while working in 2G/3G/4G modes), processing capabilities, and battery capacities [22], thus posing rigorous requirements on the traffic usage, energy consumption, speed, and latency of content distribution.

Although "heavy-cloud" seems on the other side of "light-end", it is not on the opposite of "light-end". In essence, the evolution of "heavy-cloud" is motivated by the requirements of "light-end", i.e., only with more heavy back-end clouds can front-end user devices become more light. A representative case is that every new generation of iPhone is lighter, thinner, and yet more powerful than its predecessors, while more relies on iCloud services. In the era of cloud computing and mobile Internet, cloud platforms have to collaborate more tightly with end user devices, and thus the gap between Internet content and mobile devices can be better filled.

1.3 Frontier Techniques

In recent years, various frontier techniques for Internet content distribution have emerged in both academia and industry. Below we review typical frontier techniques that are especially related to the "heavy-cloud versus light-end" scenarios:

- *Multi-CDN.* To mitigate the limitations of a single CDN, a content provider can simultaneously purchase resources from multiple CDNs and then allocate the resources on her own, as demonstrated in Fig. 1.3. A representative case of Multi-CDN is Hulu [1], a novel video content provider that makes use of three CDNs: Akamai, Limelight, and Level3. Additionally, Hulu in itself builds a relatively small-scale cloud platform for scheduling the resources from the three CDNs. With such efforts, Hulu effectively addresses the limitations of a single CDN in cost efficiency, available bandwidth, and ISP/geographical coverage.
- *Private BitTorrent* and *Bundling BitTorrent* are both extensions to the classical BitTorrent protocol. The former restricts BitTorrent's working within a more narrow, more homogeneous, and more active user group, e.g., the students in the same campus. By trading the user-group coverage for the authentication of users and shared content, private BitTorrent can remarkably enhance the engagement of users, the quality of shared content, and the performance of content distribution [24, 27, 31].

  By bundling a number of related files to a single file, the latter motivates BitTorrent users to stay longer online and share more data with others. Hence, the whole BitTorrent system can be boosted to a more healthy and prosperous status [5, 10, 26]. Typically, bundling BitTorrent combines a number of episodes of a TV series to a single, large file—this simple and useful idea has been adopted by numerous BitTorrent (and even eMule) websites.
- *Peer-to-Server&Peer* (*P2SP*). As illustrated in Fig. 1.4, P2SP allows and directs users to retrieve data from both peer swarms and content servers, so it is the integration of P2P and C/S. Till now, P2SP has been adopted by plenty of media streaming systems, such as Spotify, PPLive, PPStream, UUSee, and Funshion [6, 29]. It is worth noting that the implementation complexity of P2SP is usually higher than that of P2P or C/S. If not properly designed, P2SP can generate worse performance with higher overhead.

Fig. 1.3 Multi-CDN content distribution with a centralized cloud for scheduling the resources from multiple CDNs

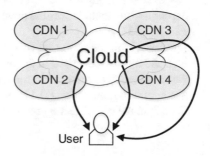

Fig. 1.4 P2SP content
distribution by integrating
P2P and C/S. (Reprinted
with permission from [12].)

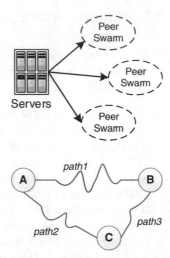

Fig. 1.5 Triangle inequality
violation in the Internet, i.e.,
path2 + path3 < path1

Furthermore, P2SP can be extended to Open-P2SP [12], which outperforms P2SP
by enabling users to retrieve data across heterogeneous protocols and content
providers. For example, a user can simultaneously download from a BitTorrent
swarm, an eMule swarm, an HTTP server, and a RTSP server. Representative examples of Open-P2SP include Xunlei, QQXuanfeng, FlashGet, Orbit, and QVoD.
Naturally, Open-P2SP is very complicated and difficult to implement, since it
involves not only technical problems but also business/copyright issues.

- *Detour routing* [25] originates from the pervasive *triangular inequality violation*
phenomena of the Internet. As depicted in Fig. 1.5, suppose we want to deliver a
file f from node A to node B in the Internet, and the shortest-hop path from A
to B is *path1*. Theoretically, delivering f along *path1* should be the fastest. But
in practice, because today's Internet is complicated by too many artificial factors,
it may be faster if we select an appropriate intermediate node C to forward f
from node A (along *path2*) to node B (along *path3*), which is referred to as detour
routing. Therefore, we observe the triangular inequality violation phenomenon
when the sum of two sides (*path2 + path3*) of a triangle is smaller the third (*path1*).
Particularly, when nodes A and B locate at different ISP networks, triangular
inequality violations would frequently occur. In this case, detour routing will be
an effective remedy for the defects of today's Internet. Representative examples of
detour routing include "offline downloading" [19] and quality improving of online
gaming [25].

- *Dynamic Adaptive Streaming over HTTP (DASH)*. HTTP (web) servers are the earliest and most widely used in the Internet. They are originally designed for serving
webpage requests rather than media streaming. However, due to their large scale
and enormous popularity, HTTP servers are often used for media streaming in practice. To make HTTP servers more suitable for media streaming, web professionals

developed DASH as an extension to the original HTTP protocol.[1] Meanwhile, web clients need adjusting so that they can adaptively select an appropriate streaming bit rate according to real-time network conditions. At present, DASH remains an active research topic and possesses considerable space for performance optimization [8, 28].

In general, all the above efforts attempt to address current issues of Internet content distribution by extending or upgrading existing techniques and frameworks. In other words, they act as remedies for defects and seek for incremental improvements. As time goes on, the "heavy-cloud versus light-end" polarization of Internet content distribution may become more and more severe, and thus we need to explore innovative techniques and frameworks. This is the basic starting point of our research presented in this book.

1.4 Overview of the Book Structure

Based on comprehensive real-world measurements and benchmarks, we observe that existing content distribution techniques often exhibit poor performance under the settings of cloud computing and mobile Internet. To address the issue, this book investigates content distribution for mobile Internet with a cloud-based approach, in the hopes of bridging the gap between Internet content and mobile devices. In particular, we propose, design, and implement a series of novel traffic-saving, energy-efficient, high-speed, and delay-tolerant content distribution techniques and frameworks that automatically adapt to mobile application scenarios.

Besides theoretical and algorithmic contributions, our research pays special attention to its *real effect*. Specifically, we discover practical problems in real systems, solve the problems under real environments, and achieve real performance enhancements. Our research stands on real-world production systems such as TrafficGuard (i.e., a cross-app cellular traffic optimization platform of Baidu), QQXuanfeng (i.e., the major content distribution platform of Tencent), CoolFish (i.e., a video streaming system of the Chinese Academy of Sciences), and Dropbox (i.e., one of the world's biggest cloud storage services). A series of useful takeaways and easy-to-follow experiences are provided to the researchers and developers working on mobile Internet and cloud computing/storage.

The main body of this book is organized in four parts: *cloud-based cellular traffic optimization* (Chap. 2), *cloud-based mobile video distribution* (Chaps. 3, 4, and 5), *cloud-assisted P2P content distribution* (Chaps. 6 and 7), and *cloud storage-oriented content distribution* (Chaps. 8 and 9). Below we provide a brief overview of each part.

Part II: Cellular traffic is the most expensive among all Internet traffic, so it is first explored in Chap. 2. As the penetration of 3G/4G/5G data networks, cellular traffic optimization has been a common desire of both cellular users and carriers. Together

---

[1] DASH is called HTTP Live Streaming (HLS) by Apple and Smooth Streaming by Microsoft.

Table 1.1 Chapter structure

Title	System	Architecture	Publication
Cross-application cellular traffic optimization (Chap. 2)	 shoujiweishi.baidu.com		NSDI'16 [17]
Cloud downloading for unpopular videos (Chap. 3)	 lixian.qq.com		JCST'15 [16] ACM-MM'11 (Long Paper) [7]
Cloud transcoding for mobile devices (Chap. 4)	 xf.qq.com		NOSSDAV'12 [13]

(continued)

Table 1.1 (continued)

Title	System	Architecture	Publication
Offline downloading: a comparative study (Chap. 5)			IMC'15 [19]
Cloud tracking or Open-P2SP (Chap. 6)	 www.xunlei.com		TPDS'13 [12] ACM-MM'11 (Doctoral Symposium) [11]
Cloud bandwidth scheduling (Chap. 7)	 www.cool-fish.org		IWQoS'12 [20]

(continued)

Table 1.1 (continued)

Title	System	Architecture	Publication
Towards network-level efficiency for cloud storage services (Chap. 8)	Google Drive · Dropbox · iDrive · iCloud · SkyDrive · SugarSync · Ubuntu One · 百度云 · 360云盘		TCC'15 [32] (Spotlight Paper) IMC'14 [14] *JTST'13* [21]
Efficient batched synchronization for cloud storage services (Chap. 9)	**Dropbox** www.dropbox.com		Middleware'13 [18] *CCCF'14* [15] (*Cover Article*)

with the Baidu PhoneGuard team, we design and deploy TrafficGuard (http://www.shoujiweishi.baidu.com), a third-party mobile traffic proxy widely used by over 10 million Android devices. TrafficGuard effectively reduces cellular traffic using a network-layer virtual private network (VPN) that connects a client-side proxy to a centralized traffic processing cloud. Most importantly, it works transparently across heterogeneous apps, so it is not constrained to any specific app.

Part III: Video content dominates the majority of Internet traffic, whose delivery deserves deep investigation. Driven by the special requirements of mobile devices on video content distribution, we measure and analyze the industrial "cloud download-ing" (Chap. 3), "cloud transcoding" (Chap. 4), and "offline downloading" (Chap. 5) services based on the Tencent Xuanfeng system (http://www.lixian.qq.com) and popular smart home routers (e.g., HiWiFi, MiWiFi, and Newifi). In particular, we diagnose their respective performance bottlenecks and propose the corresponding optimization schemes.

Part IV: P2P content distribution incurs little infrastructure cost and can scale well with the user base; however, its working efficacy can be poor and unpredictable without the assistance of cloud platforms. Through large-scale measurements and analysis of industrial cloud-assisted P2P systems, especially QQXuanfeng (http://www.xf.qq.com), we extract the basic model of "cloud tracking" content distribu-tion in Chap. 6. Further, we design the "cloud bandwidth scheduling" algorithm to maximize the cloud bandwidth multiplier effect in Chap. 7.

Part V: As an advanced paradigm of content distribution, cloud storage services like Dropbox and Google Drive have quickly gained enormous popularity in recent years. We are the first to discover the "traffic overuse problem" that pervasively exists in today's cloud storage services. Also, we propose and implement a variety of algorithms to address the problem in Chaps. 8 and 9.

At last, we summarize the major research contributions and discuss the future work in Part VI (Chap. 10). Moreover, we list and plot the title, relevant system(s), technical architecture, and resulting publications of each chapter in Table 1.1.

References

1. Adhikari, V., Guo, Y., Hao, F., Hilt, V., Zhang, Z.L.: A tale of three CDNs: an active measure-ment study of Hulu and its CDNs. In: Proceedings of the 15th IEEE Global Internet Symposium, pp. 7–12 (2012)
2. Adhikari, V., Jain, S., Ranjan, G., Zhang, Z.L.: Understanding data-center driven content dis-tribution. In: Proceedings of the ACM CoNEXT Student Workshop, p. 24 (2010)
3. Armbrust, M., Fox, A., Griffith, R., Joseph, A., Katz, R., Konwinski, A., Lee, G., Patterson, D., Rabkin, A., Stoica, I., et al.: A view of cloud computing. Commun. ACM (CACM) 53(4), 50–58 (2010)
4. Chen, G., Li, Z.: Peer-to-Peer Network: Structure. Tsinghua University Press, Application and Design (2007)
5. Han, J., Kim, S., Chung, T., Kwon, T., Kim, H., Choi, Y.: Bundling practice in Bittorrent: what, how, and why. In: Proceedings of the 12th ACM SIGMETRICS/PERFORMANCE Joint Inter-

national Conference on Measurement and Modeling of Computer Systems (SIGMETRICS), pp. 77–88 (2012)

6. Huang, Y., Fu, T.Z., Chiu, D.M., Lui, J., Huang, C.: Challenges, design and analysis of a large-scale P2P-VoD system. ACM SIGCOMM Comput. Commun. Rev. (CCR) **38**(4), 375–388 (2008)

7. Huang, Y., Li, Z., Liu, G., Dai, Y.: Cloud download: using cloud utilities to achieve high-quality content distribution for unpopular videos. In: Proceedings of the 19th ACM International Conference on Multimedia (ACM-MM), pp. 213–222 (2011)

8. Jiang, J., Sekar, V., Zhang, H.: Improving fairness, efficiency, and stability in HTTP-based adaptive video streaming with FESTIVE. In: Proceedings of the 8th ACM International Conference on Emerging Networking EXperiments and Technologies (CoNEXT), pp. 97–108 (2012)

9. Kangasharju, J., Roberts, J., Ross, K.: Object replication strategies in content distribution networks. Comput. Commun. **25**(4), 376–383 (2002)

10. Lev-tov, N., Carlsson, N., Li, Z., Williamson, C., Zhang, S.: Dynamic file-selection policies for bundling in Bittorrent-like systems. In: Proceedings of the 18th IEEE/ACM International Workshop on Quality of Service (IWQoS), pp. 1–9 (2010)

11. Li, Z., Huang, Y., Liu, G., Dai, Y.: CloudTracker: accelerating internet content distribution by bridging cloud servers and peer swarms. In: Proceedings of the 19th ACM International Conference on Multimedia (ACM-MM) Doctoral Symposium, vol. 46, p. 49 (2011)

12. Li, Z., Huang, Y., Liu, G., Wang, F., Liu, Y., Zhang, Z.L., Dai, Y.: Challenges, designs and performances of large-scale Open-P2SP content distribution. IEEE Trans. Parallel and Distrib. Syst. (TPDS) **24**(11), 2181–2191 (2013)

13. Li, Z., Huang, Y., Liu, G., Wang, F., Zhang, Z.L., Dai, Y.: Cloud transcoder: bridging the format and resolution gap between internet videos and mobile devices. In: Proceedings of the 22nd SIGMM Workshop on Network and Operating Systems Support for Digital Audio and Video (NOSSDAV), pp. 33–38 (2012)

14. Li, Z., Jin, C., Xu, T., Wilson, C., Liu, Y., Cheng, L., Liu, Y., Dai, Y., Zhang, Z.L.: Towards network-level efficiency for cloud storage services. In: Proceedings of the 14th ACM Internet Measurement Conference (IMC), pp. 115–128 (2014)

15. Li, Z., Li, J.: Deficiency of scientific research behind the price war of cloud storage services. Commun. China Comput. Fed. (CCCF) **10**(8), 36–41 (2014)

16. Li, Z., Liu, G., Ji, Z., Zimmermann, R.: Towards cost-effective cloud downloading with tencent big data. J. Comput. Sci. Technol. (JCST) **30**(6), 1163–1174 (2015)

17. Li, Z., Wang, W., Xu, T., Zhong, X., Li, X.Y., Wilson, C., Zhao, B.Y.: Exploring cross-application cellular traffic optimization with Baidu TrafficGuard. In: Proceedings of the 13th USENIX Symposium on Networked Systems Design and Implementation (NSDI), pp. 61–76 (2016)

18. Li, Z., Wilson, C., Jiang, Z., Liu, Y., Zhao, B., Jin, C., Zhang, Z.L., Dai, Y.: Efficient batched synchronization in dropbox-like cloud storage services. In: Proceedings of the 14th ACM/IFIP/USENIX International Middleware Conference (Middleware), pp. 307–327. Springer (2013)

19. Li, Z., Wilson, C., Xu, T., Liu, Y., Lu, Z., Wang, Y.: Offline downloading in China: a comparative study. In: Proceedings of the 15th ACM Internet Measurement Conference (IMC), pp. 473–486 (2015)

20. Li, Z., Zhang, T., Huang, Y., Zhang, Z.L., Dai, Y.: Maximizing the bandwidth multiplier effect for hybrid cloud-P2P content distribution. In: Proceedings of the 20th IEEE/ACM International Workshop on Quality of Service (IWQoS), pp. 1–9 (2012)

21. Li, Z., Zhang, Z.L., Dai, Y.: Coarse-grained cloud synchronization mechanism design may lead to severe traffic overuse. J. Tsinghua Sci. Technol. (JTST) **18**(3), 286–297 (2013)

22. Liu, Y., Guo, L., Li, F., Chen, S.: An empirical evaluation of battery power consumption for streaming data transmission to mobile devices. In: Proceedings of the 19th ACM International Conference on Multimedia (ACM-MM), pp. 473–482 (2011)

23. Liu, Y., Li, F., Guo, L., Shen, B., Chen, S.: A server's perspective of internet streaming delivery to mobile devices. In: Proceedings of the 31st IEEE International Conference on Computer Communications (INFOCOM), pp. 1332–1340 (2012)

24. Liu, Z., Dhungel, P., Wu, D., Zhang, C., Ross, K.: Understanding and improving incentives in private P2P communities. In: Proceedings of the 30th IEEE International Conference on Distributed Computing Systems (ICDCS), pp. 610–621 (2010)
25. Ly, C., Hsu, C., Hefeeda, M.: Improving online gaming quality using detour paths. In: Proceedings of the 18th ACM International Conference on Multimedia (ACM-MM), pp. 55–64 (2010)
26. Menasche, D.S., Rocha, D.A., Antonio, A., Li, B., Towsley, D., Venkataramani, A.: Content availability and bundling in swarming systems. IEEE/ACM Trans. Networking (TON) 21(2), 580–593 (2013)
27. Meulpolder, M., D'Acunto, L., Capota, M., Wojciechowski, M., Pouwelse, J., Epema, D., Sips, H.: Public and private bittorrent communities: a measurement study. In: Proceedings of the 9th International Workshop on Peer-to-peer Systems (IPTPS), vol. 4, p. 5. Springer (2010)
28. Tian, G., Liu, Y.: Towards agile and smooth video adaption in dynamic HTTP streaming. In: Proceedings of the 8th ACM International Conference on emerging Networking EXperiments and Technologies (CoNEXT), pp. 109–120 (2012)
29. Wu, C., Li, B., Zhao, S.: On dynamic server provisioning in multi-channel P2P live streaming. IEEE/ACM Trans. Networking (TON) 19(5), 1317–1330 (2011)
30. Yin, H., Liu, X., Zhan, T., Sekar, V., Qiu, F., Lin, C., Zhang, H., Li, B.: Design and deployment of a hybrid CDN-P2P system for live video streaming: experiences with LiveSky. In: Proceedings of the 17th ACM International Conference on Multimedia (ACM-MM), pp. 25–34 (2009)
31. Zhang, C., Dhungel, P., Wu, D., Ross, K.: Unraveling the Bittorrent ecosystem. IEEE Trans. Parallel Distrib. Syst. (TPDS) 22(7), 1164–1177 (2011)
32. Zhang, Q., Li, S., Li, Z., Xing, Y., Yang, Z., Dai, Y.: CHARM: a cost-efficient multi-cloud data hosting scheme with high availability. IEEE Trans. Cloud Comput. (TCC) 3(3), 372–386 (2015)

Part II
Cloud-Based Cellular Traffic Optimization

Chapter 2
Cross-Application Cellular Traffic Optimization

Abstract As mobile cellular devices and traffic continue growing rapidly, providers are putting more efforts to optimize traffic, with the hopes of improving user experiences while reducing congestion and bandwidth costs. This chapter presents the design, deployment, and experiences with Baidu TrafficGuard, a cloud-based mobile proxy that reduces cellular traffic using a network-layer VPN. The VPN connects a client-side proxy to a centralized traffic processing cloud. TrafficGuard works transparently across heterogeneous applications, and effectively reduces cellular traffic by 36% and overage instances by 10.7 times for roughly 10 million Android users in China. We discuss a large-scale cellular traffic analysis effort, how the resulting insights guided the design of TrafficGuard, and our experiences with a variety of traffic optimization techniques over one year of deployment.

2.1 Introduction

Mobile cellular devices are changing today's Internet landscape. Growth in cellular devices today greatly outpaces that of traditional PCs, and global cellular traffic is growing by double digits annually, to an estimated 15.9 Exabytes in 2018 [1]. This growing traffic demand has led to significant congestion on today's cellular networks, resulting in bandwidth caps, and throttling at major wireless providers. The challenges are more dramatic in developing countries, where low-capacity cellular networks often fail to deliver basic quality of service needed for simple applications [2–4].

While this is a well-known problem, only recently have we seen efforts to address it at scale. Google took the unprecedented step of prioritizing mobile-friendly sites in its search algorithm [5]. This will likely spur further efforts to update popular websites for mobile devices. Recent reports estimate that most enterprise webpages are designed for PCs, and only 38% of webpages are mobile-friendly [6]. More recently, Google released details on their Flywheel proxy service for compressing content for the Chrome mobile browser [7].

Competition in today's mobile platforms has led to numerous "walled-gardens," where developers build their own suites of applications that keep users within their

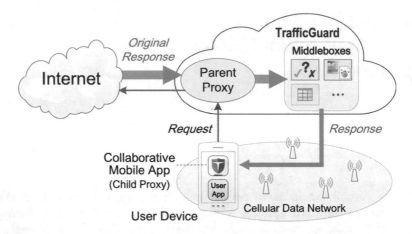

Fig. 2.1 Architectural overview of TrafficGuard. (Reprinted with permission from [22].)

ecosystem. The ongoing trend limits the benefits of application-specific proxies, even ones with user bases as large as Google Chrome [7–13]. In contrast, an alternative approach is to transparently intercept and optimize network traffic across all apps at the OS/network layer. Although some examples of this approach exist [14–17], little is known about their design or impact on network performance.

This chapter describes the design, deployment, and experiences with Baidu Traf-ficGuard, a third-party cellular traffic proxy widely deployed for Android devices in China.[1] As shown in Fig. 2.1, TrafficGuard is a cloud-based proxy that redirects traffic through a VPN to a client-side mobile app (http://shoujiweishi.baidu.com). It currently supports all Android 4.0+ devices, and does not require root privileges. Inside the cloud, a series of software middleboxes are utilized to monitor, filter, and reshape cellular traffic. TrafficGuard was first deployed in early 2014, and its Android app has been installed by roughly 10 million users. The average number of daily active users is around 0.2 million.

In designing a transparent mobile proxy for cellular traffic optimization, Traffic-Guard targets four key goals:

- First, traffic optimization should not harm user experiences. For example, image compression through pixel scaling often distorts webpage and UI (user interface) rendering in user apps. Similarly, traffic processing should not introduce unaccept-able delays.
- Second, our techniques must generalize to different apps, and thus proprietary APIs or data formats should be avoided. For example, Flywheel achieves significant traffic savings by transcoding images to the WebP format [23]. Though WebP offers high compression, not all apps support this format.

---

[1]Cellular data usage in Asia differs from that of US/European networks, in that HTTP traffic dominates 80.4 % of cellular traffic in China and 74.6 % in South Korea [18]. In comparison, HTTPS accounts for more than 50 % of cellular traffic in the US [19–21].

- Third, we wish to limit client-side resource consumption, in terms of memory, CPU, and battery. Note that the client needs to collaborate well with the cloud using a certain amount of resources.
- Finally, we wish to reduce system complexity, resource consumption, and monetary costs on the cloud side. In particular, the state information maintained for each client should be carefully determined.

In this chapter, we document considerations in the design, implementation, and deployment of TrafficGuard. *First*, we analyze aggregate cellular traffic measurements over 110 K users to understand the characteristics of cellular traffic in China. This gave us insights on the efficacy and impact of traditional data compression, as well as the role of useless content like broken images in cellular traffic. *Second*, we adopt a lightweight, adaptive approach to image compression, where more considerate compression schemes are constructed to achieve a sweet spot on the image-quality versus file-size tradeoff. This helps us achieve traffic savings comparable to Flywheel (27 %) at roughly 10–12 % of the computation overhead. *Third*, we develop a customized VPN tunnel to efficiently filter users' unwanted traffic, including overnight, background, malicious, and advertisement traffic. *Finally*, we implement a cloud-client paired proxy system, and integrate best-of-breed caching techniques for duplicate content detection. The cloud-client paired design allows us to finely tune the tradeoff between traffic optimization and state maintenance.

TrafficGuard is the culmination of these efforts. For installed users, it reduces overall cellular traffic by an average of 36 %, and instances of traffic overage (i.e., going beyond the users' allotted data caps) by 10.7 times. Roughly 55 % of users saw more than a quarter reduction in traffic, and 20 % of users saw their traffic reduced by half. TrafficGuard introduces relatively small latency penalties (median of 53 ms, mean of 282 ms), and has little to no impact on the battery life of user devices.

While already successful in its current deployment, TrafficGuard can achieve even higher efficiency if cellular carriers (are willing to) integrate it into their infrastructure. As demonstrated in Fig. 2.2, carriers could deploy TrafficGuard between the GGSN (Gateway GPRS Support Node) and SGSN (Serving GPRS Support Node). Then the optimized traffic is further transferred to the RNC (Radio Network Controller) and BTS (Base Transceiver Station). This would greatly simplify both the cloud-side and client-side components of TrafficGuard, and further reduce latency penalties for users.

Finally, we note that while Baidu does not have an internal IRB (institutional review board [24]) review process, all reasonable steps were taken at Baidu to protect

Fig. 2.2 Potential integration of TrafficGuard into a 3G cellular carrier. Integration for 4G would be similar. (Reprinted with permission from [22].)

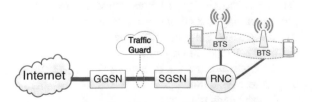

user privacy during this study. All users who participated in the study opted-in as volunteers with informed consent, and full traffic traces were limited to one week of measurements (all other datasets are anonymized logs). Wherever possible, analysis was limited to anonymized metadata only. When necessary, content analysis was done on aggregate data, and fully decoupled from any user identifiers or personally identifiable information.

2.2 State-of-the-Art Systems

This section briefly surveys state-of-the-art mobile traffic proxy systems. As listed in Table 2.1, we compare seven systems with TrafficGuard. We focus on five of the most important and ubiquitous features supported by these systems: (1) image compression, (2) text compression, (3) content optimization, (4) traffic filtering, and (5) caching. In each case, we highlight the strengths of different approaches, as well as the shortcomings, which motivated our design of TrafficGuard.

Since most mobile traffic proxy systems are closed-source, we rely on a variety of methods to determine their features. The implementation of Google Flywheel is described in [7]. For Opera Turbo, UCBrowser (proxy), and QQBrowser (proxy), we are able to uncover most of their features through carefully controlled experiments. Specifically, we set up our own web server, used these proxies to browse our own content hosted by the server, and carefully compared the data sent by the server with what was received by our client device. Unfortunately, Opera Max, Microsoft Data Sense, and Onavo Extend use encrypted proxies, and thus we can only discover a subset of their implementation details.

First, we examine the image compression techniques. Three systems transcode images to WebP, which effectively reduces network traffic [7]. However, this only works for user apps that support WebP (e.g., Google Chrome). Similarly, Opera Max and Onavo Extend transcode PNGs to JPEGs, and Onavo Extend also transcodes large GIFs to JPEGs. Taking a different approach, UCBrowser rescales large images ($>700 \times 700$ pixels) to small images ($<150 \times 150$ pixels). Although rescaling reduces traffic, it could harm user experiences by significantly degrading image qualities. In contrast to these systems, TrafficGuard uses an adaptive quality reduction approach that is not CPU intensive, reduces traffic across apps, and generally does not harm user experiences (see Sect. 2.5.1).

Second, we find that all the seven systems compress textual content, typically with gzip. However, our large-scale measurement findings (in Sect. 2.3.2.2) reveal that the vast majority of textual content downloaded by smartphone users is very short, meaning that compression would be ineffective. Thus, TrafficGuard does not compress texts, since the CPU overhead of decompression is not worth the low (1.36 %) HTTP traffic savings.

Third, we explore the *content optimization* strategies employed by mobile traffic proxies. We define *content optimization* as attempts to reduce network traffic by altering the semantics or functionality of content. For example, Flywheel replaces

Table 2.1 Comparison of state-of-the-art mobile traffic proxy systems

System	Image compression	Text compression	Content optimization	Traffic filtering	Caching
Google Flywheel	Transcoding to WebP	Yes	Lightweight error page	Safe Browsing	Server-side
Opera Turbo	Transcoding to WebP	Yes	Pre-executing JavaScript	Ad blocking	?
UCBrowser	Pixel Scaling	Yes	No	Ad blocking	?
QQBrowser	Transcoding to WebP	Yes	No	Ad blocking	?
Opera Max [17] (China's version)	Transcoding PNG to JPEG	Yes	No	Restricting overnight traffic	?
Microsoft Data Sense	?	Yes	No	Restricting background traffic, and ad blocking	?
Onavo Extend	Transcoding PNG and large GIF to JPEG	Yes	No	No	Client-side
TrafficGuard	Adaptive quality reduction	No	Attempting to discard useless content	Restricting overnight and background traffic, ad blocking, Safe Browsing	Server side, and VBWC on both sides

"?" means unknown. (Reprinted with permission from [22].)

HTTP 404 error pages with a lightweight version. More aggressively, Opera Turbo executes JavaScript objects at the proxy, so that clients do not need to download and execute them. Although this can reduce traffic, it often breaks the original functionality of websites and user apps, e.g., in the controlled experiments we often noticed that JavaScript functions like onscroll() and oninput() were not properly executed by Opera Turbo. Rather than adopt these approaches, TrafficGuard validates HTTP content and attempts to discard useless content like broken images (see Sect. 2.5.2).

Fourth, we observe that many of the target systems implement traffic filtering. Four systems block advertisements, plus Flywheel using Google Safe Browsing [25] to block malicious content. Opera Max attempts to restrict apps' traffic usage during the night, when users are likely to be asleep. Microsoft Data Sense takes things a step further by also restricting traffic from background apps, under the assumption that apps which are not currently interactive should not be downloading lots of data. We discover that all these filtering techniques are beneficial to users (see Sect. 2.3.2.4), and thus we incorporate all of them into TrafficGuard (see Sect. 2.5.3).

Finally, we study the caching strategies of existing systems. Flywheel maintains a server-side cache of recently accessed objects, while Onavo Extend maintains a local cache (of 100 MB by default). In contrast, TrafficGuard adopts server-side strategies by maintaining a cache at the proxy (see Sect. 2.4), as well as implementing Value-based web caching (VBWC) between the client and server (see Sect. 2.5.4). Although we evaluated other sophisticated caching strategies, we ultimately chose VBWC because it offers excellent performance and is straightforward to implement.

2.3 Measuring Cellular Traffic

In this section, we present a large-scale measurement study of cellular traffic usage by Android smartphone users. Unlike prior studies [18, 26–30], our analysis focuses on content and metadata. Using this dataset, we identify several key performance issues and tradeoffs that guide the design of TrafficGuard.

2.3.1 Dataset Collection

The ultimate goal of TrafficGuard is to improve smartphone users' experiences by decreasing network usage and filtering unwanted content. To achieve this goal, we decided to take a measurement-driven methodology, i.e., we first observed the actual cellular traffic usage patterns of smartphone users, and then used the data to drive our design and implementation decisions.

When we first deployed TrafficGuard between Jan. 5 and Mar. 31, 2014, the system only monitored users' cellular traffic; it did not filter or reshape traffic at all. We randomly invited users to test TrafficGuard from ~100M existing mobile users of Baidu. We obtained informed consent from volunteers by prominently informing them that full traces of their cellular traffic would be collected and analyzed. We assigned a unique ClientToken to each user device that installed the mobile app of TrafficGuard.

We used two methods to collect packet traces from volunteers. For an HTTP request, the TrafficGuard app would insert the ClientToken into the HTTP header. The TrafficGuard cloud would then record the request, remove the injected header, complete the HTTP request, and store the server's response. However, for non-HTTP requests (most of which are HTTPS), it was not possible for the TrafficGuard cloud to read the injected ClientToken (we did not attack secure connections via man-in-the-middle). Thus, the TrafficGuard app locally recorded the non-HTTP traffic, and uploaded it to the cloud in a batch along with the ClientToken once per week. These uploads were restricted to WiFi,[2] in order to avoid wasting volunteers' cellular data traffic. In both cases, we also recorded additional metadata like the specific app

---

[2]Certainly TrafficGuard also has the *capability* of helping mobile users save WiFi traffic, just like what Google Flywheel does. However, at the moment TrafficGuard only targets at saving cellular traffic for two reasons. First, WiFi users generally do not care about the traffic usage since they

Table 2.2 General statistics of our collected TGdataset

Collection period	03/21–03/27, 2014
Unique users	111,910
Total requests	162M
Dataset size	1324 GB (100%)
Non-HTTP traffic (plus TCP/IP)	259 GB (19.6%)
HTTP traffic (plus TCP/IP)	1065 GB (80.4%)
HTTP header traffic	107 GB (8.1%)
HTTP body traffic	875 GB (66.1%)

(Reprinted with permission from [22].)

that initiated each request, and whether that app was working in the foreground or background.

We collected packet traces from volunteers for one week, between Mar. 21 and 27, 2014. In total, this dataset contains 320M requests from 0.65M unique ClientTokens. However, we observe that many user devices in the dataset only used their cellular connections for short periods of time. These *short-term* users might have good WiFi availability, or might be using their cellular connections but did not (remember to) run the mobile app of TrafficGuard. To avoid bias, we focus on the traces belonging to 111,910 *long-term* users who used their cellular connections in at least four days during the collection period. This final dataset is referred to as TGdataset, whose general statistics are listed in Table 2.2.

2.3.2 Content Analysis

Below, we analyze the content and metadata contained in TGdataset. In particular, we observe that today's cellular traffic can be effectively optimized in multiple ways.

2.3.2.1 General Characteristics

We begin by presenting some general characteristics of TGdataset. As listed in Table 2.2, 80.4% of TGdataset is HTTP traffic, most of which corresponds to the bodies of HTTP messages. This finding is positive for two reasons. First, it means content metadata (e.g., Content-Length and Content-Type) is readily available for us to analyze. Second, it is clear that the TrafficGuard system will be able to analyze and modify the vast majority of cellular traffic, since it is in plaintext.

Table 2.3 presents information about the types of HTTP content in TGdataset. We observe that images are the second most frequent type of content, but consume 71% of

(Footnote 2 continued)
do not pay for their Internet access in terms of traffic usage. Second, proxy-based traffic saving inevitably leads to latency penalty and thus would impact WiFi users' experiences.

Table 2.3 Statistics of HTTP content in TGdataset

Type	Percentage of requests (%)	Percentage of HTTP traffic (%)	Size (KB)	
			Median	Mean
Image	**32**	**71**	**5.7**	**15.5**
Text	**49**	**15.7**	**0.2**	**2.2**
Octet-stream	10	5.5	0.4	3.8
Zip	8.1	5.1	0.5	4.3
Audio and video	0.03	2.6	407	614
Other	0.87	0.1	0.3	0.7

(Reprinted with permission from [22].)

the entire HTTP traffic. Textual content is the most frequent, while nonimage binary content accounts for the remainder of HTTP traffic. We manually analyzed many of the octet-streams in our dataset and found that they mainly consist of software and video streams.

2.3.2.2   Size and Quality of Content

Next, we examine the size and quality of content in TGdataset, and relate these characteristics to the compressibility of content.

Images. Four image types dominate in our dataset: JPEG, WebP, PNG, and GIF. Certainly, all four types of images are already compressed. However, we observe that 40 % of images are *large*, which we define as images of $w \times h$ pixels such that $w \times h \geq 250,000 \wedge w \geq 150 \wedge h \geq 150$ (refer to Sect. 2.5.1 for more details of image categorization). Some images even have over 4000×4000 pixels (exceeding 10 MB in size) in extreme cases.

More importantly, we observe that many JPEGs have high *quality factors* (QFs). QF determines the strength of JPEG's lossy-compression algorithm, with QF $= 100$ causing minimal loss but a larger file size. The median QF of JPEGs in TGdataset is 80 while the average is 74. Such high-quality images are unnecessary for most cellular users, considering their limited data plans and screen sizes. This presents us with an optimization opportunity that TrafficGuard takes advantage of (see Sect. 2.5.1).

Textual content. The six most common types of textual content in TGdataset are: JSON, HTML, PLAIN, JavaScript, XML, and CSS. Compared with images, textual content is much smaller: the median size is merely 0.2 KB. Compressing the short texts with the size less than 0.2 KB (e.g., with gzip, bzip2, or 7-zip) cannot decrease their size; in fact, the additional compression metadata may even *increase* the size of such textual data.

Surprisingly, we find that compressing the other, larger half ($>$0.2 KB) of textual content with gzip brings limited benefits—it only reduced the HTTP traffic of texts by 8.7 %, equal to 1.36 % (= 8.7 % × 15.7 %) of total HTTP traffic. Similarly, using bzip2 and 7-zip could not significantly increase the compression rate. However, decompressing texts on user devices does necessitate additional computation and thus causes battery overhead. Given the limited network efficiency gains and the toll on battery life, we opt to not compress texts in TrafficGuard, unlike all other systems as listed in Table 2.1.

Other content. For the remaining octet-stream, zip, audio and video content, we find that compression provides negligible benefits, since almost all of them are already compressed (e.g., MP3 and VP9). Although it is possible to reduce network traffic by transcoding, scaling, or reducing the quality of multimedia content [12], we do not explore these potential optimizations in this work.

2.3.2.3 Content Validation

Delving deeper into the content downloaded by our volunteers, we discover a surprisingly high portion of useless content, particularly *broken* images. We define an image to be broken if it cannot be decoded by any of the three widely used image decoders: imghdr [31], Bitmap [32], and dwebp [33]. As shown in Table 2.4, 10.6 % of images in TGdataset are broken, wasting 3.2 % of all image traffic in our dataset (their average size is much smaller than that of correct images). Note that we also observe a small fraction of *blank* and *incomplete* images that we can decode, as well as a few *inconsistent* images that are actually not images, but we do not consider to obey our strict definition of correctness.

2.3.2.4 Traffic Filtering

As we note in Sect. 2.2, existing mobile traffic proxies have adopted multiple strategies for traffic filtering. In this section, we investigate the potential of four particular filtering strategies by analyzing TGdataset.

Table 2.4 Validity and usefulness of images

Type	Percentage of requests (%)	Percentage of image traffic (%)	Image size (KB):	
			Median	Mean
Correct	87	95.9	5.4	14.8
Broken	**10.6**	**3.2**	**0.13**	**3.2**
Blank	2.3	0.57	0	0
Incomplete	0.1	0.21	0.01	5.0
Inconsistent	0.04	0.16	4.8	33

(Reprinted with permission from [22].)

Overnight traffic. Prior studies have observed that many smartphones generate data traffic late at night, even when users are not using the devices [26, 28, 30]. If we conservatively assume that our volunteers are asleep between 0 and 6 AM, then 11.4 % of traffic in our dataset can potentially be filtered without noticeable impact on users. Based on this finding, we implemented a feature in TrafficGuard that allows users to specify a night time period during which cellular traffic is restricted (see Sect. 2.5.3).

Background traffic. Users expect foreground apps to consume data since they are interactive, but background apps may also consume network resources. Although this is expected in some cases (e.g., a user may stream music while also browsing the web), undesirable data consumption by background apps has become such a common complaint that numerous articles exist to help mitigate this problem [34–37]. In TGdataset, we observe that 26.7 % of cellular traffic is caused by background apps. To this end, we implemented dual filters in TrafficGuard specifically designed to reduce the network traffic of background apps (see Sect. 2.5.3).

Malicious traffic. A recent measurement study of Google Play reveals that more than 25 % of Android apps are malicious, including spammy, re-branded, and cloned apps [38]. We compare all the HTTP requests in TGdataset against a proprietary blacklist containing 29M links maintained by major Internet companies (including Baidu, Google, Microsoft, Symantec, Tencent, *etc.*), and find that 0.85 % of requests were issued for malicious content. We addressed this issue in TrafficGuard by filtering out HTTP requests for blacklisted URLs.

Advertisement traffic. In addition to malicious content, we also find that 4.15 % of HTTP requests in TGdataset were for ads. We determined this by comparing all the requested HTTP URLs in our dataset against a proprietary list of 102M known advertising URLs (similar to the well-known EasyList [39]). Ad blocking is a morally complicated practice, and thus we give TrafficGuard users the choice of whether to opt-in to ad filtering. Users' configuration data reveal that the majority (67 %) of users have chosen to block ads. On the other hand, we did get pushback from a small number of advertisers; when this happened, usually, we would remove the advertisers from our ad block list after verification.

2.3.2.5 Caching Strategies

Finally, we explore the feasibility of two common caching strategies. Unfortunately, we find neither technique offers satisfactory performance, which motives us to implement a more sophisticated caching strategy.

Name-based. Traditional web proxies like Squid [40] implement *name-based* caching of objects (i.e., objects are indexed by their URLs). However, this approach is known to miss many opportunities for caching [41–43]. To make matters worse, we observe that over half of the content in TGdataset is not cacheable by Squid due to HTTP protocol issues. This situation is further exacerbated by the fact that many start-of-the-art HTTP libraries do not support caching at all [44]. Thus, although TrafficGuard uses Squid in the back-end cloud, we decided to augment it with an additional, object-level caching strategy (known as VBWC, see Sect. 2.5.4).

HTTP ETag. The HTTP ETag [45] was introduced in HTTP/1.1 to mitigate the shortcomings of named-based caching. Unfortunately, the effectiveness of ETag is still limited by two constraints. First, as ETags are assigned arbitrarily by web servers, they do not allow clients to detect identical content served by multiple providers. This phenomenon is called content *aliasing* [46]. We observe that 14.16 % of HTTP requests in TGdataset are for aliased content, corresponding to 7.28 % of HTTP traffic. Second, we find that ETags are sparsely supported: only 5.76 % of HTTP responses include ETags.

2.4 System Overview

Our measurement findings in Sect. 2.3.2 provide useful guidelines for optimizing cellular traffic across apps. Additionally, we observe that some techniques used by prior systems (e.g., text compression) are not useful in practice. These findings guide the design of TrafficGuard for optimizing users' cellular traffic.

This section presents an overview of TrafficGuard, which consists of a front-end mobile app on users' devices and a set of back-end services. Below, we present the basic components of each end, with an emphasis on how these components support various traffic optimization mechanisms. Additional details about specific traffic optimization mechanisms are explained in Sect. 2.5.

Mobile app: the client-side support. The TrafficGuard mobile app is comprised of a user interface and a *child proxy*. The user interface is responsible for displaying cellular usage statistics, and allows users to configure TrafficGuard settings. The settings include enabling/disabling specific traffic optimization mechanisms, as well as options for specific mechanisms (the details are discussed in Sect. 2.5). We also leverage the user interface to collect feedback from users, which help us continually improve the design of TrafficGuard.

The child proxy does the real work of traffic optimization on the client side. It intercepts incoming and outgoing HTTP requests at the cellular interface, performs computations on them, and forwards (some) requests to the back-end cloud via a customized VPN tunnel. As shown in Fig. 2.3, the client-side VPN tunnel is implemented using the TUN virtual network-level device [47] that intercepts traffic from or injects traffic to the TCP/IP stack. HTTP GET requests[3] are captured by the child proxy, encapsulated, and then sent to the back-end cloud for further process-

---

[3]Non-GET HTTP requests (e.g., POST, HEAD, and PUT) and non-HTTP requests do not benefit from TrafficGuard's filtering and caching mechanisms, so the child proxy forwards them to the TCP/IP stack for regular processing. Furthermore, TrafficGuard makes no attempt to analyze SSL/TLS traffic for privacy reasons.

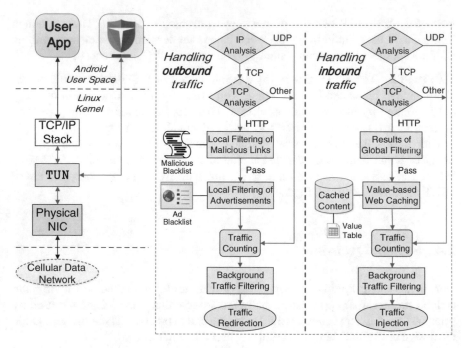

Fig. 2.3 Basic design of the child proxy. (Reprinted with permission from [22].)

ing. Accordingly, the child proxy is responsible for receiving responses from the back-end.

The mobile app provides client-side support for traffic optimization. First, it allows users to monitor and restrict cellular traffic at night and from background apps in a real-time manner. Users are given options to control how aggressively TrafficGuard filters these types of traffic. Second, it provides local filtering of malicious links and unwanted ads using two small blacklists of the most frequently visited malicious and advertising URLs. Requests for malicious URLs are dropped; users are given a choice of whether to enable ad blocking, in which case requests for ad-related URLs are also dropped.

Third, the child proxy acts as the client-side of a value-based web cache [46] (VBWC, see Sect. 2.5.4 for details). At a high level, the child proxy maintains a key-value store that maps MD5 hashes to pieces of content. The back-end cloud may return "VBWC Hit" responses to the client that contain the MD5 hash of some content, rather than the content itself. In this case, the child proxy retrieves the content from the key-value store using the MD5 hash, and then locally constructs an HTTP response containing the cached content. The reconstructed HTTP response is then returned to the corresponding user app. This process is fully transparent to user apps.

Web proxy: the back-end support. As shown in Fig. 2.4, the cloud side of Traffic-Guard consists of two components: a cluster of parent proxy servers that decapsulate

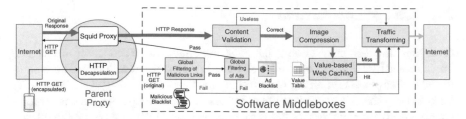

Fig. 2.4 Cloud-side overview of TrafficGuard. HTTP requests are generally processed from *left* to *right* by a cluster of parent proxy servers and a series of software middleboxes implemented on *top* of Nginx. (Reprinted with permission from [22].)

users' HTTP GET requests and fetch content from the Internet; and a series of software middleboxes that process HTTP responses.

Once an HTTP GET request sent by the child proxy is received, the parent proxy decapsulates it and extracts the *original* HTTP GET request. Next, middleboxes compare the original HTTP GET request against large blacklists of known malicious and ads-related URLs. Note that this HTTP GET request has passed the client-side filtering with small blacklists. Together, this two-level filtering scheme prevents TrafficGuard users from wasting memory loading large blacklists on their own devices. If a URL hits either blacklist, it is reported back to the mobile app so the user can be notified.

An HTTP request that passes the blacklist filters is forwarded to a Squid proxy, which fetches the requested content from the original source. The Squid proxy implements name-based caching of objects using an LRU (Least Recently Used) scheme, which helps reduce latency for popular objects. Once the content has been retrieved by Squid, it is further processed by middleboxes that validate content (Sect. 2.5.2) and compress images (Sect. 2.5.1).

Lastly, before the content is returned to users, it is indexed by VBWC (Sect. 2.5.4). VBWC maintains a separate index of content for every active user, which contains the MD5 hash of each piece of content recently downloaded by that user. For a given user, if VBWC discovers that some content is already indexed, it returns that MD5 in a "VBWC Hit" response to the mobile app, instead of the actual content. As described above, the child proxy then constructs a valid HTTP response message containing the cached content. Otherwise, the MD5 is inserted into the table and the actual content is sent to the user.

2.5 Mechanisms

This section presents the details of specific traffic optimization mechanisms in TrafficGuard. Since many of the mechanisms include user-configurable parameters, we gathered users' configuration data between Jul. 4 and Dec. 27, 2014. This dataset is referred to as TGconfig.

2.5.1 Image Compression

Overview. Image compression is the most important traffic reduction mechanism implemented by TrafficGuard, since our TGdataset shows that cellular traffic is dominated by images. Based on our observation that the majority of JPEGs have quality factors (QFs) that are excessively high for display on smartphone screens, Traffic-Guard adaptively compresses JPEGs by reducing their QFs to an acceptable level. Additionally, TrafficGuard transcodes PNGs and GIFs to JPEGs with an acceptable QF. Note that TrafficGuard does *not* transcode PNGs with transparency data or animated GIFs, to avoid image distortion. TrafficGuard ignores WebP images, since they are already highly compressed.

TrafficGuard's approach to image compression has three advantages over alternative strategies. First, as JPEG is the dominant image format supported by almost all (>99% to our knowledge) user apps, TrafficGuard does not need to transcode images back to their original formats on the client side. Second, our approach costs only 10–12% as much CPU as Flywheel's WebP-based transcoding method (see Sect. 2.6.3). Finally, our approach does not alter the pixel dimensions of images. This is important because many UI layout algorithms (e.g., CSS) are sensitive to the pixel dimensions of images, so rescaling images may break webpage and app UIs.

Categorizing Images. The challenge of implementing our adaptive QF reduction strategy is deciding how much to reduce the QFs of images. Intuitively, the QFs of large images can be reduced more than small images, since the resulting visual artifacts will be less apparent in larger images. Thus, following the approach of Ziproxy [48] (an open-source HTTP proxy widely used to compress images), we classify images into four categories according to their width (w) and height (h) in pixels:

- *Tiny* images contain <5000 pixels, i.e., $w \times h < 5000$.
- *Small* images include images with less than 50,000 pixels (i.e., $5000 \leq w \times h < 50,000$), as well as "slim" images with less than 150 width or height pixels (i.e., $w \times h \geq 5000 \wedge (w < 150 \vee h < 150)$).
- *Mid-size* images contain less than 250,000 pixels, that is $50,000 \leq w \times h < 250,000 \wedge w \geq 150 \wedge h \geq 150$.
- *Large* images contain no less than 250,000 pixels, that is $w \times h \geq 250,000 \wedge w \geq 150 \wedge h \geq 150$.

QF Reduction Scheme. After images are divided into the above four categories, we need to determine a proper *QF (reduction) scheme* for transcoding images in each category. Our goal is to maximize compression by reducing QF, while also minimizing the reductions of user-perceived image quality. To measure quality, we use structural similarity (SSIM) [49], which assesses the visual similarity between a compressed image and the original (1 means the two images are identical). Quantitatively, we calculate the SSIM and *compression ratio* ($= \frac{\text{Size of images after compression}}{\text{Size of images before compression}}$) corresponding to consecutive QFs, based on all the correct images in TGdataset. The results are plotted in Figs. 2.5 and 2.6.

Fig. 2.5 Average SSIM corresponding to consecutive QFs. (Reprinted with permission from [22].)

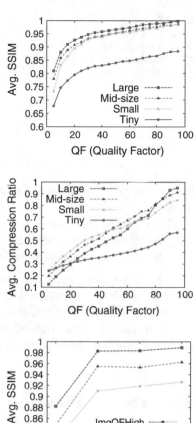

Fig. 2.6 Average compression ratio corresponding to consecutive QFs. (Reprinted with permission from [22].)

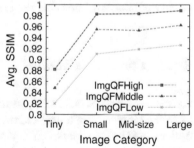

Fig. 2.7 Average SSIM corresponding to the three QF schemes. (Reprinted with permission from [22].)

Specifically, we define a QF scheme *ImgQFScheme* = {*T*, *S*, *M*, *L*} to mean that tiny, small, mid-size, and large images are compressed to QF = *T*, *S*, *M*, and *L*, respectively. In practice, we constructed three QF schemes that vary from high compression, less quality to low compression, high quality: *ImgQFLow* = {30, 25, 25, 20}, *ImgQFMiddle* = {60, 55, 50, 45}, and *ImgQFHigh* = {90, 90, 85, 80}. We then compressed all the correct images in TGdataset using each scheme to evaluate their impact on image quality and size.

Figure 2.7 examines the impact of each QF scheme on image quality. Prior work has shown that image compression with SSIM ≥0.85 is generally considered acceptable by users [7]. As shown in Fig. 2.7, all three QF schemes manage to stay above the 0.85 quality threshold for small, mid-size, and large images. The two cases where image quality becomes questionable concern tiny images, which are the hardest case for any compression strategy. Overall, these results suggest that in most cases, even

Fig. 2.8 Average compressed size corresponding to the three QF schemes. (Reprinted with permission from [22].)

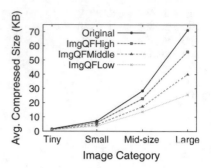

the aggressive *ImgQFLow* scheme will produce images with an acceptable level of fidelity.

Figure 2.8 examines the image size reduction enabled by each QF scheme, as compared to the original images. As expected, more aggressive QF schemes provide more size reduction, especially for large images.

User Behavior. The mobile app of TrafficGuard allows users to choose their desired QF scheme. Users must select a scheme after they install TrafficGuard. The data in TGconfig reveal that 95.4 % of users selected the *ImgQFMiddle* scheme. Also, qualitative feedback from TrafficGuard users suggests that they are satisfied with the quality of images while using the system.

2.5.2 Content Validation

As mentioned in Sect. 2.3.2.3, TrafficGuard users encounter a nontrivial amount of broken images when using apps. The back-end cloud of TrafficGuard naturally notices most broken images during the image analysis, transcoding, and compression process. In these cases, the cloud simply discards the broken image and sends a "Broken Warning" response to the client. From the requesting app's perspective, broken images appear to be missing due to a network error, and are handled as such.

2.5.3 Traffic Filtering

In this section, we present the implementation details of the four types of filters employed by TrafficGuard. Most traffic filtering in our system occurs on the client side (in the child proxy), including first-level filtering of malicious URLs and ads, and throttling of overnight and background traffic. Only second-level filtering of malicious URLs and ads occurs on the cloud side.

Restricting overnight traffic. The mobile app of TrafficGuard automatically turns the user's cellular data connection off between the hours of t_1 and t_2, which are configurable by the user. This feature is designed to halt device traffic during the night, when the user is likely to be asleep. TrafficGuard pops-up a notification just before t_1, alerting the user that her cellular connection will be turned off in ten seconds. Unless the user explicitly cancels the action, her cellular data connection will not be resumed until t_2. According to TGconfig, nearly 20% of users have enabled the overnight traffic filter, and 84% of them adopt the default night duration of 0–6 AM.

Throttling background traffic. To prevent malicious or buggy apps from draining users' limited data plans, TrafficGuard throttles traffic from background apps. Specifically, the TrafficGuard app has a configurable *warning bound* (B_1) and a *disconnection bound* (B_2), with $B_2 \gg B_1$. TrafficGuard also maintains a count c of the total bytes transferred by background apps. If c increases to B_1, TrafficGuard notifies the user that background apps are consuming a significant volume of traffic. If c reaches B_2, another notification is created to alert the user that her cellular data connection will be closed in ten seconds. Unless the user explicitly cancels this action or manually reopens the cellular data connection, her cellular data connection will not be resumed. After the user responds to the B_2 notification, c is reset to zero.

According to TGconfig, 97.6% of users have enabled the background traffic filter, indicating that users actually care about background traffic usage. Initially, we set the default warning bound $B_1 = 1.0$ MB. However, we observed over 57% of users decreased B_1 to 0.5 MB, indicating that they wanted to be reminded of background traffic usage more frequently. Conversely, the initial disconnection bound was $B_2 = 5$ MB, but 69% of users raised B_2 to 20 MB, implying that the initial default setting was too aggressive. Based on this implicit feedback, we changed the default values of B_1 and B_2 to 0.5 and 20 MB. In comparison, Microsoft Data Sense only maintains a disconnection bound (B_2) to restrict background traffic, and there is no default value provided.

Two-level filtering of malicious links and ads. To avoid wasting cellular traffic on unwanted content, TrafficGuard always prevents users from accessing malicious links, while giving users the choice of whether to opt-in to ad blocking. In Sect. 2.4, we have presented high-level design of the two-level filtering. Here we talk about two more nuanced implementation issues.

The first issue is about the sizes of the local, small blacklists. Both lists have to be loaded in memory by the child proxy for quick searching, so they must be much shorter than the cloud-side large blacklists (which contain 29M malicious URLs and 102M ads-related URLs). To balance memory overhead with effective local traffic filtering, we limit the maximum size of the local blacklists to 40 MB. Consequently, the local blacklists usually contain around 1M links in total, which we observe are able to identify 72–78% of malicious and ads links.

The second issue concerns updates to blacklists. As mentioned in Sect. 2.3.2.4, the large blacklists are maintained by an industrial union that typically updates them once per month. Accordingly, the TrafficGuard cloud automatically creates updated small blacklists and pushes them to mobile users.

2.5.4   Value-Based Web Caching (VBWC)

Early in 2003, Rhea et al. proposed VBWC to overcome the shortcomings of traditional HTTP caching [46]. The key idea of VBWC is to index objects by their *hash
values* rather than their URLs, since an object may have many *aliases*. VBWC has
a much better hit rate than HTTP caching because it handles aliased content. However, prior to TrafficGuard, VBWC has not been widely deployed in practice due
to two problems: (1) the *complexity* of segmenting an object into KB-sized blocks
and choosing proper block boundaries; (2) its *incompatibility* with the HTTP protocol, since VBWC requires that the proxy and the client maintain significant state
information, i.e., a mapping from hash values to cached content.

Reducing complexity. To determine whether TrafficGuard's VBWC implementation should segment content into blocks (and if so, at what granularity), we conduct trace-driven simulations using the content in TGdataset. Specifically, we played
back each user's log of requests, and inserted the content into VBWC using 8,
32, 128 KB, and full content segmentation strategies. To determine segment boundaries, we ran experiments with simple fixed-size segments [46] and variable-sized,
Rabin-fingerprinting based segments [50]. We also examined the handprinting-based
approach that combines Rabin-fingerprinting and deterministic sampling [51].

Through these simulations, we discovered that 13 % of HTTP requests would hit
the VBWC cache if we stored content whole, i.e., with no segmentation. Surprisingly, even if we segmented content into 8 KB blocks using the Rabin-fingerprinting
(the most aggressive caching strategy we evaluated), the hit rate only increased to
15 %. The handprinting-based approach exhibited similar performance to Rabin-
fingerprinting when a typical number ($k = 4$) of handprint samples are selected,
while incurring a bit lower computation overhead. By carefully analyzing the cache-
hit results, we find that the whole-content hashing is good enough for two reasons:
(1) images dominate the size of cache-hit objects in TGdataset; (2) there are almost
no partial matches among images. Thus, we conclude that a simple implementation
of content-level VBWC is sufficient to achieve high hit rates.

Addressing incompatibility. As discussed above, VBWC is incompatible with standard HTTP clients and proxies. Fortunately, we have complete control over the
TrafficGuard system, particulary the cloud-client paired proxies, which enabled us
to implement VBWC. The front-end child proxy takes care of encapsulating HTTP
requests from user apps and decapsulating responses from the back-end cloud, meaning that VBWC is transparent to user apps. In practice, the mobile app of TrafficGuard
maintains a 50-MB content cache on the client's file system, along with an in-memory
table mapping content hashes to filenames that is a few KB large.

Ideally, every change to the cloud-side mapping table triggers a change to the
client-side mapping table accordingly. But in practice, for various reasons (e.g.,
network packet loss) this pair of tables may be different at some time, so we need
to synchronize them with proper overhead. In TrafficGuard, the client-side mapping
table is loosely synchronized with the cloud-side mapping table on an hourly basis,
making the synchronization traffic negligible and VBWC mostly effective.

2.6 Evaluation

In this section, we evaluate the traffic reduction, system overhead, and latency penalty brought by TrafficGuard.

2.6.1 Data Collection and Methodology

We evaluate the performance of TrafficGuard using both real-system logs and trace-driven simulations. We collect working logs from TrafficGuard's back-end cloud servers between Dec. 21 and 27, 2014, which include traces of 350M HTTP requests issued from 0.6M users, as well as records of CPU and memory utilization over time on the cloud servers. We refer to this dataset as TGworklog.

On the other hand, as the client-side traffic optimization mechanisms mainly help users reduce traffic by suppressing unwanted requests, it is not possible to accurately record the corresponding saved traffic (which never occurred in reality). Instead, we rely on trace-driven simulations using TGdataset to estimate the client-side and overall traffic savings.

2.6.2 Traffic Reduction

Client-side. First, we examine the effectiveness of TrafficGuard's client-side mechanisms at reducing traffic. In TGdataset, 11.4 % of cellular traffic is transferred at night, and according to TGconfig, 20 % of users have enabled overnight traffic filtering. Thus, we estimate that users eliminate 2.3 % (=11.4 % × 20 %) of cellular traffic using the overnight traffic filter.

Moreover, we observe that 1 % of users in TGdataset regularly exceed the disconnection bound $B_2 = 20$ MB per day of background traffic. The resulting overage traffic amounts to 5.33 % of cellular traffic. In TGconfig, 97.6 % of users have enabled background traffic filtering. Therefore, we estimate that the background traffic filter reduces cellular traffic by 5.2 % (=5.33 % × 97.6 %). Note that this background traffic saving is an *under-estimation*, since we do not take the potential effect of B_1 (=0.5 MB, the warning bound) into account.

Additionally, in TGdataset malicious content accounts for 0.8 % of HTTP traffic while ads account for 4 %. According to TGconfig, 67 % of users have chosen to drop ads. Consequently, after all malicious content and unwanted ads are filtered, 3.48 % (=0.8 % + 4 % × 67 %) of HTTP traffic can be saved. This is equal to 2.8 % (=3.48 % × 80.4 %) of total cellular traffic.

Overall. Next, we evaluate how much traffic TrafficGuard is able to reduce overall through trace-driven simulations. Specifically, we play back all the requests in TGdataset, and record how many bytes are saved by each mechanism: traffic filtering,

Fig. 2.9 Total cellular traffic usage optimized by each mechanism. (Reprinted with permission from [22].)

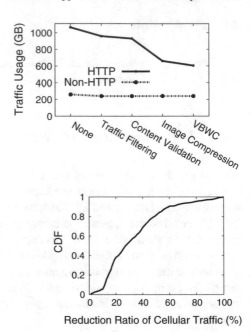

Fig. 2.10 Distribution of users' cellular traffic reduction ratios. (Reprinted with permission from [22].)

content validation, image compression, and VBWC. As shown in Fig. 2.9, Traffic-Guard is able to reduce HTTP traffic by 43 % and non-HTTP traffic by 7.4 % when all four mechanisms are combined. In summary, the overall cellular traffic usage is reduced by 36 %, from 1324 to 845 GB.

As expected, image compression is the most important mechanism when used in isolation. 38 % of the image traffic is reduced by our implemented adaptive quality reduction approach. In other words, our approach saves a comparable portion (27 % = 38 % × 71 %) of HTTP traffic as compared to Flywheel's WebP-based transcoding method, at a small fraction of the CPU cost (see Sect. 2.6.3).

To understand how traffic savings are spread across users, we plot the distribution of cellular traffic reduction ratios for our users in Fig. 2.10. We observe that 55 % of users saved over a quarter of cellular traffic, and 20 % users saved over a half (most of whom benefit a lot from traffic filtering and VBWC). These results demonstrate that most users received significant traffic savings.

Using TrafficGuard's built-in user-feedback facility, we asked users to report their cellular data caps. 95 % of the long-term volunteers in TGdataset reported their caps to us. Using this information, we plot Fig. 2.11, which shows the percentage of each user's data cap that would be used with and without TrafficGuard (again, based on trace-driven simulations). We observe that 58.2 % of users exceed their usage caps under normal circumstances, and that TrafficGuard grants significant practical benefits for these users, e.g., users who would normally be using 200–300 % of their allocation (and thus pay overage fees) are able to stay below 100 % usage with

Fig. 2.11 Users' cellular traffic usage relative to their data caps. (Reprinted with permission from [22].)

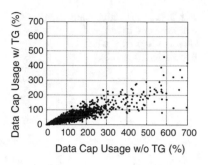

Table 2.5 Top-10 applications served by TrafficGuard, ordered by popularity and by greatest traffic reduction

By User Ratio (UR)			By Traffic Saving Ratio (TSR)		
App name	UR (%)	TSR (%)	App name	UR (%)	TSR (%)
WeChat	74	22	Android Browser	0.11	84
QQ	66	22	Zhihu Q&A	0.15	81
Baidu Search	29	21	iAround	0.03	63
Taobao	23	42	No.1 Store	0.26	61
QQBrowser	22	27	Baidu news	0.45	57
Sogou Pinyin	20	12	Tiexue military	0.01	56
Baidu Browser	16	30	WoChaCha	0.34	54
Toutiao News	14	22	Mogujie store	0.91	53
Sohu News	10	30	Koudai store	0.26	53
QQ Zone	10	33	Papa photo	0.02	52

(Reprinted with permission from [22].)

TrafficGuard. Overall, TrafficGuard reduces the number of users who exceed their data caps by 10.7 times.

At last, we wonder how TrafficGuard's traffic reduction gains are spread across user apps. Table 2.5 lists the top-10 apps ordered by popularity (the fraction of users with the app) as well as by the fraction of traffic eliminated. We observe that TrafficGuard is able to eliminate 12–42 % of traffic for popular apps, but that the apps with the greatest traffic savings (52–84 %) tend to be unpopular. This indicates that the developers of popular apps may already be taking steps to optimize their network traffic, while most unpopular apps can hardly become mobile-friendly in the near future.

Fig. 2.12 CPU and memory
overhead of the back-end
servers. (Reprinted with
permission from [22].)

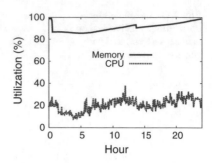

2.6.3   System Overhead

Cloud-side overhead. The major cost of operating TrafficGuard lies in provisioning
back-end cloud servers and supplying them with bandwidth. TrafficGuard has been
able to support ∼0.2M users who send ∼90M requests per day using only 23 commodity servers (HP ProLiant DL380). The configuration of each server is: 2*4-core
Xeon CPU E5-2609 @2.50GHz, 4*8-GB memory, and 6*300-GB 10K-RPM SAS
disk (RAID-6).

Figure 2.12 illustrates the CPU/memory utilization of cloud servers on a typical
day. Mainly thanks to our lightweight image compression strategy, the CPU utilization stays below 40 %. Further, to compare the computation overhead of our
image compression strategy with Flywheel's WebP-based transcoding (based on
the cwebp [52] encoder), we conduct offline experiments on two identical server
machines using 1M correct images randomly picked from TGdataset as the workload. Images are compressed one by one without intermission. The results in Fig. 2.13
confirm that the computation overhead (= average CPU utilization × total running
time) of TrafficGuard image compression is only a small portion (10–12 %) of that
of WebP-based transcoding.

Memory utilization is typically >90 % since content is in-memory cached whenever possible. Using a higher memory capacity, say 1 TB per server, can accelerate the
back-end processing and thus decrease the corresponding latency penalty. Nonethe-
less, as shown in Fig. 2.25, the back-end processing latency constitutes only a minor
portion of the total latency penalty, so we do not consider extending the memory
capacity in the short term.

Figure 2.14 reveals the inbound/outbound bandwidth for back-end servers. Interestingly, we observe that a back-end server uses more outbound bandwidth than
inbound, though inbound traffic has been optimized. This happens because the back-
end has a 38 % cache-hit rate (with 4 TB of disk cache), so many objects are downloaded from the Internet once but then downloaded by many clients.

Client-side overhead. The client-side overhead of TrafficGuard comes from three
sources: memory, computation, and battery usage. The memory usage is mod-
est, requiring 40 MB for local blacklists, and 10–20 MB for the VBWC mapping
table. Similarly, while running on a typical (8-core ARM CPU @1.7GHz) Android

Fig. 2.13 CPU overhead of
different image compression
strategies. (Reprinted with
permission from [22].)

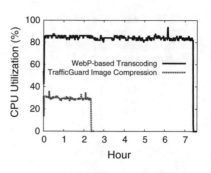

Fig. 2.14 Inbound and
outbound bandwidth for
back-end servers. (Reprinted
with permission from [22].)

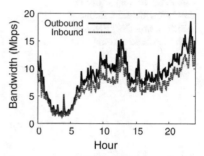

Fig. 2.15 Distribution of
client-side battery power
consumption. (Reprinted
with permission from [22].)

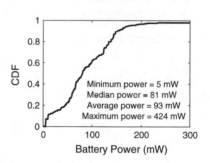

smartphone, TrafficGuard's single-core CPU usage is generally below 20 % when
the cellular modem is active, and almost zero when the network is inactive.

To understand the impact of TrafficGuard on battery life, we record the battery
power consumption of its mobile app when the child proxy is processing data packets.
As shown in Fig. 2.15, its working-state battery power is 93 mW on average, given
that the battery capacity of today's smartphones lies between 5–20 Wh and their
working-state battery power lies between 500 mW and a few watts [53, 54].

To understand specific facets of TrafficGuard's battery consumption, we conduct micro-benchmarks on the client side with three popular, diverse user apps:
the stock Android Browser, WeChat (the most popular app in China, similar to
WhatsApp), and Youku (China's equivalent of YouTube). In each case, we drove
the app for five minutes with and without TrafficGuard enabled while connected
to a 4G network. Figures 2.16, 2.17 and 2.18 show the battery usage in each

Fig. 2.16 Battery usage of
Android Browser with and
w/o TrafficGuard. (Reprinted
with permission from [22].)

Fig. 2.17 Battery usage of
WeChat with and without
TrafficGuard. (Reprinted
with permission from [22].)

Fig. 2.18 Battery usage of
Youku with and without
TrafficGuard. (Reprinted
with permission from [22].)

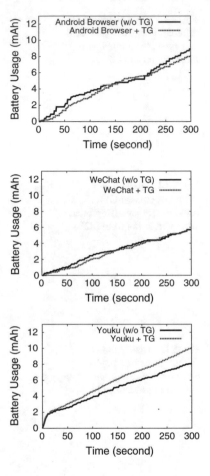

experiment. Meanwhile, Figs. 2.19, 2.20 and 2.21 depict the corresponding CPU
usage; Figs. 2.22, 2.23 and 2.24 plot the corresponding memory usage. All these
results reveal that in cases where TrafficGuard can effectively reduce network traffic (e.g., while browsing the web), it also saves battery life or has little impact on
battery life, because the user app needs to process less traffic; accordingly, Traffic-
Guard does not increase CPU/memory usage on the whole. However, in cases where
TrafficGuard can hardly reduce any traffic (e.g., Youku video streaming), it reduces
battery life and increases CPU/memory usage. Thus, we are planning to improve
the design of TrafficGuard, in order that it can recognize and bypass the traffic from
audio/video streams.

Fig. 2.19 CPU usage of
Android Browser with and
w/o TrafficGuard. (Reprinted
with permission from [22].)

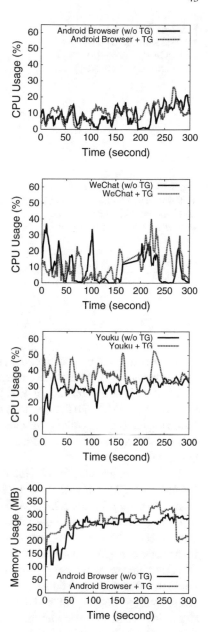

Fig. 2.20 CPU usage of
WeChat with and without
TrafficGuard. (Reprinted
with permission from [22].)

Fig. 2.21 CPU usage of
Youku with and without
TrafficGuard. (Reprinted
with permission from [22].)

Fig. 2.22 Memory usage of
Android Browser with and
w/o TrafficGuard. (Reprinted
with permission from [22].)

2.6.4 Latency Penalty

As TrafficGuard forwards HTTP GET requests to a back-end proxy rather than
directly to the source, it may add response latency to clients' requests. In addition,
client-side packet processing by the child proxy also brings extra latency. To put the

Fig. 2.23 Memory usage of
WeChat with and without
TrafficGuard. (Reprinted
with permission from [22].)

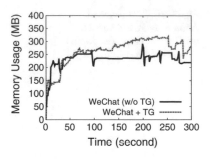

Fig. 2.24 Memory usage of
Youku with and without
TrafficGuard. (Reprinted
with permission from [22].)

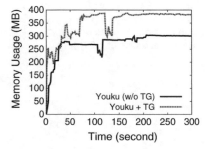

latency penalty into perspective, first, we note three mitigating factors that effectively reduce latency: (1) TrafficGuard filters out ∼10.3 % of requests locally, which eliminates all latency except for client-side processing; (2) the ∼21.2 % of traffic that is not owing to HTTP GET requests is delivered over the Internet normally, thus only incurring the latency penalty for client-side processing; and (3) 38 % of HTTP GET requests hit the back-end Squid cache, thus eliminating the time needed to fetch the content from the Internet.

Next, to understand TrafficGuard's latency penalty in the worst-case scenario (unfiltered HTTP GETs that do not hit the Squid cache), we examine latency data from TGworklog. Figure 2.25 plots the total latency of requests that go through the TrafficGuard back-end and miss the cache, as well as the individual latency costs of four aspects of the system: (1) processing time on the client side, (2) processing time in the back-end, (3) time for the back-end to fetch the desired content, and (4) the RTT from the client to the back-end. Figure 2.25 shows that both client-side processing and back-end processing add little delay to requests. Instead, the majority of delay comes from fetching content, and the RTT from clients to the back-end cloud. Interestingly, Fig. 2.26 reveals that the average processing time of an outbound packet is longer than that of an inbound packet, although outbound packets are usually smaller than inbound packets. This is because the client-side filtering of malicious links and ads is the major source of client-side latency penalty.

In the worst-case scenario, we see that TrafficGuard does add significant latency to user requests. If we conservatively assume that clients can fetch content with the same latency distribution as Baidu's servers, then TrafficGuard adds 131 ms of latency in the median case and 474 ms of latency in the average case. However, if we

Fig. 2.25 Latency for each phase content processing and retrieval. (Reprinted with permission from [22].)

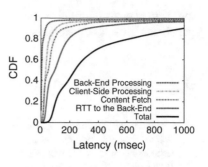

Fig. 2.26 Latency for clients' processing data packets. (Reprinted with permission from [22].)

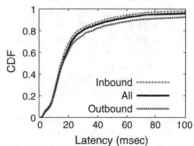

take into account the three mitigating factors listed at the beginning of this section (which all reduce latency), the median latency penalty across all traffic is reduced to merely 53 ms, and the average is reduced to 282 ms.

2.7 Conclusion

Traffic optimization is a common desire of today's cellular users, carriers, and service developers. Although several existing systems can optimize the cellular traffic for specific apps (typically web browsers), cross-app systems are much rarer, and have not been comprehensively studied. In this chapter, we share our design approach and implementation experiences in building and maintaining TrafficGuard, a real-world cross-app cellular traffic optimization system used by 10 million users.

To design TrafficGuard, we took a measurement-driven methodology to select optimization strategies that are not only high-impact (i.e., they significantly reduce traffic) but also efficient, easy to implement, and compatible with heterogenous apps. This methodology led to some surprising findings, including the relative ineffectiveness of text compression. Real-world performance together with trace-driven experiments indicates that our system meets its stated goal of reducing traffic (by 36 % on average), while also being efficient (23 commodity servers are able to handle the entire workload). In the future, we plan to approach cellular carriers about integrating TrafficGuard into their networks, since this will substantially decrease latency penalties for users and simplify the overall design of the system.

References

1. Cisco Visual Networking Index: Global Mobile Data Traffic Forecast Update 2014-2019 White Paper. http://www.cisco.com/c/en/us/solutions/collateral/service-provider/visual-networking-index-vni/white_paper_c11-520862.html
2. Isaacman, S., Martonosi, M.: Low-infrastructure methods to improve internet access for mobile users in emerging regions. In: Proceedings of the 20th International World Wide Web Conference (WWW), pp. 473–482 (2011)
3. Johnson, D., Pejovic, V., Belding, E., van Stam, G.: Traffic characterization and internet usage in Rural Africa. In: Proceedings of the 20th International World Wide Web Conference (WWW), pp. 493–502 (2011)
4. Li, Z., Wilson, C., Xu, T., Liu, Y., Lu, Z., Wang, Y.: Offline downloading in China: a comparative study. In: Proceedings of the 15th ACM Internet Measurement Conference (IMC), pp. 473–486 (2015)
5. Google to websites: be mobile-friendly or get buried in search results. http://mashable.com/2015/04/21/google-mobile-search-2/#UbuurRKFaPqU
6. The State Of Digital Experience Delivery (2015). https://www.forrester.com/The+State+Of+Digital+Experience+Delivery+2015/fulltext/-/E-RES120070
7. Agababov, V., Buettner, M., Chudnovsky, V., Cogan, M., Greenstein, B., McDaniel, S., Piatek, M., Scott, C., Welsh, M., Yin, B.: Flywheel: Google's data compression proxy for the mobile web. In: Proceedings of the 12th USENIX Symposium on Networked Systems Design and Implementation (NSDI), pp. 367–380 (2015)
8. Opera Turbo mobile web proxy. http://www.opera.com/turbo
9. QQBrowser. http://browser.qq.com
10. UCBrowser. http://www.ucweb.com
11. Cui, Y., Lai, Z., Wang, X., Dai, N., Miao, C.: QuickSync: improving synchronization efficiency for mobile cloud storage services. In: Proceedings of the 21st ACM International Conference on Mobile Computing and Networking (MobiCom), pp. 592–603 (2015)
12. Li, Z., Huang, Y., Liu, G., Wang, F., Zhang, Z.L., Dai, Y.: Cloud transcoder: bridging the format and resolution gap between internet videos and mobile devices. In: Proceedings of the 22nd SIGMM Workshop on Network and Operating Systems Support for Digital Audio and Video (NOSSDAV), pp. 33–38 (2012)
13. Li, Z., Jin, C., Xu, T., Wilson, C., Liu, Y., Cheng, L., Liu, Y., Dai, Y., Zhang, Z.L.: Towards network-level efficiency for cloud storage services. In: Proceedings of the 14th ACM Internet Measurement Conference (IMC), pp. 115–128 (2014)
14. Data Sense for Windows Phone apps. http://www.windowsphone.com/en-us/how-to/wp8/connectivity/use-data-sense-to-manage-data-usage
15. Onavo Extend for Android. http://www.onavo.com/apps/android_extend
16. Opera Max. http://www.operasoftware.com/products/opera-max
17. Opera Max, China's version. http://www.oupeng.com/max
18. Woo, S., Jeong, E., Park, S., Lee, J., Ihm, S., Park, K.: Comparison of caching strategies in modern cellular backhaul networks. In: Proceedings of the 11th ACM International Conference on Mobile Systems, Applications, and Services (MobiSys), pp. 319–332 (2013)
19. Naylor, D., Schomp, K., Varvello, M., Leontiadis, I., Blackburn, J., Lopez, D., Papagiannaki, K., Rodriguez, P., Steenkiste, P.: Multi-context TLS (mcTLS): enabling secure in-network functionality in TLS. In: Proceedings of the 2015 ACM Conference on Special Interest Group on Data Communication (SIGCOMM), pp. 199–212 (2015)

20. Rao, A., Kakhki, A., Razaghpanah, A., Tang, A., Wang, S., Sherry, J., Gill, P., Krishnamurthy, A., Legout, A., Mislove, A., Choffnes, D.: Using the Middle to Meddle with Mobile. Technical report NEU-CCS-2013-12-10, CCIS, Northeastern University

21. Sherry, J., Lan, C., Popa, R., Ratnasamy, S.: BlindBox: deep packet inspection over encrypted traffic. In: Proceedings of the 2015 ACM Conference on Special Interest Group on Data Communication (SIGCOMM), pp. 213–226 (2015)

22. Li, Z., Wang, W., Xu, T., Zhong, X., Li, X.Y., Wilson, C., Zhao, B.Y.: Exploring cross-application cellular traffic optimization with Baidu trafficguard. In: Proceedings of the 13th USENIX Symposium on Networked Systems Design and Implementation (NSDI), pp. 61–76 (2016)

23. WebP: a new image format for the Web. http://developers.google.com/speed/webp

24. Institutional review board (IRB). https://en.wikipedia.org/wiki/Institutional_review_board

25. Google Safe Browsing. http://developers.google.com/safe-browsing

26. Aucinas, A., Vallina-Rodriguez, N., Grunenberger, Y., Erramilli, V., Papagiannaki, K., Crowcroft, J., Wetherall, D.: Staying online while mobile: the hidden costs. In: Proceedings of the 9th ACM Conference on emerging Networking EXperiments and Technologies (CoNEXT), pp. 315–320 (2013)

27. Falaki, H., Lymberopoulos, D., Mahajan, R., Kandula, S., Estrin, D.: A first look at traffic on smartphones. In: Proceedings of the 10th ACM Internet Measurement Conference (IMC), pp. 281–287 (2010)

28. Huang, J., Qian, F., Mao, Z., Sen, S., Spatscheck, O.: Screen-off traffic characterization and optimization in 3G/4G networks. In: Proceedings of the 12th ACM Internet Measurement Conference (IMC), pp. 357–364 (2012)

29. Lumczanu, C., Guo, K., Spring, N., Bhattacharjee, B.: The effect of packet loss on redundancy elimination in cellular wireless networks. In: Proceedings of the 10th ACM Internet Measurement Conference (IMC), pp. 294–300 (2010)

30. Qian, F., Wang, Z., Gao, Y., Huang, J., Gerber, A., Mao, Z., Sen, S., Spatscheck, O.: Periodic transfers in mobile applications: network-wide origin, impact, and optimization. In: Proceedings of the 21th International World Wide Web Conference (WWW), pp. 51–60 (2012)

31. imghdr—Determine the type of an image. http://docs.python.org/2/library/imghdr.html

32. System.Drawing.Bitmap class in the .NET Framework. http://msdn.microsoft.com/library/system.drawing.bitmap(v=vs.110).aspx

33. dwebp—Decompress a WebP file to an image file. http://developers.google.com/speed/webp/docs/dwebp

34. Android OS background data increase since 4.4.4 update. http://forums.androidcentral.com/moto-g-2013/422075-android-os-background-data-increase-since-4-4-4-update-please-help.html

35. Android OS is continuously downloading something in the background. http://android.stackexchange.com/questions/28100/android-os-is-continuously-downloading-something-in-the-background-how-can-i

36. How to Minimize Your Android Data Usage and Avoid Overage Charges. http://www.howtogeek.com/140261/how-to-minimize-your-android-data-usage-and-avoid-overage-charges

37. Vergara, E., Sanjuan, J., Nadjm-Tehrani, S.: Kernel level energy-efficient 3G background traffic shaper for android smartphones. In: Proceedings of the 9th IEEE International Wireless Communications and Mobile Computing Conference (IWCMC), pp. 443–449 (2013)

38. Viennot, N., Garcia, E., Nieh, J.: A measurement study of google play. ACM SIGMETRICS Perform. Eval. Rev. **42**(1), 221–233 (2014)

39. Adblock Plus EasyList for ad blocking. http://easylist.adblockplus.org

40. Wessels, D.: Squid: The Definitive Guide. O'Reilly Media, Inc. (2004)

41. Fielding, R., Gettys, J., Mogul, J., Frystyk, H., Masinter, L., Leach, P., Berners-Lee, T.: Hypertext transfer protocol—HTTP/1.1 (1999)

42. Qian, F., Sen, S., Spatscheck, O.: Characterizing resource usage for mobile web browsing. In: Proceedings of the 12th ACM International Conference on Mobile Systems, Applications, and Services (MobiSys), pp. 218–231 (2014)

43. Spring, N., Wetherall, D.: A protocol-independent technique for eliminating redundant network traffic. In: Proceedings of the 2000 ACM Conference on Special Interest Group on Data Communication (SIGCOMM), pp. 87–95 (2000)

44. Qian, F., Quah, K., Huang, J., Erman, J., Gerber, A., Mao, Z., Sen, S., Spatscheck, O.: Web caching on smartphones: ideal vs. reality. In: Proceedings of the 10th ACM International Conference on Mobile Systems, Applications, and Services (MobiSys), pp. 127–140 (2012)

45. HTTP ETag. http://en.wikipedia.org/wiki/HTTP_ETag

46. Rhea, S., Liang, K., Brewer, E.: Value-based web caching. In: Proceedings of the 12th International World Wide Web Conference (WWW), pp. 619–628 (2003)

47. Universal TUN/TAP device driver. http://www.kernel.org/doc/Documentation/networking/tuntap.txt

48. Ziproxy: the HTTP traffic compressor. http://ziproxy.sourceforge.net

49. Wang, Z., Bovik, A., Sheikh, H., Simoncelli, E.: Image quality assessment: from error visibility to structural similarity. IEEE Trans. Image Process. (TIP) **13**(4), 600–612 (2004)

50. Rabin, M.: Fingerprinting by Random Polynomials. Technical report TR-15-81, Center for Research in Computing Technology, Harvard University (1981)

51. Pucha, H., Andersen, D., Kaminsky, M.: Exploiting similarity for multi-source downloads using file handprints. In: Proceedings of the 4th USENIX Conference on Networked Systems Design and Implementation (NSDI), pp. 2–2 (2007)

52. cwebp—Compress an image file to a WebP file. http://developers.google.com/speed/webp/docs/cwebp

53. Carroll, A., Heiser, G.: An analysis of power consumption in a smartphone. In: Proceedings of the 2010 USENIX Annual Technical Conference (ATC), pp. 21–21 (2010)

54. Liu, Y., Xiao, M., Zhang, M., Li, X., Dong, M., Ma, Z., Li, Z., Chen, S.: GoCAD: GPU-assisted online content adaptive display power saving for mobile devices in internet streaming. In: Proceedings of the 25th International World Wide Web Conference (WWW), pp. 1329–1338 (2016)

Part III
Cloud-Based Mobile Video Distribution

Chapter 3
Cloud Downloading for Unpopular Videos

Abstract Video content distribution dominates the Internet traffic. The state-of-the-art techniques generally work well in distributing popular videos, but do not provide satisfactory content distribution service for *unpopular videos* due to low data health or low data transfer rate. In recent years, the worldwide deployment of cloud utilities provides us with a novel perspective to consider the above problem. We propose and implement the *cloud download* scheme, which achieves high-quality video content distribution by using cloud utilities to *guarantee the data health* and *enhance the data transfer rate*. Specifically, a user sends his video request to the cloud which subsequently downloads the video from the Internet and stores it in the cloud cache. Then the user can usually retrieve his requested video (whether popular or unpopular) from the cloud with a high data rate in any place at any time via the intra-cloud data transfer acceleration. Running logs of our real deployed commercial system (named VideoCloud) confirm the effectiveness and efficiency of cloud download. The users' average data transfer rate of unpopular videos exceeds 1.6 Mbps, and over 80 % of the data transfer rates are more than 300 Kbps which is the basic playback rate of online videos. Our study provides practical experiences and valuable heuristics for making use of cloud utilities to achieve efficient Internet video delivery.

3.1 Introduction

Video content distribution dominates the Internet traffic. A recent Cisco report [1] says that nearly 90 % of all the consumer IP traffic is expected to consist of video content distribution. Therefore, achieving *high-quality* video content distribution over the Internet is of great significance for both academia and industry. Here the meaning of *high quality* is twofold: *high data health* and *high data transfer rate*. The metric *data health* is initially used in the BitTorrent protocol [2]. It denotes the number of available full copies of the shared file in a BitTorrent swarm. For example, the data health 1.0 means one full copy is available, and a swarm with data health less than 1.0 is called an *unhealthy* swarm because no peer in the swarm can get a full copy. In this chapter, we keep using *data health* to represent the data redundancy level of a video file. High data health implies that the user is able to obtain a full

© Springer Science+Business Media Singapore 2016   51
Z. Li et al., *Content Distribution for Mobile Internet: A Cloud-based Approach*,
DOI 10.1007/978-981-10-1463-5_3

copy of the video, and high data transfer rate enables the advanced function of online video streaming (including live streaming [3] and on-demand streaming [4]).

The state-of-the-art techniques of video content distribution mainly include CDN (content distribution network like Akamai) and P2P. CDN is the traditional technique that optimizes the performance of Internet content distribution by strategically deploying edge servers at multiple locations (often over multiple ISP networks). These edge servers cooperate with each other by replicating or moving data according to data popularity and server load. An end user usually obtains a copy of data from a nearby edge server, so that the data transfer rate is greatly enhanced and the load on the original data source is reduced. However, for the sake of limited storage and bandwidth capacity, it is not cost-effective for CDN to replicate unpopular videos to edge servers [5], considering that there are many more unpopular videos than popular videos over the Internet. Moreover, CDN is a charged facility that only serves the content providers who have paid, rather than a public utility of the Internet. Consequently, it is impractical to count on CDN for efficient distribution of unpopular videos.

Different from CDN, P2P content distribution mainly relies on the unstable but numerous end users to form peer-to-peer data swarms, where data is directly exchanged between neighboring peers. The real strength of P2P shows when a popular video is distributed, because a popular video is shared by a number of peers and more peers usually imply higher data health and higher degree of download parallelism, which further lead to higher data transfer rate. As to an unpopular video, it is often difficult to find a corresponding peer swarm. Even if the peer swarm exists, the few peers are unlikely to have high data health or high data transfer rate, and thus each peer has to stay online for long hours to wait for the download completion—a tedious process of low efficiency. In a word, although CDN and P2P generally work well in distributing popular videos, neither of them is able to provide satisfactory content distribution service for unpopular videos, due to low data health or low data transfer rate.

In recent years, the worldwide deployment of cloud utilities provides us with a novel perspective to consider the above problem. In this chapter, we propose and implement the *cloud download* scheme, which achieves high-quality video content distribution by using cloud utilities to *guarantee the data health* and *enhance the data transfer rate*. The principle of cloud download is depicted in Fig. 3.1. First, a user sends his video request to the cloud (see Arrow 1 in Fig. 3.1). The video request contains a file link which can be an HTTP/FTP link, a BitTorrent/eMule link, and so on.[1] Subsequently, the cloud *downloads* the requested video from the file link and stores it in the cloud cache (see Arrow 2 in Fig. 3.1) to guarantee the data health of the video ≥ 1.0 (each video also has a duplicate in the cloud cache for redundancy). Then the cloud notifies the user (see Arrow 3 in Fig. 3.1) and the user can usually

---

[1]The cloud does not accept keywords as the video request, because one keyword or a combination of several keywords may correspond to multiple videos with different contents in the Internet.

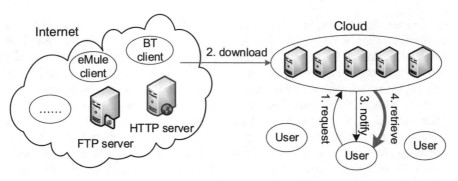

Fig. 3.1 Working principle of cloud download. (Reprinted with permission from [6].)

retrieve[2] his requested video (whether popular or unpopular) from the cloud with a high data rate (see Arrow 4 in Fig. 3.1) in any place at any time, via the intra-cloud data transfer acceleration (which will be addressed in detail in Sect. 3.3.2). In practice, the cloud does not need to notify the user when his requested video is available. Instead, the user actively checks the download progress by himself and takes corresponding actions. That is to say, Arrow 3 in Fig. 3.1 can also be replaced by "3. check".

Besides, an important derivative advantage brought by cloud download is the *user-side energy efficiency*. An Internet user often has to keep his computer (and network interface card) powered on for long hours (says t_1) only to download an unpopular video [7]. During this process, a lot of energy is wasted because the major components (including CPU, memory, disk, and so forth) keep working but are not efficiently used. Cloud download uses the cloud servers to download the requested videos, so its users do not need to be online; in fact, they do not need to open their computers at all—this is the reason why we also call "cloud download" as "offline download." When the requested video is available in the cloud, the user can usually retrieve it in short time (says t_2). Thus, cloud download significantly reduces the user-side energy cost (by the ratio $\frac{t_1-t_2}{t_1}$). The detailed energy efficiency analysis will be presented in Sect. 3.4.5.

The only drawback of cloud download lies in that for some videos, the user must wait for the cloud to finish the downloading and thus he cannot view the video at once. The above-mentioned wait time is denoted as the *view startup delay*. Note that CDN and P2P also have their view startup delay to buffer a certain amount of data for a smooth view startup of the video (e.g., buffer the first several minutes' data for a 100-min video). This drawback is effectively alleviated by the *implicit and secure data reuse among the users* of cloud download. For each video, the cloud only downloads it from the Internet when it is requested for the first time, and the subsequent requests are directly satisfied by using the cached copy with a very low view startup delay (except when the cached copy is replaced). Such data reuse is

---

[2]Here we use *retrieve* to distinguish with *download*. In this chapter, *download* means the cloud obtains data from the Internet while *retrieve* means the user obtains data from the cloud.

more secure than the explicit data reuse among P2P users (which is susceptible to
the Sybil attack [8], Eclipse attack [9], DHT attack [10], and so on), because it is
completely handled by the cloud and is oblivious to users. According to the real
system performance, the data reuse rate among the users reaches 87 %, indicating
that most video requests are satisfied instantly with a very low view startup delay.

Since June 2010, we have deployed a large-scale commercial cloud download
system named VideoCloud (http://xf.qq.com/help_video.html), using a "micro" data
center composed of 426 commodity servers. VideoCloud has attracted over 6 million
registered users and supports most of the mainstream content distribution protocols
like HTTP, FTP, BitTorrent, eMule, and so on. Currently, VideoCloud receives over
0.2 million video requests sent from around 50,000 users per day, and most of the
requests are issued for unpopular videos. The data center of VideoCloud has been
deployed across four major ISPs in China and is planned to cover more domains.
The user's monetary cost for cloud download service differs from Amazon S3 and
Microsoft Azure, and it is more similar to Dropbox. Specifically, the user of Video-
Cloud is charged according to the cloud storage capacity and regardless of the bandwidth consumed. Any registered user is allocated with 5-GB free storage, and extra
storage is charged in the unit of 5 GB.

The system running logs confirm the effectiveness and efficiency of cloud download. For example, the users' average data transfer rate of unpopular videos exceeds
1.6 Mbps, and over 80 % of the data transfer rates are more than 300 Kbps which is
the basic playback rate of online videos. In comparison, when the *common download
method* is used, the average data transfer rate is merely 0.57 Mbps, and 70 % of the
data transfer rates are less than 300 Kbps. The common download method denotes
the common way in which a user downloads video content from the Internet, e.g.,
using a web browser or a P2P client software to download a video. Besides, compared
with the common download method, cloud download reduces the user-side energy
cost by around 92 %.

In conclusion, our contributions in this chapter are as follows:

1. We analyze the state-of-the-art techniques of video content distribution (i.e., CDN
   and P2P) and discover that neither of them is able to provide satisfactory content
   distribution service for unpopular videos. Driven by this problem, we propose
   and implement the novel cloud download scheme, which achieves high-quality
   video content distribution by using cloud utilities to guarantee the data health and
   enhance the data transfer rate. The only drawback of cloud download, i.e., the
   view startup delay, is effectively alleviated by the implicit and secure data reuse
   among the users.

2. We have deployed VideoCloud, a large-scale commercial cloud download system.
   And we present its system architecture and design techniques, as well as our
   observations, analysis, and insights. Our study provides practical experiences and
   valuable heuristics for making use of cloud utilities to achieve efficient Internet
   services.

3. We evaluate the performance of VideoCloud via its running logs using three major metrics: data transfer rate, view startup delay, and energy efficiency. The evaluation results confirm the effectiveness and efficiency of cloud download.

3.2 Related Work

As the bandwidth in the core (backbone) and access networks for end users continuously grows, people have been putting forward higher and higher demand on video content distribution. The pixel resolution has improved from CIF (common intermediate format, 352*288), VGA (video graphics array, 640*480), to HD (high-definition, 1280*720), and the playback mode has evolved from view after download to view as download. In the past 15 years, high-quality video content distribution has been a research hot-spot in both industry and academia [11], in particular the state-of-the-art techniques: CDN and P2P. The advantages and disadvantages of CDN, P2P, and cloud download have been briefly addressed in the previous section. Recently, some researchers have recognized the limitations of both CDN and P2P, and thus proposed many novel schemes by combining or optimizing CDN and P2P.

Based on ChinaCache, the biggest commercial CDN service provider in China, Yin et al. developed a *hybrid CDN-P2P* live streaming system (named LiveSky [12]) to incorporate the strengths on both sides: the scalability of P2P, and the quality control capability and reliability of CDN. Although the hybrid CDN-P2P architecture inevitably brings extra deployment complication and maintenance cost, LiveSky achieves lower burden on the CDN network and higher efficiency of peer streaming for popular videos. However, for unpopular files, it is difficult and inefficient for the limited number of users to form a peer swarm, and the performance of LiveSky resembles that of a common CDN.

Wu et al. refocused on the importance of servers in P2P streaming systems and thus proposed the *server-assisted P2P* streaming scheme named Ration [13]. Based on a 7-month running trace of a commercial P2P live streaming system named UUSee, they found that the total available bandwidth of the 150 streaming servers could not meet the increasing demand of download bandwidth from hundreds of channels (a channel can be seen as a peer swarm), although the total upload bandwidth of peers also increased with download demand. So they proposed an allocation algorithm of server bandwidth, named Ration, which could proactively predict the minimum server bandwidth demand of each channel, based on historical information. Therefore, each channel can be guaranteed with desirable streaming quality. Ration has the similar shortcoming as LiveSky because every channel of UUSee can be seen as a very popular video. For unpopular videos, Ration would work like the traditional client–server video streaming scheme too.

During past years there have been a strong trend in *extremely high-quality* video content distribution like online HDTV (high-definition TV) and cinematic-quality VoD (video on demand) [14]. Undoubtedly, extremely high-quality videos can provide Internet users with wonderful viewing experiences; however, the content

distribution of extremely high-quality videos (in particular those unpopular videos
without powerful CDN support) over the highly dynamic Internet environments has
still been a big challenge. The latest practical solution may be Novasky [14], an operational "P2P storage cloud" for on-demand streaming of cinematic-quality videos
over a high-bandwidth network (i.e., the campus network of Tsinghua University).
The limitation of Novasky is obvious: it works on a high-bandwidth campus network
which is much more stable and homogeneous than the real Internet. Cloud download
uses cloud utilities to guarantee the data health of videos and meanwhile enhance
the data transfer rate to quite high and stable. Thus, cloud download is a promising solution to the future extremely high-quality video content distribution over the
Internet.

3.3 System Design

In this section, we present the system architecture and enabling techniques of Video-
Cloud, as well as our observations, analysis, and insights.

3.3.1 System Overview

As depicted in Fig. 3.2, the architecture of VideoCloud is mainly composed of five
building blocks: (1) *ISP Proxies*, (2) *Task Manager*, (3) *Task Dispatcher*, (4) *Downloaders*, and (5) *Cloud Cache*. The detailed hardware composition of each building
block is listed in Table 3.1. Note that all the information of Memory, Storage, and
Bandwidth refers to one server. We do not list the CPU information since the performance of CPU is not important for our system which is data (bandwidth and
storage) intensive rather than computation intensive. In total, the system utilizes 426

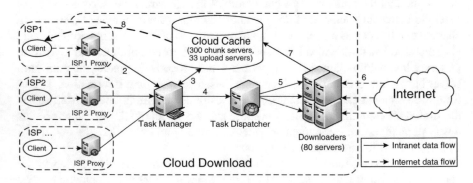

Fig. 3.2 System architecture of cloud download. (Reprinted with permission from [6].)

Table 3.1 Hardware composition of VideoCloud

Building block	Number of servers	Memory	Storage	Bandwidth
ISP Proxy	4	8 GB	250 GB	1 Gbps (Intranet), 0.3 Gbps (Internet)
Task Manager	4	8 GB	250 GB	1 Gbps (Intranet)
Task Dispatcher	3	8 GB	460 GB	1 Gbps (Intranet)
Downloaders	80	8 GB	460 GB	1 Gbps (Intranet), 0.325 Gbps (Internet)
Cloud Cache	300 chunk servers, 33 upload servers, and 2 index servers	8 GB	4 TB (chunk server), and 250 GB (upload server)	1 Gbps (Intranet), and 0.6 Gbps (Internet)

Reprinted with permission from [6]

commodity servers, including 300 chunk servers making up a 600-TB cloud cache, 80 download servers with 26 Gbps of Internet bandwidth, and 33 upload servers with 20 Gbps of Internet bandwidth. Every server runs the Suse Linux v10.1 operating system. Now we describe the organization and working process of the system by following the message and data flows of a typical cloud download task.

The user of VideoCloud should have installed its client software. The client software is able to recognize which ISP the user locates at from the user's IP address (with the help of an embedded and periodically updated IP-ISP mapping file), so the video request is firstly sent to the corresponding ISP Proxy by the client software (see Arrow 1 in Fig. 3.2). Each ISP Proxy maintains a *request queue* to control the number of requests sent to the Task Manager (see Arrow 2 in Fig. 3.2), so that the Task Manager is resilient to request upsurge in any ISP. Presently, VideoCloud has set four ISP Proxies in the four major ISPs in China: China Telecom, China Unicom, China Mobile, and CERNET (China Education and Research Network). If the user does not locate at any of the four major ISPs (such users take a small portion), his video request is sent to a random one of the four ISP Proxies. We plan to set more ISP Proxies in more ISPs in the future.

On receiving a video request, the Task Manager first checks whether the requested video has a copy in the Cloud Cache (see Arrow 3 in Fig. 3.2). If the video request is a BitTorrent/eMule link, the Task Manager examines whether the Cloud Cache contains a video which has the same hash code with that contained in the BitTorrent/eMule link.[3] Otherwise, the Task Manager directly examines whether the file link is repeated in the Cloud Cache. If the requested video actually has a copy, the user can directly and instantly retrieve the video from the Cloud Cache (see Arrow

[3] A BitTorrent/eMule link contains the hash code of its affiliated file in itself, while an HTTP/FTP link does not.

8 in Fig. 3.2). Otherwise, the Task Manager forwards the video request to the Task Dispatcher (see Arrow 4 in Fig. 3.2).

The Task Dispatcher assigns the video request to one server (called a "down-loader") in the Downloaders for data downloading (see Arrow 5 in Fig. 3.2). For example, if the video request is a P2P request, the assigned downloader will act like a common peer to join the corresponding peer swarm. The Task Dispatcher is mainly responsible for balancing the bandwidth loads of the 80 downloaders. The number of downloaders (80) is empirically determined to guarantee that the total download bandwidth (26 Gbps) exceeds the peak load of download tasks (nearly 20 Gbps till now). Each downloader executes multiple download tasks in parallel in order to fully utilize its download bandwidth (around 0.325 Gbps) (see Arrow 6 in Fig. 3.2), and the Task Dispatcher always assigns a newly incoming video request to the downloader which has the lowest download data rate.

As long as the downloader accomplishes a download task, it computes the hash code of the downloaded video and attempts to store the video in the Cloud Cache (see Arrow 7 in Fig. 3.2). The downloader first checks whether the video has a copy in the Cloud Cache (using the hash code). If the video is repeated, the downloader simply discards it. Otherwise, the downloader checks whether the Cloud Cache has enough unused space to store the new video. If the Cloud Cache does not have enough unused space, it deletes some cached videos to get enough unused space to store the new video. The concrete cache architecture, cache capacity planning, and cache replacement strategy will be investigated in Sect. 3.3.2, Sect. 3.3.4, and Sect. 3.3.5, respectively.

When the above-mentioned video store process is finished, the user can usually retrieve the requested video from the Cloud Cache (see Arrow 8 in Fig. 3.2) in any place at any time. Since the user's ISP information can be acquired from his video retrieve message (see Arrow 4 in Fig. 3.1), the Cloud Cache takes advantage of the intra-cloud ISP-aware data upload technique to restrict the retrieve data flow within the same ISP as the user's, so as to enhance the data transfer rate and avoid the inter-ISP traffic cost.

3.3.2   Data Transfer Acceleration

A critical problem of cloud download is how to accelerate the data transfer (i.e., retrieve) process so that the user can obtain his requested video (whether popular or unpopular) from the cloud with a high data rate in any place at any time. Considering that the cross-ISP data transfer performance degrades seriously and the inter-ISP traffic cost is often expensive [15, 16], we solve this problem via the intra-cloud ISP-aware data upload technique. Since the user's real-time ISP information can be acquired from his video retrieve message, the Cloud Cache takes advantage of its ISP-aware upload servers to restrict the retrieve data flow within the same ISP as the user's, so as to enhance the retrieve data rate and avoid inter-ISP traffic cost. Specifically, as shown in Fig. 3.3, the Cloud Cache consists of 300 chunk servers,

Fig. 3.3 Architecture of the cloud cache. (Reprinted with permission from [6].)

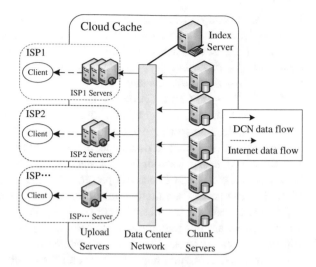

33 upload servers, and 2 index servers which are connected by a DCN (data center network). A specific number of upload servers are placed in each ISP, proportional to the data traffic volume in each ISP. The video requests come from tens of ISPs, but most of them come from the four major ISPs in China. Figure 3.4 demonstrates the number of users, the number of video requests, and the data traffic volume in each ISP in 1 day. Thereby, the Cloud Cache places 21, 10, 1, and 1 upload servers in the four major ISPs respectively at the moment. If the user locates at other ISPs, we randomly choose an upload server to transfer the corresponding data.

Every video is segmented into chunks of equal size to be stored in the chunk servers, and every chunk has a duplicate for redundancy, so the 300 chunk servers can accommodate a total of $\frac{300 \times 4 \text{ TB}}{2} = 600$ TB unique data. In order to achieve load balance and exploit the chunk correlation in the same file, all the chunks of a video are stored together into the chunk server with the biggest available storage capacity.

Fig. 3.4 Number of users, number of video requests, and data traffic volume in each ISP in 1 day. (Reprinted with permission from [6].)

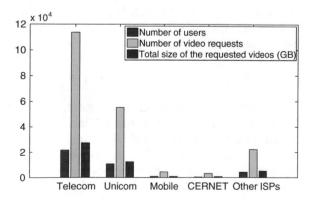

The duplicate chunks of a video must be stored in another chunk server. There exists an index server (as well as a backup index server) which maintains the metadata of chunks for chunk search and validation. The metadata is a list of n-tuples like $<$*file hash code, file link, number of chunks, physical location of the first chunk, physical location of the first duplicate chunk*$>$.

The DCN in the Cloud Cache adopts the traditional three-tier tree structure to organize the switches, composed of a core tier in the root of the tree, an aggregation tier in the middle, and an edge tier at the leaves of the tree. The index servers, chunk servers, upload servers, and downloaders are connected to the switches at the edge tier. Suppose a user A locating at ISP1 wants to retrieve a video f stored in a chunk server S, and the Cloud Cache has placed 10 upload servers (U_1, U_2, $\cdots$, U_{10}) in ISP1. The chunks of f are firstly transferred from S to a random upload server (says U_4) in ISP1, and then transferred from U_4 to the user A. The transfer process is not store and forward but pass through: as soon as U_4 gets a complete chunk of f, U_4 transfers the chunk to A. f would not be cached in U_4 because the intra-cloud end-to-end bandwidth is quite high (1 Gbps) and we do not need to make things more complicated than necessary.

3.3.3 Download Success Rate Improvement

Although cloud download guarantees the data health of the requested video (≥ 1.0) after the video is downloaded by the cloud, it cannot guarantee to download every requested video successfully. In this part, we construct a simple model to analyze the download success rates of cloud download and *common download* (the data reuse among users is not considered). *Common download* is the common way in which a user downloads video content from the Internet. Considering the highly dynamic and complicated Internet environments, the target of our model is to illustrate the long-term expected trend, rather than the accurate prediction in a short period.

Whether we use common download or cloud download, the download success rate of a requested HTTP/FTP file only depends on the accessibility of the file link (1-accessible or 0-inaccessible). According to our measurements of the accessibility of numerous HTTP/FTP file links submitted to VideoCloud, the average download success rate of HTTP/FTP files is:

$$R_1 = R_1' = 0.414.$$

The download success rate of a requested P2P file is much more complicated because the accessibility of a peer is a stochastic variable. Consider a P2P swarm consisting of n peers sharing a file f. The time limit is T hours, that is to say, each peer must draw his conclusion in T hours: 1-download success or 0-download failure. In average, each peer stays online for t hours in the time limit (T hours) and the data health of a single peer is h ($h < 1.0$). For a common peer P, during the t hours when P is online, P is expected to encounter $\frac{n \cdot t}{T}$ online peers (n is the average number of peers in a peer swarm), assuming the online time of each peer is independent. Since the data health of a single peer is h, the download success rate of P is expected to be:

$$R_2 = 1 - (1 - h)^{\frac{n \cdot t}{T}}.$$

Cloud download uses a stable peer P' (in fact, P' is a cloud server) to join in the P2P swarm, so the online duration t for P' is $t = T$. Then the download success rate of P' is expected to be:

$$R_2' = 1 - (1 - h)^n.$$

Among all the video requests, let α denote the fraction of HTTP/FTP file requests, and β denote the fraction of P2P file requests. Thus, the overall download success rates of common download and cloud download are expected to be:

$$R = \alpha \cdot R_1 + \beta \cdot R_2, \text{ and } R' = \alpha \cdot R_1' + \beta \cdot R_2'.$$

Our 17-day measurements of VideoCloud show that $h = 0.4$, $n = 5.4$, $\frac{t}{T} = 0.12$, $\alpha = 27.4\%$, and $\beta = 72.6\%$. As a result,

$$R = 31.8\%, \text{ and } R' = 79.3\%.$$

The expected download success rates (R and R') are depicted in Fig. 3.5 to compare with the real performance of VideoCloud. The real system average download success rate is 81.4%.

Fig. 3.5 Download success rate in each day. (Reprinted with permission from [6].)

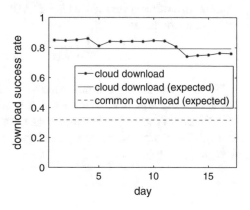

3.3.4 Cache Capacity Planning

The biggest hardware and energy cost of the VideoCloud system comes from the Cloud Cache, in particular the 300 chunk servers making up a 600-TB cloud cache. In this part, we address the reason why the cache capacity is planned as 600 TB.

VideoCloud has over 6 million registered users. It is impossible to allocate each user with unlimited cloud cache capacity. Instead, each registered user is allocated with a 5-GB free cloud cache at the moment, because 5 GB is around the size of a common TV play series.[4] Given that the average size of requested videos is 379 MB, we regard a cloud cache which accommodates more than 13 videos (5 GB/379 MB = 13.5) as basically enough to satisfy a common user's requirement. Extra storage is charged in unit of 5 GB. According to our statistics, almost all the users of VideoCloud are 5-GB free users, which is quite similar to the situation of Amazon Cloud Drive. Consequently, over 6 million registered users need more than 29000 TB of cache capacity *in the worst case*. The *worst case* happens under the following three conditions: (1) Every user fully utilizes its 5-GB cloud cache[5]; (2) There is no data reuse among the users; and (3) The data in a user's cloud cache is stored *forever* unless it is retrieved by the user (this condition will be replaced by a more practical and economical condition later on). It is difficult to predict the extent of the first and second conditions because they depend on users' behaviors and may vary enormously as time goes by. Therefore, to change the third condition is our only choice. The third condition is replaced by a practical and economical condition: (3) The data in a user's cloud cache is stored *for 1 week* unless it is retrieved by the user. The store period (1 week) is an empirical parameter according to our operating experiences of VideoCloud, i.e., almost all the users (over 95%) retrieve their requested videos within 1 week after the requested video is available. Currently, VideoCloud receives around 0.22 million video requests per day and the average size of requested videos is 379 MB, so the total cloud cache capacity *in the worst case* should be:

$$C = 379 \text{ MB} \times 0.22 M \times 7 = 584 \text{ TB}.$$

To cope with the fluctuations in the daily number of video requests, the total cloud cache capacity is planned as $C' = 600$ TB, slightly larger than $C = 584$ TB. Via the 600-TB cloud cache, the data reuse rate among the users reaches 87%, indicating that most video requests are satisfied instantly (i.e., with a very low view startup delay).

---

[4] Amazon Cloud Drive also sets 5 GB as the basic cloud storage capacity provided to its users.

[5] Since almost all the users of VideoCloud are 5-GB free users at the moment, we regard every user as a 5-GB free user for computation convenience.

3.3.5 Cache Replacement Strategy

Although the current cloud cache capacity (600 TB) can well handle the current daily number of video requests (around 0.22 million), it is quite likely that the number of video requests will be much higher than 0.22 million in some day. For example, if the daily number of video requests increases to 2.2 million, what shall we do? Obviously, it is impossible for us to construct a 6000-TB cloud cache made up of 3000 chunk servers—the hardware and energy cost are far beyond our affordability. As a result, some data must be replaced to make efficient utilization of the limited cloud cache capacity, where the cache replacement strategy plays a critical role. In this part, we investigate the performance of the most commonly used cache replacement strategies, i.e., FIFO (first in first out), LRU (least recently used), and LFU (least frequently used) via real-trace driven simulations. The trace is a 17-day system log (refer to Sect. 3.4.1 for detailed information) of VideoCloud. The metrics are twofold: (1) *cache hit rate*; and (2) *size of replaced data*, which illustrates the I/O cost of chunk servers. We hope the cache hit rate to be as high as possible, while the size of replaced data to be as small as possible.

As shown in Figs. 3.6 and 3.7, among the three cache replacement strategies, FIFO performs the worst, and LFU performs the best to achieve the highest cache hit rate and the smallest size of replaced data. The cache capacity is set to 70 TB, and using other cache capacities rather than 70 TB generates the similar results. Therefore, the Cloud Cache of VideoCloud adopts the LFU cache replacement strategy for future scalability. Delving more deeply, LFU has been recognized to be especially suitable for a system where the popularity of data objects does not change very much over a specific time period (1 day or 1 week) [17]. VideoCloud has the abovementioned property because most of the data objects are unpopular videos whose popularity hardly changes much.

Fig. 3.6 Cache hit rate. (Reprinted with permission from [6].)

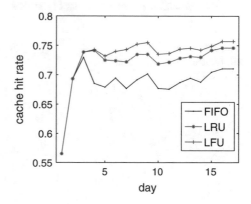

Fig. 3.7   Size of replaced
data. (Reprinted with
permission from [6].)

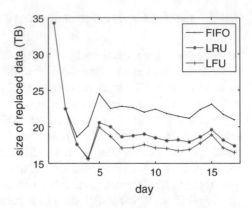

3.4   Performance Evaluation

3.4.1   Dataset

We use the complete running log of the VideoCloud system in 17 days, from January
1, 2011 to January 17, 2011 to evaluate the performance of cloud download. The
log includes the performance information of around 3.87 million video requests,
involving around one million unique videos. Most of the videos are .rmvb (around
40 %) and .avi files (around 20 %). 27.4 % of the requested videos are HTTP/FTP
files, and the remaining are BitTorrent/eMule files. The total size of the requested
videos is 1400 TB, and the total size of the unique videos is 280 TB. The daily
statistics are plotted in Fig. 3.8. For each video request, we record its *user id*, *file
link*, *file hash code*, *file type*, *file size*, *video request time*, *download duration time* (of
the cloud downloader), *retrieve duration time* (of the users), *cache hit status* (1-hit,
0-miss), *download success status* (1-success, 0-failure), and so on.

Fig. 3.8   Daily statistics.
(Reprinted with permission
from [6].)

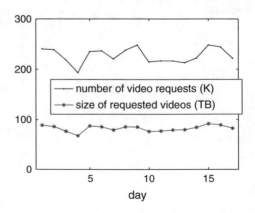

Fig. 3.9 Popularity
distribution of videos.
(Reprinted with permission
from [6].)

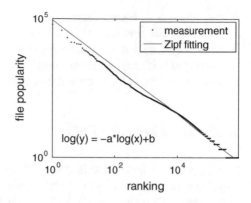

Figure 3.9 indicates that the popularity distribution of the requested videos in 17 days is highly skewed, approximately following the Zipf model [18]. Let x denote the popularity ranking of a video file, and let y denote the popularity of the file. Then we have the following fitting equation:

$$log(y) = -a \cdot log(x) + b,$$

which is equal to

$$y = 10^b \cdot x^{-a},$$

where $a = 0.8464$ and $b = 11.3966$. More in detail, 97.1 % of the videos receive less than one request per day while merely 0.09 % of the videos receive more than ten requests per day (we empirically use the indicator "ten requests per day" as the boundary between popular and unpopular videos), demonstrating that almost all the requested videos in VideoCloud are unpopular. Besides, around 83 % of the requests are issued for unpopular videos. As mentioned in Sect. 3.1, our cloud download scheme aims to provide efficient content distribution service for unpopular videos, so we only evaluate the performance corresponding to unpopular videos in the following parts.

3.4.2 Metrics

We use three major metrics as follows to evaluate the performance of a cloud download system.

1. *Data transfer rate* denotes the data rate when a user retrieves his requested video from the cloud. Specifically, data transfer rate $= \frac{\text{file size}}{\text{retrieve duration time}}$.
2. *View startup delay* denotes how long a user must wait for the cloud to download his requested video. For a video request, if the cache hit status is 1-hit, the view

startup delay is taken as 0; otherwise, the view startup delay is regarded as the
download duration time of the cloud downloader.

3. *Energy efficiency* denotes how much energy is saved by using cloud download,
   compared with the common download method. In particular, we consider the
   user-side energy efficiency and the *overall* energy efficiency, respectively.

3.4.3 Data Transfer Rate

Since the data transfer rate is computed by dividing the file size by the retrieve
duration time, in this part we first present the CDF of file size (in Fig. 3.10), the CDF
of retrieve duration time (in Fig. 3.11) and the CDF of data transfer rate (in Fig. 3.12),
and then try to discover their relations.

The average file size is 379 MB, which is close to the common size of a 100-min
video, given the fact that around 60 % of the requested videos are .rmvb and .avi
files. From Fig. 3.10, we find that 16 % of the files are smaller than 8MB, most of
which are demo videos, pictures, and documents. The reason lies in that many video
content providers like to attach the introductions, snapshots, or advertisements to the
videos.

Fig. 3.10 CDF of file size.
(Reprinted with permission
from [6].)

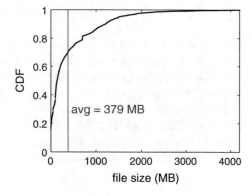

Fig. 3.11 CDF of retrieve
duration time. (Reprinted
with permission from [6].)

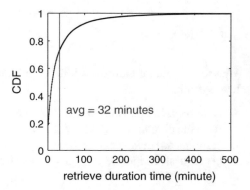

Fig. 3.12 CDF of data transfer rate. (Reprinted with permission from [6].)

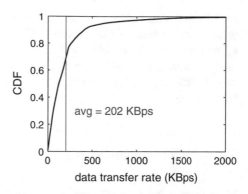

The average retrieve duration time is 32 min. From Fig. 3.11, we see that 73 % of the files are retrieved in less than 32 min, and 93 % of the files are retrieved in less than 100 min so that if the file is a 100-min video, it can be viewed with high playback continuity (the user can choose either mode: view as download or view after download).

The average data transfer rate is 202 KBps ($>$1.6 Mbps). As shown in Fig. 3.12, over 80 % of the data transfer rates are more than 37.5 KBps (=300 Kbps) which is the basic playback rate of online videos. The main reason why around 20 % of the data transfer rates are less than 300 Kbps is that the user does not locate at the four major ISPs in China (as mentioned in Sect. 3.3.2) and thus his video retrieve data flow crosses multiple ISPs. More in detail, the data transfer rate in each ISP is plotted in Fig. 3.13.

We discover a simple but accurate relation among the average file size, the average data transfer rate, and the average retrieve duration time, that is

$$\frac{\text{the avg file size (379 MB)}}{\text{the avg data transfer rate (202 KBps)}} = \quad (3.1)$$

$$\text{the avg retrieve duration time (32 min).}$$

Fig. 3.13 Data transfer rate in each ISP. (Reprinted with permission from [6].)

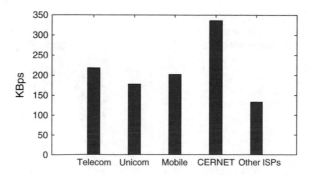

This is a very useful equation which illustrates that if we take some measures (e.g., to invest more upload servers with higher upload bandwidth, or deploy more upload servers in more ISPs) to further enhance the data transfer rate, the retrieve duration time is expected to decrease inverse proportionally. Thereby, we can find a proper tradeoff point between the data transfer rate and the retrieve duration time for future design.

3.4.4   View Startup Delay

View startup delay is effectively alleviated by the implicit and secure data reuse among the users in VideoCloud. For a video request, if the cache hit status is 1-hit (i.e., the requested video has been stored in the cloud cache), the view startup delay is taken as 0; otherwise, the view startup delay is the download duration time. Thus, we firstly present the CDF of download duration time (in Fig. 3.14) and the CDF of download data rate (in Fig. 3.15), and then get the amortized view startup delay.

The average download duration time is 433 min and the average download data rate is 71 KBps (=0.57 Mbps). In the previous subsection, we discover the relationship

Fig. 3.14 CDF of download duration time. (Reprinted with permission from [6].)

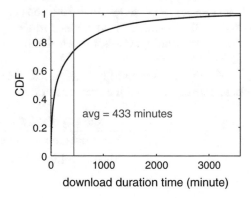

Fig. 3.15 CDF of download data rate. (Reprinted with permission from [6].)

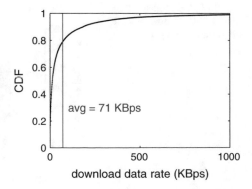

(see Eq. (3.1)) among the average file size, the average data transfer rate, and the average retrieve duration time. However, this relationship does not exist as to the download duration time and the download data rate:

$$\frac{\text{the avg file size (379 MB)}}{\text{the avg download data rate (71 KBps)}} = 91 \text{ min}$$

$$\ll \text{the avg download duration time (433 min)}.$$

(3.2)

The reason is that most download events have too low download data rates, e.g., 22 % of the download rates are less than 2 KBps, 45 % less than 10 KBps, and 70 % less than 37.5 KBps (=300 Kbps). In particular, 79 % of the download data rates are less than the average download data rate (71 KBps).

As mentioned in Sect. 3.3.4, the data reuse rate among the users in Video-Cloud reaches 87 %, so the amortized view startup delay = 87 % · 0 + 13 %· 433 min = 56 min. We will make efforts to further reduce the amortized view startup delay, although this may be a challenging work.

3.4.5 Energy Efficiency

It is difficult for VideoCloud to record the accurate energy cost of each user, so we leverage the approximate power consumption of a PC (personal computer) to estimate the average energy cost of the users. According to a recent IDC report [19], laptop sales have occupied about 70 % of the PC sales. Based on the average statistics of PCs in 2011, the power consumption of a laptop is about 50 W and that of a desktop is about 250 W. Thereby, the average power consumption of a PC is estimated as

$$P_1 = 50 \text{ W} \cdot 70\% + 250 \text{ W} \cdot 30\% = 110 \text{ W}.$$

Our 17-day system log includes the performance information of $N = 3.87M$ video requests. Without cloud download, the energy cost for the users to accomplish all the video requests is denoted as E_1. To properly estimate E_1, the *download parallelism* of each user must be taken into account. As shown in Fig. 3.16, in the common download way, suppose the user i starts Task 1 at the time s_1 and finishes Task 1 at the time f_1, and then the download duration time of Task 1 is $t_1 = f_1 - s_1$. The meanings of the symbols for Task 2/3/4/5 are similar. Then the *download parallelism* of the user i is computed as

$$p_i = (\sum_{j=1}^{5} t_j)/(f_3 - s_1 + f_5 - s_5),$$

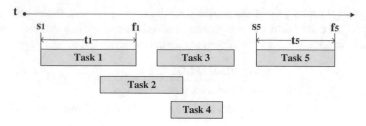

Fig. 3.16 Download parallelism of a user i. (Reprinted with permission from [6].)

and the energy cost of the user i is computed as

$$e_i = P_1 \cdot (f_3 - s_1 + f_5 - s_5) = P_1 \cdot \left(\sum_{j=1}^{5} t_j\right)/p_i.$$

As a result, E_1 is estimated as

$$E_1 = \sum_{i=1}^{m} e_i = 2.21\,M \text{ KWH},$$

where m denotes the total number of users and KWH = Kilowatt Hour.

By using cloud download, the energy cost of the whole system is:

$$E_2 = E_c + E_u,$$

where E_c denotes the energy cost of the cloud utilities and E_u denotes the energy cost of the users. Since each server in the cloud works in all the time and the average power consumption of a server is $P_2 = 700$ W, E_c is estimated as:

$$E_c = P_2 \cdot S \cdot 17\,\text{days} = 700\,\text{W} \cdot 426 \cdot 17\,\text{days} = 0.12\,M \text{ KWH},$$

where S is the total number of servers in VideoCloud. And E_u is estimated in the same way we estimate E_1:

$$E_u = \sum_{i=1}^{m} e_i' = 0.18\,M \text{ KWH},$$

where e_i' is the energy cost of the user i in retrieving his requested videos from the cloud. Therefore,

$$E_2 = E_c + E_u = 0.12\,M \text{ KWH} + 0.18\,M \text{ KWH} = 0.3\,M \text{ KWH}.$$

In conclusion, the *user-side* energy efficiency is

$$\frac{E_1 - E_u}{E_1} = \frac{2.21\,M - 0.18\,M}{2.21\,M} = 92\,\%, \tag{3.3}$$

and the *overall* energy efficiency of the total cloud download system (cloud + users) is

$$\frac{E_1 - E_2}{E_1} = \frac{2.21\,M - 0.3\,M}{2.21\,M} = 86\,\%. \tag{3.4}$$

3.5   Conclusion and Future Work

Video content distribution is becoming a kill application of the Internet owing to the users' inflating requirements on both video quantity and quality, so it is of great importance to investigate how to achieve high-quality content distribution for both popular and unpopular videos. In this chapter, we firstly analyze the state-of-the-art techniques. We find they generally work well in distributing popular videos, but do not provide satisfactory content distribution service for unpopular videos. In fact, there are many more unpopular videos than popular videos over the Internet. Therefore, we propose and implement the novel cloud download scheme, which utilizes cloud utilities to achieve high-quality content distribution for unpopular videos. Running logs of our real deployed commercial system confirm the effectiveness and efficiency of cloud download. Our study provides practical experiences and valuable heuristics for making use of cloud utilities to achieve efficient Internet services.

Still some future work remains. First, it is possible to extend the application of cloud download to smaller or private organizations. In our opinion, even a company or a university can build a cloud download system like VideoCloud as its private cloud system to facilitate its users. For example, we discover that in many companies some employees may keep their computers all night on to continue an unfinished download task after they leave the company, which is rather energy-*inefficient*. Since the design of cloud download (described in Sect. 3.3) is quite simple and practical, a company can invest in building a private (small-scale) cloud download system and then encourage its employees to send every download request to the cloud.

Secondly, as mentioned in Sect. 3.3.3, although cloud download has improved the download success rate of requested videos to 81.4 %, download failure still exists. In fact, it is very difficult to judge the download failure of a video request. Given that the most powerful web search engine has just discovered less than 1 % of all the things existing in the Internet [20], it is impossible to tell a user whether his requested video can be obtained at last if we keep on trying. Consequently, we have to tell the user his video request is *judged to have failed* at the "right" time. Then the key point is: what is the "right" time? In another words, what is the rule to judge the failure of a video request? Presently, we choose a simple judging rule which takes into account both the download duration time and the download progress (i.e., the download completion fraction of the requested video). The rule is: check the download progress periodically; if the download progress does not change in the latest period, the video request is judged to have failed. The current period is empirically set to be 24 h. Next step we plan to further analyze the system log to discover more factors that influence the failure of video requests and consider a more accurate failure judging algorithm.

Finally, as a large-scale commercial system in its first version, VideoCloud tends to adopt traditional/straightforward design in constructing each component so that the deployment and debugging are easy to handle. We realize there is still considerable optimization space for novel design to take effect. This chapter is the first step of our efforts, and we are dedicated to accumulating experiences and gaining insights on the way.

References

1. The Cisco Visual Networking Index report. http://newsroom.cisco.com/dlls/2008/ekits/Cisco_Visual_Networking_Index_061608.pdf
2. The BitTorrent protocol specification. http://www.BitTorrent.org/beps/bep_0003.html
3. Zhang, X., Liu, J., Li, B., Yum, T.S.P.: CoolStreaming/DONet: a data-driven overlay network for peer-to-peer live media streaming. In: Proceedings of the 24th IEEE International Conference on Computer Communications (INFOCOM), pp. 2102–2111 (2005)
4. Huang, C., Li, J., Ross, K.W.: Can internet video-on-demand be profitable? ACM SIGCOMM Comput. Commun. Rev. (CCR) **37**(4), 133–144 (2007)
5. Kangasharju, J., Roberts, J., Ross, K.W.: Object replication strategies in content distribution networks. Comput. Commun. **25**(4), 376–383 (2002)
6. Huang, Y., Li, Z., Liu, G., Dai, Y.: Cloud download: using cloud utilities to achieve high-quality content distribution for unpopular videos. In: Proceedings of the 19th ACM International Conference on Multimedia (ACM-MM), pp. 213–222 (2011)
7. Roth, K.W., McKenney, K., Association, C.E., et al.: Energy Consumption by Consumer Electronics in U.S. Residences. TIAX LLC (2007)
8. Douceur, J.R.: The Sybil attack. In: Proceedings of the 1st International Workshop on Peer-to-Peer Systems (IPTPS), pp. 251–260. Springer (2002)
9. Singh, A., Ngan, T.W.J., Druschel, P., Wallach, D.S.: Eclipse attacks on overlay networks: threats and defenses. In: Proceedings of the 25th IEEE International Conference on Computer Communications (INFOCOM), pp. 1–12. IEEE (2006)
10. Sit, E., Morris, R.: Security considerations for peer-to-peer distributed hash tables. In: Proceedings of the 1st International Workshop on Peer-to-Peer Systems (IPTPS), pp. 261–269. Springer (2002)
11. Wu, D., Hou, Y.T., Zhu, W., Zhang, Y.Q., Peha, J.M.: Streaming video over the internet: approaches and directions. IEEE Trans. Circuits Syst. Video Technol. (TCSVT) **11**(3), 282–300 (2001)
12. Yin, H., Liu, X., Zhan, T., Sekar, V., Qiu, F., Lin, C., Zhang, H., Li, B.: Design and deployment of a hybrid CDN-P2P system for live video streaming: experiences with LiveSky. In: Proceedings of the 17th ACM International Conference on Multimedia (ACM-MM), pp. 25–34 (2009)
13. Wu, C., Li, B., Zhao, S.: On dynamic server provisioning in multichannel P2P live streaming. IEEE/ACM Trans. Networking (TON) **19**(5), 1317–1330 (2011)
14. Liu, F., Shen, S., Li, B., Li, B., Yin, H., Li, S.: Novasky: cinematic-quality VoD in a P2P storage cloud. In: Proceedings of the 30th IEEE International Conference on Computer Communications (INFOCOM), pp. 936–944 (2011)

15. Choffnes, D.R., Bustamante, F.E.: Taming the torrent: a practical approach to reducing cross-isp traffic in peer-to-peer systems. ACM SIGCOMM Comput. Commun. Rev. (CCR) **38**(4), 363–374 (2008)

16. Xie, H., Yang, Y.R., Krishnamurthy, A., Liu, Y.G., Silberschatz, A.: P4P: provider portal for applications. ACM SIGCOMM Comput. Commun. Rev. (CCR) **38**(4), 351–362 (2008)

17. Podlipnig, S., Böszörmenyi, L.: A survey of web cache replacement strategies. ACM Comput. Surv. (CSUR) **35**(4), 374–398 (2003)

18. Breslau, L., Cao, P., Fan, L., Phillips, G., Shenker, S.: Web caching and Zipf-like distributions: evidence and implications. In: Proceedings of the 18th IEEE International Conference on Computer Communications (INFOCOM), vol. 1, pp. 126–134 (1999)

19. The IDC Desktop and Laptop Sales report. http://news.techworld.com/sme/3227696/desktop-and-laptop-sales-to-grow-this-year

20. Croft, W.B., Metzler, D., Strohman, T.: Search Engines: Information Retrieval in Practice. Addison-Wesley Reading (2010)

Chapter 4
Cloud Transcoding for Mobile Devices

Abstract Despite its increasing popularity, Internet video streaming to mobile devices confronts many challenging issues. One such issue is the format and resolution gap between Internet videos and mobile devices: many videos available on the Internet are encoded in formats not supported by mobile devices, or in resolutions not best suited for streaming over cellular/WiFi networks. Hence video transcoding for specific devices (and to be streamed over cellular/WiFi networks) is needed. As a computation-intensive task, video transcoding directly on mobile devices is not desirable because of their limited battery capacity. In this chapter, we propose and implement Cloud Transcoder, which utilizes an intermediate cloud platform to bridge the format/resolution gap by performing video transcoding in the cloud. Specifically, Cloud Transcoder only requires the user to upload a video request (i.e., a URL link to the video available on the public Internet as well as the user-specified transcoding parameters) rather than the video content. After receiving the video request, Cloud Transcoder downloads the original video from the Internet, transcodes it on the user's demand, and delivers the transcoded video back to the user. Therefore, the mobile device only consumes energy during the last step—but generally with much less energy consumption than downloading the original video from the Internet, due to faster delivery of transcoded video from the cloud platform. Running logs of our real-deployed system validate the efficacy of Cloud Transcoder.

4.1 Introduction

Recent years have seen wide adoption of smart mobile devices such as smartphones and tablets. Gartner reports that worldwide sales of mobile devices have far exceeded the PC shipments [1]. Apart from the conventional web surfing, users are increasingly using their mobile devices for Internet video streaming. It is predicted that mobile video traffic will likely dominate the total mobile Internet traffic in the near future [2]. Despite its increasing popularity, Internet video streaming to mobile devices confronts many challenging issues, one of which is the format and resolution gap between Internet videos and mobile devices.

© Springer Science+Business Media Singapore 2016   75
Z. Li et al., *Content Distribution for Mobile Internet: A Cloud-based Approach*,
DOI 10.1007/978-981-10-1463-5_4

Due to their relatively small screen sizes but diverse screen resolutions, embedded processors and limited battery capacities, mobile devices usually support a range of video formats and resolutions [3] which are often different from many videos available on the public Internet that are captured and encoded primarily for streaming to desktop and laptop PCs. For example, iPhone4S, one of the most popular and powerful smartphones at present, typically supports MP4 videos up to $640 * 480$ pixels and does not support Adobe Flash videos (FLV). However, today's Internet videos, either uploaded by common users or supplied by large video content providers, are still PC oriented—most videos possess a single format and very limited resolutions. For instance, Youtube usually transcodes its own videos into three resolutions (240p, 360p and 480p) in FLV format in advance to *approximate* its users' devices and bandwidths. As to a mobile device, it often still has to transcode the downloaded video to *match* its specific playback capability, i.e., to *fill the gap* between Internet videos and mobile devices.

Because of the aforementioned gap, there is a growing demand for *video transcoding* so that videos of any format and resolution available on the public Internet can be transcoded *on-demand* to the format and resolution supported by a specific mobile device. One simple solution is to perform video transcoding locally and directly at the user's mobile device (e.g., via a downloadable video transcoding app [4, 5] designed for mobile devices). Unfortunately, video transcoding is a highly computation-intensive task—in [6, 7] it is shown that the computation cost of video transcoding is equivalent to that of simultaneously viewing (decoding) multiple videos. Hence locally performing video transcoding on mobile devices will consume a significant amount of energy on mobile devices, draining their limited battery capacity. Alternatively, a user may first download the original videos to her PC, utilize specialized video transcoding software (e.g., iTunes or AirVideo [8]) to transcode the videos to the format and resolution supported by her mobile device, and then upload the transcoded videos to her mobile device. Clearly, such an approach is rather inconvenient, and may not always be possible. For instance, when the user is out of office/home, and does not have access to her PC.

The emergence of cloud computing provides a more promising alternative to address this format and resolution gap problem: it is natural to imagine using cloud-based video transcoding utilities to perform video transcoding for mobile users on demand. To provide such an *on-demand* video transcoding service, the existing cloud-based transcoding solution [9–11] typically lets the user upload a video (≤ 100 MB) to the cloud, which subsequently transcodes the original video based on the user's format and resoultion specification, and then delivers the transcoded video back to the user. This solution may work well for transcoding audios and short videos, but is not fit for transcoding *long videos* such as feature-length movies. The main difficulty lies in that it is both time-consuming and energy-consuming for a user to upload a video of long duration (and of higher resolution) to the cloud. This problem is further exacerbated by the asymmetric nature of the Internet access—the uplink bandwidth is generally far lower than the downlink bandwidth, as well as by the fact that the size of the original video is usually larger than that of the transcoded one.

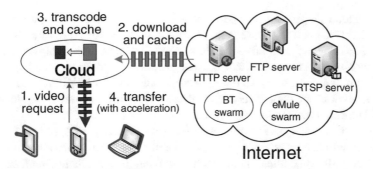

Fig. 4.1 Working principle of Cloud Transcoder. (Reprinted with permission from [12].)

Taking all above into consideration, in this chapter we propose and implement Cloud Transcoder which utilizes an intermediate cloud platform to bridge the format and resolution gap between Internet videos and mobile devices. As depicted in Fig. 4.1, Cloud Transcoder *only requires* a user to upload a *video (transcoding) request* rather than the video content. The *video request* contains a *video link* and the *user-specified transcoding parameters* including the format, resolution, etc. An example is shown below

$$< video\ link; format, resolution, \cdots > \ ,$$

where the *video link*[1] can be an HTTP/FTP/RTSP link or a BitTorrent/eMule/Magnet [13] link. After receiving the video request, Cloud Transcoder downloads the original video (says v) using the video link (from the Internet, e.g., an HTTP/FTP/RTSP server or a P2P swarm where the original video is stored) and stores v in the cloud cache, then transcodes v on the user's demand and caches the transcoded video (says v'), and finally transfers v' back to the user *with a high data rate* via the intra-cloud data transfer acceleration. Nowadays, web/P2P download has become the major way in which people obtain video content, so it is reasonable for Cloud Transcoder to require its users to upload their video requests rather than the video content. Therefore, the mobile user only consumes energy during the last step—fast retrieving the transcoded video from the cloud. In a nutshell, Cloud Transcoder provides energy-efficient on-demand video transcoding service to mobile users via its special and practical designs trying to minimize the user-side energy consumption.

Since Cloud Transcoder moves all the video download and transcoding works from its users to the cloud, a critical problem is how to handle the resulting heavy *download bandwidth pressure* and *transcoding computation pressure* on the cloud. To solve this problem, we utilize the *implicit data reuse* among the users and the *explicit transcoding recommendation and prediction techniques*. First of all, for each

---

[1] For a "naive" user who cannot decide what format and resolution he should specify, he can leave the transcoding parameters empty and then Cloud Transcoder will recommend some possible choices to him.

video v, Cloud Transcoder only downloads it from the Internet when it is requested for the first time, and the subsequent download requests for v are directly satisfied by using its copy in the cloud cache. Such implicit data reuse is completely handled by the cloud and is thus oblivious to users. Meanwhile, the transcoded videos of v (note that v may correspond to multiple transcoded videos in different formats and resolutions which are collectively denoted as $T(v)$) are also stored in the cloud cache to avoid repeated transcoding operations.

Moreover, when a user issues a video (transcoding) request for a video v and the cloud cache has already stored several transcoded versions of v, but the user's transcoding specification does not match any of the existing versions, Cloud Transcoder will *recommend* one of the transcoded videos (with the transcoding parameters closest to what the user has requested) to the user as a possible alternative. If the user accepts the recommended choice, the transcoded video can be delivered to the user immediately. The goal here is to reduce the unnecessary load on the transcoding service; it also speeds up the whole transcoding process for the users. Finally, when the transcoding computation load falls down at night, we also utilize the video popularity based *prediction* to perform video transcoding *in advance*. Namely, we proactively transcode the (predicted) most popular videos into a range of formats and resolutions supported by widely held mobile devices, so as to meet the potential user demand and reduce the transcoding load during the peak day time. Based on the real-world performance of Cloud Transcoder, the cache hit rate of the download tasks reaches 87 %, while the cache hit rate of the transcoding tasks reaches 66 %.

Since May 2011, we have implemented Cloud Transcoder as a novel production system[2] that employs 244 commodity servers deployed across multiple ISPs. It supports popular mobile devices, popular video formats and user-customized video resolutions. Still at its startup stage, Cloud Transcoder receives nearly 8,600 video requests sent from around 4,000 users per day, and 96 % of the original videos are long videos (≥ 100 MB). But its system architecture (in particular the cloud cache) is generally designed to serve 100,000 daily requests. Real-system running logs of Cloud Transcoder confirm its efficacy. As an average case, a mobile user needs around 33 min to retrieve a transcoded video of 466 MB. The above process typically consumes around 9 %/5 % of the battery capacity of an iPhone4S/iPad2 ($\approx 0.47/1.25$ WH, 1 WH = 1 Watt Hour = 3600 J). And the average data transfer rate of transcoded videos reaches 1.9 Mbps, thus enabling the users' view-as-download function. In conclusion, the system architecture, design techniques and real-world performance of Cloud Transcoder provides practical experiences and valuable heuristics to other cloud system designers planning to offer video transcoding service to its users.

The remainder of this chapter is organized as follows. Section 4.2 describes the system design of Cloud Transcoder. Section 4.3 evaluates the performance of Cloud Transcoder. We discuss about the possible future work in Sect. 4.4.

---

[2]The implementation of Cloud Transcoder is based on a former production system [14] which only downloads videos on behalf of users.

4.2 System Design

4.2.1 System Overview

The system architecture of Cloud Transcoder is composed of six building blocks: (1) *ISP Proxies*, (2) *Task Manager*, (3) *Task Dispatcher*, (4) *Downloaders*, (5) *Transcoders* and (6) *Cloud Cache*, as plotted in Fig. 4.2. It utilizes 244 commodity servers, including 170 chunk servers making up a 340-TB cloud cache, 20 download servers with 6.5 Gbps of Internet bandwidth, 15 transcoding servers with 60 processing cores @2.4 GHz, 23 upload servers with 6.9 Gbps of Internet bandwidth, etc. Such hardware composition (in particular the cloud cache) is generally designed to serve 100K (K = 1000) daily requests, though the current number of daily requests is usually below 10K. Below we describe the organization and working process of Cloud Transcoder by following the message and data flows of a typical video request.

First, a user uploads her video transcoding request to the corresponding ISP Proxy (see Arrow 1 in Fig. 4.2). Each ISP Proxy maintains a *task queue* to control the number of tasks (video requests) sent to the Task Manager (see Arrow 2 in Fig. 4.2), so that the Task Manager is resilient to task upsurge in any ISP. Presently, Cloud Transcoder maintains ten ISP Proxies in the ten biggest ISPs in China: Telecom, Unicom, Mobile, CERNET, and so on. If a user (occasionally) does not locate at any of the ten ISPs, her video request is sent to a random ISP Proxy. On receiving a video request, the Task Manager checks whether the requested video has a copy in the Cloud Cache in two steps (see Arrow 3 in Fig. 4.2):

Step 1. Checking the video link. Inside the Cloud Cache, each original video v has a unique hash code and a series of video links pointing to v in its corresponding metadata m_v. If the video link contained in the video request is a P2P link, the Task Manager examines whether the Cloud Cache contains a video that has the same hash

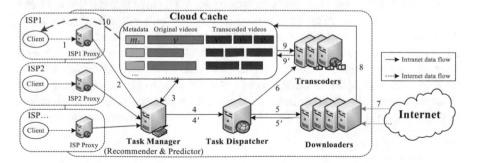

Fig. 4.2 System architecture of Cloud Transcoder. (Reprinted with permission from [12].)

code with that contained in the P2P link.[3] Otherwise, the Task Manager directly examines whether the video link is repeated in the Cloud Cache. If the video link is not found, the Task Manager initiates a *video download task* and sends it to the Task Dispatcher (see Arrow 4 in Fig. 4.2).

Step 2. Checking the transcoded video. If the video link (pointing to the original video v) is found in the Cloud Cache, the Task Manager further checks whether $T(v)$[4] contains an existing transcoded video that matches the user-customized transcoding parameters. If the requested video actually has a copy, the user can directly and instantly retrieve the video from the Cloud Cache (see Arrow 10 in Fig. 4.2). Otherwise, the Task Manager recommends $T(v)$ to the user for a possible choice so as to reduce the transcoding computation pressure on the cloud; thereby, the Task Manager also acts as the Task Recommender. If the user does not accept any recommendation but insists on her customized transcoding parameters, the Task Manager initiates a *video transcoding task* and sends it to the Task Dispatcher (see Arrow 4' in Fig. 4.2).

On receiving a video download task from the Task Manager, the Task Dispatcher assigns the download task to one server (called a downloader) in the Downloaders (see Arrow 5 in Fig. 4.2). For example, if the video link contained in the download task is a P2P link, the assigned downloader will act as a common peer to join the corresponding peer swarm. On receiving a video transcoding task from the Task Manager, the Task Dispatcher assigns the transcoding task to one server (called a transcode) in the Transcoders for video transcoding (see Arrow 6 in Fig. 4.2).

The Task Dispatcher is mainly responsible for balancing the download bandwidth pressure of the 20 downloaders and the transcoding computation pressure of the 15 transcoders. Each downloader executes multiple download tasks in parallel (see Arrow 7 in Fig. 4.2), and the Task Dispatcher always assigns a newly incoming video download task to the downloader with the lightest download bandwidth pressure. Likewise, a newly incoming video transcoding task is always assigned to the transcoder with the lightest computation pressure.

As long as the downloader accomplishes a download task, it computes the hash code of the downloaded video and attempts to store the video into the Cloud Cache (see Arrow 8 in Fig. 4.2). The downloader first checks whether the downloaded video has a copy in the Cloud Cache (using the hash code).[5] If the video is repeated, the downloader simply discards it. Otherwise, the downloader checks whether the Cloud Cache has enough spare space to store the new video. If the Cloud Cache does not have enough spare space, it deletes some cached videos to get enough spare space to store the new video. The concrete cache capacity planning and cache replacement strategy will be investigated in Sect. 4.2.3. When the above-mentioned video store

---

[3] A P2P (BitTorrent/eMule/Magnet) link contains the hash code of its affiliated file in itself, while an HTTP/FTP/RTSP link does not.

[4] $T(v)$ denotes all the existing transcoded videos of v in different formats and resolutions stored in the Cloud Cache.

[5] It is possible that multiple downloaders are downloading the same video content with different video links.

process is finished, the downloader notifies the Task Dispatcher (see Arrow 5' in Fig. 4.2) for further processing.

When a transcoder receives a video transcoding task, it first reads the corresponding original video from the Cloud Cache (see Arrow 9 in Fig. 4.2) and then transcodes it according to the transcoding parameters contained in the video transcoding task. Specifically, each transcoder employs the classic open-source FFmpeg codec software for video transcoding and it supports most popular video formats like MP4, AVI, FLV, WMV and RMVB, as well as user-customized video resolutions. After finishing the transcoding task, the transcoder also checks whether the Cloud Cache has enough spare space to store the new transcoded video (see Arrow 9' in Fig. 4.2).

Finally, the requested video is available in the Cloud Cache and the user can retrieve it as she likes (see Arrow 10 in Fig. 4.2). Since the user's ISP information can be acquired from her video retrieve message, the Cloud Cache takes advantage of the intra-cloud ISP-aware data upload technique (elaborated in Sect. 4.2.4) to accelerate the data transfer process.

4.2.2 Transcoding Prediction

When the *computation pressure* of the transcoders stays below a certain threshold during a certain period (currently the threshold is empirically set as 50 % and the period is set as one hour), the Task Manager starts to predict which videos are likely to be requested for transcoding into which formats and resolutions, based on the video popularity information. The *transcoding computation pressure* is indicated by the *average CPU utilization of the transcoders*. Such prediction often happens at night, when the Task Manager (now behaving as the Task Predictor) first updates the video popularity information using the user requests received in the latest 24 h. The video popularity information is twofold: (1) the number of request times of each video and (2) the most popular transcoding parameters. Currently, the Task Manager picks the top-1000 popular videos and top-3 popular transcoding parameters to initiate transcoding tasks. If a certain popular video has been transcoded into a certain popular format and resolution in the past, the corresponding transcoding task should not be repeated.

Each predicted (non-repeated) transcoding task is sent to the Task Dispatcher to satisfy future potential requests of users, so that part of the transcoding computation pressure in "hot" time has been moved to "cold" time for load balancing (see Fig. 4.3). Besides, we discover the average CPU utilization of the 15 transcoders in the whole day (with prediction) is 34.13 %, indicating that 15 transcoders can support at most $\frac{8600}{34.13\%} \approx 25K$ daily requests (8600 is the total number of video requests received in the whole day). Consequently, in order to support 100K daily video requests, we still need to add at least 45 more transcoders in the future.

Fig. 4.3 Average CPU
utilization of the transcoders
in one day (with prediction)
and the other day (without
prediction), respectively.
(Reprinted with permission
from [12].)

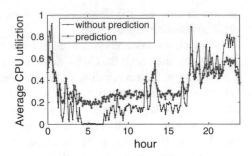

4.2.3   Cloud Cache Organization

Cloud Cache plays a kernel role in the system architecture of Cloud Transcoder by
storing (caching) all the videos and their metadata and meanwhile transferring the
transcoded videos back to users. As depicted in Fig. 4.4, the Cloud Cache consists
of 170 chunk servers, 23 upload servers and 3 index servers, connected by a DCN
(data center network). The DCN adopts the traditional 3-tier tree structure to organize the switches, comprising a core switch in the root of the tree, an aggregation
tier in the middle and an edge tier at the leaves of the tree. All the chunk servers,
upload servers, index servers, downloaders, and transcoders are connected to edge
switches. A specific number of *upload servers* are placed in each ISP, approximately
proportional to the data traffic volume in each ISP.

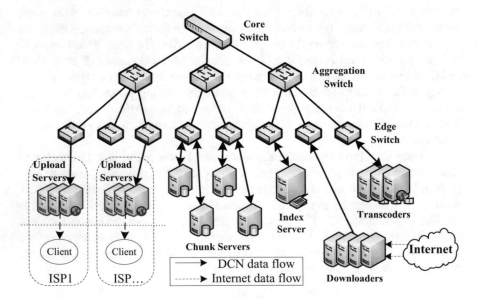

Fig. 4.4 Hardware organization of Cloud Cache. (Reprinted with permission from [12].)

Every video (whether original or transcoded) is segmented into chunks of equal size to be stored in the chunk servers, and every chunk has a duplicate for redundancy, so the 170 chunk servers can accommodate a total of $C = \frac{170 \times 4\,\text{TB}}{2} = 340\,\text{TB}$ unique data. In order to achieve load balance and exploit the chunk correlation in the same file, all the chunks of a video are stored together into the chunk server with the biggest available storage capacity. The duplicate chunks of a video must be stored in another chunk server. There is an index server (as well as two backup index servers) which maintains the metadata of videos.

The 340-TB cloud cache accommodates both original and transcoded videos. Below we first present the cache capacity planning and then discuss the cache replacement strategies. Cloud Transcoder is designed to handle up to 100K daily video requests. Since the average size of original videos is 827 MB (see Fig. 4.8) and every video is stored in the cloud cache for at most 12 days (refer to the user service policy [15]), the total storage capacity of the original videos should be: 827 MB × 100 K × 12 = 969 TB to well handle 100 K daily requests *when there is no data reuse among the users*. According to the running logs of Cloud Transcoder, the current data reuse rate of original videos is about 87 % and thus the storage capacity of the original videos is planned as: $C_1 = 827\,\text{MB} \times 100\,\text{K} \times 12 \times (1 - 87\,\%) = 126$ TB. On the other hand, an original video is associated with three transcoded videos in average and the average size of transcoded videos is 466 MB (see Fig. 4.9), so the storage capacity of the transcoded videos is planned as: $C_2 = 3 \times 466\,\text{MB} \times 100\,\text{K} \times 12 \times (1 - 87\,\%) = 213$ TB. As a result, the total cache capacity should be $C = C_1 + C_2 \approx 340$ TB.

Although the current number of daily video requests is much smaller than 100K, it is possible that this number will exceed 100K some day. If the huge upsurge in request number really happens, some data must be replaced to make efficient utilization of the limited cloud cache capacity, where the cache replacement strategy plays a critical role. Here we investigate the performance of the most commonly used cache replacement strategies for both original and transcoded videos via real-trace driven simulations, i.e., FIFO (first in first out), LRU (least recently used) and LFU (least frequently used). The trace is a 23-day system log (refer to Sect. 4.3 for detailed information) of all the video requests and the simulated cloud cache storage is 30

Fig. 4.5 Cache hit rates for original videos in simulations. (Reprinted with permission from [12].)

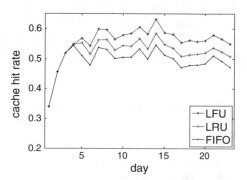

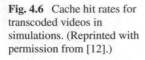

Fig. 4.6 Cache hit rates for transcoded videos in simulations. (Reprinted with permission from [12].)

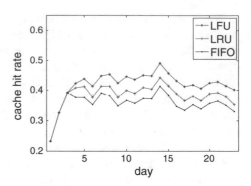

TB ($\approx \frac{8600}{100K}$ · 340 TB, where 8600 is the current average number of daily requests). From Figs. 4.5 and 4.6, we discover that for both original and transcoded videos, FIFO performs the worst and LFU performs the best to achieve the highest cache hit rate.

4.2.4   Accelerating the Data Transfer of Transcoded Videos

A critical problem of Cloud Transcoder is how to accelerate the transfer process of the transcoded videos from the cloud to the user in order to save the users' energy consumption in retrieving their requested videos. Considering that the cross-ISP data transfer performance degrades seriously and the inter-ISP traffic cost is often expensive, we solve this problem via the *intra-cloud ISP-aware data upload technique*. Since the user's real-time ISP information can be acquired from her video retrieve message, the Cloud Cache takes advantage of its ISP-aware upload servers to restrict the data transfer path within the same ISP as the user's, so as to enhance the data transfer rate and avoid inter-ISP traffic cost. Specifically, suppose a user A locating at ISP1 wants to retrieve a video v' stored in a chunk server S, and the Cloud Cache has placed 3 upload servers (U_1, U_2 and U_3) in ISP1 (see Fig. 4.4). The chunks of v' are first transferred from S to a random upload server (says U_3) in ISP1, and then transferred from U_3 to the user A. The transfer process is not store-and-forward but pass-through: as soon as U_3 gets a complete chunk of v', U_3 transfers the chunk to A. v' would not be cached in U_3 because the intra-cloud end-to-end bandwidth is quite high (1 Gbps) and we do not want to make things unnecessarily complicated.

4.3   Performance Evaluation

We use the complete running log of Cloud Transcoder in 23 days (Oct. 1–23, 2011) to evaluate its performance. The log includes the performance information of 197,400 video transcoding tasks involving 76,293 unique videos. The daily statistics are plotted in Fig. 4.7. For each task, we record its *user device type*, *video link*, *transcoding parameters*, *original size*, *transcoded size*, *download duration time* (of the cloud downloader), *transcoding time*, *retrieve duration time* (of the user) and so on. 85 % of the video links sent from users are P2P links. The most popular transcoding parameters include MP4-1024*768 (10 %, mostly coming from iPad users), MP4-640*480 (38 %, mostly coming from iPhone and Android smartphone users) and 3GP-352*288 (27 %, mostly coming from Android smartphone users). As shown in Figs. 4.8 and 4.9, the average file size of the original videos is 827 MB, as 1.77 times as that of the transcoded videos (466 MB). 96 % of the original videos are long videos ($\geq$ 100 MB).

As an average case, a mobile user needs around 33 min to retrieve a transcoded video (see Fig. 4.10) with the help of the intra-cloud data transfer acceleration. The above process may consume 6.1/5.5 % of the battery capacity of an iPhone4S/iPad2 *in theory*, given that the battery of iPhone4S/iPad2 is claimed to support about 9–10 h WiFi data transfer. To check the practical energy consumption, we use our own iPhones/iPads to retrieve a long enough transcoded video from Cloud Transcoder (via WiFi) for 33 min and then record their battery consumptions. All the other user applications are closed, and the screen brightness is set to 25 % with "auto-adjustment" disabled. The results are listed in Table 4.1, indicating that the iPhone4S

Fig. 4.7 Daily statistics. (Reprinted with permission from [12].)

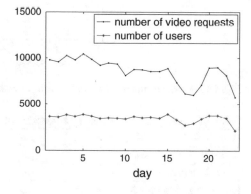

Fig. 4.8 Original file size. (Reprinted with permission from [12].)

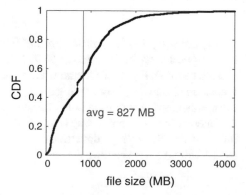

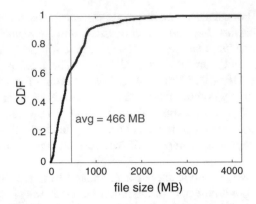

Fig. 4.9 Transcoded file size. (Reprinted with permission from [12].)

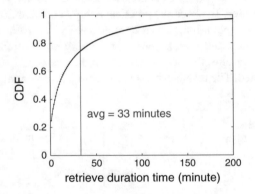

Fig. 4.10 Retrieve duration. (Reprinted with permission from [12].)

Table 4.1 Battery consumptions of iPhone4S and iPad2 with different data transfer rates

Data transfer rate ($\approx$KBps)	50	100	200	300
iPhone4S battery consumption (%)	8.7	8.9	9.0	9.2
iPad2 battery consumption (%)	4.5	4.8	5.0	5.1

Reprinted with permission from [12]

battery consumption is typically around 9 % ($\approx$0.47 WH) while the iPad2 battery consumption is typically around 5 % ($\approx$1.25 WH).

As a contrast, Fig. 4.11 illustrates the average download duration time for a downloader (in Cloud Transcoder) to get an original video is 189 min (as 5.72 times as the average retrieve duration time), because each downloader directly gets data from the Internet in the common way (without designated acceleration). Finally, Fig. 4.12 indicates that the average data transfer rate of transcoded videos reaches 238 KBps (= 1.9 Mbps), thus enabling the users' view-as-download function.

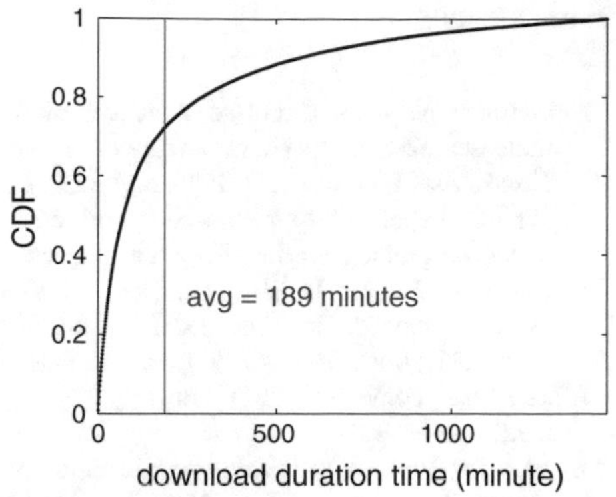

Fig. 4.11 Download
duration. (Reprinted with
permission from [12].)

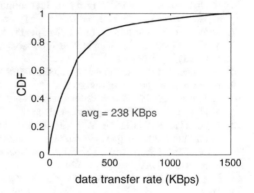

Fig. 4.12 Data transfer rate.
(Reprinted with permission
from [12].)

4.4 Future Work

Still some future work remains. First, as a novel production system still at its startup
stage, Cloud Transcoder tends to adopt straightforward and solid designs in constructing each component so that the deployment and debugging works are easy to
handle. We realize there is still considerable space for a better design to take effect
and this chapter is the first step of our efforts.

Second, some web browsers also start to provide video transcoding service. For
example, UCBrowser, the most popular mobile web browser in China, has employed
cloud utilities to transcode web flash videos into three resolutions: 144 * 176,
176 * 208 and 240 * 320, in order to facilitate its mobile users. Amazon has recently
claimed that its novel Silk web browser will transcode Internet videos to certain
formats and resolutions (especially fit for its 7-inch Kindle Fire Tablet) by using its
EC2 cloud platform. We have started to integrate the service of Cloud Transcoder to
the QQ web browser.

References

1. Gartner says sales of mobile devices grew 5.6% in third quarter of 2011; Smartphone sales increased 42%. http://www.gartner.com/it/page.jsp?id=1848514
2. Cisco Visual networking index: global mobile data traffic forecast update, 2015–2020 White Paper. http://www.cisco.com/c/en/us/solutions/collateral/service-provider/visual-networking-index-vni/mobile-white-paper-c11-520862.html
3. Liu, Y., Li, F., Guo, L., Shen, B., Chen, S.: A server's perspective of Internet streaming delivery to mobile devices. In: Proceedings of the 31st IEEE International Conference on Computer Communications (INFOCOM), pp. 1332–1340 (2012)
4. The file converter PRO. http://play.google.com/store/apps/details?id=com.ghostmobile.mediaconverter
5. VLC for Android. http://play.google.com/store/apps/details?id=org.videolan.vlc
6. Huang, Z., Mei, C., Li, L.E., Woo, T.: CloudStream: delivering high-quality streaming videos through a cloud-based SVC proxy. In: Proceedings of the 30th IEEE International Conference on Computer Communications (INFOCOM), pp. 201–205 (2011)
7. Ostermann, J., Bormans, J., List, P., Marpe, D., Narroschke, M., Pereira, F., Stockhammer, T., Wedi, T.: Video coding with H.264/AVC: tools, performance, and complexity. IEEE Circuits Syst. 4(1), 7–28 (2004)
8. Air Video. http://itunes.apple.com/app/id306550020
9. Mov-avi. http://online.movavi.com
10. Online-convert. http://www.online-convert.com
11. YouConvertIt. http://www.youconvertit.com
12. Li, Z., Huang, Y., Liu, G., Wang, F., Zhang, Z.L., Dai, Y.: Cloud Transcoder: bridging the format and resolution gap between Internet videos and mobile devices. In: Proceedings of the 22nd SIGMM Workshop on Network and Operating Systems Support for Digital Audio and Video (NOSSDAV), pp. 33–38 (2012)
13. Magnet URI scheme. http://en.wikipedia.org/wiki/Magnet_URI_scheme
14. Huang, Y., Li, Z., Liu, G., Dai, Y.: Cloud download: using cloud utilities to achieve high-quality content distribution for unpopular videos. In: Proceedings of the 19th ACM International Conference on Multimedia (ACM-MM), pp. 213–222 (2011)
15. User service policy of Cloud Transcoder. http://xf.qq.com/help_video.html

Chapter 5
Offline Downloading: A Comparative Study

Abstract Although Internet access has become more ubiquitous in recent years, most users in China still suffer from low-quality connections, especially when downloading large files. To address this issue, hundreds of millions of China's users have resorted to technologies that allow for *"offline downloading,"* where a proxy is employed to pre-download the user's requested file and then deliver the file at her convenience. In this chapter, we examine two typical implementations of offline downloading: the *cloud-based approach* and the *smart AP* (access point) *based approach*. Using a large-scale dataset collected from a major cloud-based system and comprehensive benchmarks of popular smart APs, we find that the two approaches are complementary while also being subject to distinct performance bottlenecks. Driven by these results, we design and implement a proof-of-concept middleware called ODR (Offline Downloading Redirector) to help users get rid of performance bottlenecks. We feel that offline downloading has broad applicability to other areas of the world that lack broadband penetration. By deploying offline downloading technologies, coupled with our proposed ODR middleware, the Internet experiences for users in many parts of the world can be improved.

5.1 Introduction

Although Internet access has become more ubiquitous in recent years, many users still suffer from low-quality (i.e., low-bandwidth, intermittent, or restricted) network connections [1–6]. In particular, there is a huge gap of high-speed, fixed broadband penetration between developed and developing countries. By the end of 2014, the penetration rate of fixed broadband access in the developed world has reached 27.5 % with as high as 25 Mbps of download bandwidth [7]. On the other hand, the broadband penetration rate is merely 6.1 % in the developing world with relatively limited, unstable download bandwidth [8].

This digital divide prevents many Internet users in developing countries from accessing the full wealth of data and services available online, especially those *large files* (e.g., HD videos and large software) which require high-quality connections to download [9]. Researchers have studied various approaches to making the

© Springer Science+Business Media Singapore 2016   89
Z. Li et al., *Content Distribution for Mobile Internet: A Cloud-based Approach*,
DOI 10.1007/978-981-10-1463-5_5

Internet more accessible, performant and affordable, such as delay-tolerant networking (DTN) [10, 11]. Nevertheless, to date these technologies have not been widely deployed or evaluated in practice.

Modern China exemplifies both the promise and challenges of increasing Internet penetration [12]. In the last ten years, 46 % of China's population has come online [13], and China is now home to world-class Internet companies like Tencent, Baidu, Alibaba, and Sina Weibo. However, the majority (over 72 %) of China's Internet users have low-quality connections [14], due to low access bandwidth, unreliable/unstable data connection, and poor interconnectivity between ISPs (a well-known problem in China known as the *ISP barrier*). The disparity between those who have access to high-speed, fixed broadband and those who do not is likely to increase over the next few years as more of China's rural population comes online.

To deal with the problems caused by low-quality Internet connections, hundreds of millions of China's users have resorted to technologies that allow for "*offline downloading*" of large files [16–22]. Offline downloading implements ideas from DTNs by outsourcing long downloads to a proxy, as demonstrated in Fig. 5.1. Specifically, when a user wants to acquire a file, the user first *requests* a proxy to *pre-download* the file on her behalf (typically using an HTTP/FTP/P2P link via a low-quality network connection). The proxy may have access to faster, cheaper, or more reliable connectivity than the user, so it is better suited to downloading the file from the Internet. The user can then *fetch* the file from the proxy at a later point in time, when local network conditions are conducive to the task.

In this chapter, we examine two implementations of offline downloading that are extremely popular in China [23, 24] (Sect. 5.3):

- *The cloud-based approach* leverages a geo-distributed, massive cloud storage pool as the proxy [21, 22, 25], which usually caches petabytes of files in a datacenter that is within or directly peered with the requesting user's ISP. This approach is adopted by Tencent Xuanfeng [19], Baidu CloudDisk [17], and Xunlei [20]. As it

Fig. 5.1 Basic working principle of offline downloading, as well as the corresponding timing diagram. (Reprinted with permission from [15].)

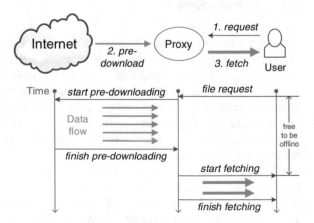

requires expensive cloud infrastructure for data storage and delivery, it is mostly operated by big Internet companies like Tencent and Baidu.

- *The smart AP-based approach* relies on a local smart WiFi AP (access point, also known as home router) as the proxy. It is adopted by HiWiFi [26], MiWiFi [27], Newifi [28], etc. A traditional AP only forwards data for its connected end devices like laptops and smartphones. In contrast, a smart AP, if requested, also pre-downloads and caches data on an embedded/connected storage device (e.g., an SD card, a USB flash drive, or a hard disk drive). The user can then fetch the requested file at her convenience once it is successfully pre-downloaded. This approach incurs almost zero infrastructure cost, but requires smart AP devices with redesigned hardware, OS, and application software.

Currently, there is a dispute over which approach better suits the best-effort Internet [29, 30]. This *selection dilemma* confuses the users of offline download-ing services, especially those who have little expertise in Internet content deliv-ery. The key argument lies in the performance of the two approaches, in terms of (pre-)downloading *speed*, *delay*, and *failure ratio*. Both approaches have advocates that express complaints in news media and marketing reports. However, all these disputes are either limited to one particular offline downloading service/product [21, 22, 31–33], or rely on oversimplified workloads and network environments [25, 34–36]. The former make it hard to form a general and unified view of the factors that may affect offline downloading performance, while the latter do not present comprehensive or objective results.

In this chapter, we address the issue in a *quantitative* and *comparative* manner. First, we measure the workload characteristics of offline downloading (Sect. 5.4), based on a large-scale dataset collected from a major cloud-based system called Xuanfeng [19]. Our analysis of this dataset provides useful insights on the opti-mization of offline downloading services. Second, we identify the key performance bottlenecks of both approaches, based on the complete running logs of Xuanfeng (Sect. 5.5) and comprehensive benchmarks of three popular smart APs (Sect. 5.6). Some of our key results include:

1. *The users' fetching processes are often impeded.* The cloud-based approach can usually accelerate downloading by 7–11 times, but performs *poorly* (i.e., the user's fetching speed falls below 1 Mbps, or 125 KBps, and is thus unfit for HD video streaming) once there is a bandwidth bottleneck in the network path between the cloud and the user. Specifically, a high portion (28 %) of Xuanfeng users suffer from this bottleneck, which is mainly caused by cross-ISP data delivery, low user-side access bandwidth, or lack of cloud-side upload bandwidth. These users should utilize an additional smart AP to mitigate these impediments.
2. *The cloud's upload bandwidth is being overused.* The cloud-based approach is threatened by running out of its upload bandwidth due to *unnecessarily* sending *highly popular* files. A small percentage (0.84 %) of highly popular files account for a large part (39 %) of all downloads. As the user base grows, the cloud of Xuanfeng will have to reject more (> 1.5 %) users' fetching requests. Because the majority (87 %) of requested files are hosted in peer-to-peer data swarms [37],

many highly popular files can be directly downloaded by users with as good or greater performance than what is provided by cloud-based offline downloading services.

3. *Smart APs frequently fail during pre-downloading.* Although smart APs are immune to the above performance bottlenecks of the cloud-based approach, they frequently (42 %) fail while pre-downloading *unpopular* files. This is mainly caused by insufficient seeds in a P2P data swarm and poor HTTP/FTP connections. Note that 36 % of offline downloading requests are issued for unpopular files. Therefore, users who need to download unpopular files should choose the cloud-based approach, which is better at downloading unpopular files—the failure ratio (13 %) is much lower owing to *collaborative caching* (refer to Sect. 5.3.1) in the massive cloud storage pool.

4. *Smart APs can be slower due to hardware/filesystem restrictions.* Surprisingly, a smart AP's pre-downloading speed can be restricted by its hardware and filesystem. This is because some types of storage devices (e.g., USB flash drive) and filesystems (e.g., NTFS) do not fit the pattern of frequent, small data writes during the pre-downloading process. These smart APs would benefit from upgraded storage devices and/or alternate filesystems, so as to release the full potential of offline downloading.

Driven by these results, we design and implement a proof-of-concept middleware called ODR (Offline Downloading Redirector, available at http://odr.thucloud.com) to help users get rid of performance bottlenecks (Sect. 5.7). As illustrated in Fig. 5.2, the basic idea of ODR is to adaptively redirect the user's file request to where the best performance is expected to be achieved, including the cloud (we use the Xuanfeng cloud in our implementation), the smart AP, the user's local device, or a combination. ODR's primary goal is to minimize the downloading time and failure ratio; its secondary goal is to minimize the upload bandwidth burden on the cloud.

ODR makes redirection decisions based on two types of information. First, after receiving an offline downloading request, ODR queries the content database of Xuanfeng to obtain the popularity information of the requested file. Then, ODR examines

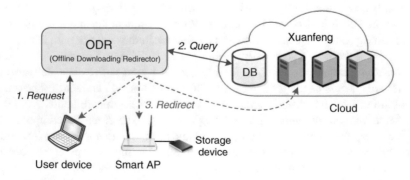

Fig. 5.2 Basic working principle of ODR. (Reprinted with permission from [15].)

whether there is a potential bandwidth bottleneck by analyzing the user's IP address, access bandwidth, storage device, and so forth. Note that ODR requires no modification to existing cloud-based systems or smart AP devices. As a result, it is easy to deploy in practice.

To validate the efficacy of ODR, we replay an unbiased sample of Xuanfeng users' offline downloading requests using a prototype ODR system. The evaluation results indicate that ODR is able to effectively overcome the performance bottlenecks. First, the percentage of impeded fetching processes is reduced from 28 to 9 %. Second, the cloud's upload bandwidth burden is reduced by 35 % and thus no fetching request will need to be rejected. Third, the percentage of smart APs' failures in pre-downloading unpopular files is reduced from 42 to 13 %. Last, the hardware/filesystem restrictions on smart APs' pre-downloading speeds are almost completely avoided.

Finally, we feel that offline downloading has broad applicability to other areas of the world that lack broadband penetration. By deploying offline downloading technologies, coupled with our proposed ODR middleware, the Internet experiences for users in many parts of the world can be significantly improved.

5.2 Related Work

This section reviews previous studies of offline downloading, including both the cloud and smart AP-based approaches. We also discuss the hybrid approach which directly connects the smart AP to the cloud and compare it with our ODR. In addition, we describe a few offline downloading (based) services outside China. Finally, we briefly survey the state-of-the-art downloading techniques and compare them with offline downloading.

Cloud-based approach. With the proliferation of cloud-based services, a number of studies have investigated the design and implementation of cloud-based offline downloading systems and their performance measurements.

Huang et al. [22] presented the early-stage system design of Xuanfeng in 2011, which focuses on guaranteeing data health and accelerating the downloading speed of unpopular videos. However, perhaps due to the startup stage of the system at that time (with a relatively small user base), their study did not notice the two critical performance bottlenecks, i.e., Bottleneck 1 and Bottleneck 2 uncovered in this chapter.

Ao et al. [21] conducted a long-term measurement study of Xuanfeng in 2012, and predicted that the system would be short of cloud-side upload bandwidth in the near future. Complementary to their study, our work provides in-depth insights into the cloud-side upload bandwidth burden, and recognizes Bottleneck 2—the root cause of cloud bandwidth shortage. Furthermore, our proposed ODR middleware can significantly reduce cloud-side bandwidth consumption by asking users to download highly popular P2P files directly from their data swarms.

Zhou et al. [25] made a theoretical analysis of offline downloading service models, including the cloud-based model and the peer-assisted model. They argue that the former can help scale with file population and the latter should be used to deal with popular files. An adaptive algorithm called AMS (Automatic Mode Selection) is proposed for selecting an appropriate model. Compared with AMS, ODR is more general and applicable: it requires no modification on the cloud side. Additionally, ODR is a deployed system rather than a theoretical algorithm.

Smart AP-based approach. Since the history of smart APs is extremely short (just two years), we are not aware of any systematic study on their downloading performances. Most of the existing evaluations [31–36] are based on simplified network environments and unrealistic workloads (e.g., a few popular files). This is probably the reason why Bottleneck 3 in our study had not been discovered yet. Furthermore, Bottleneck 4 had never been identified in existing evaluations of smart APs.

Hybrid approach. HiWiFi, MiWiFi, and Newifi all provide hybrid solutions for offline downloading [38–40]. In these hybrid solutions, user-requested files are first downloaded by the cloud, and then the smart AP fetches the files from the cloud. That is to say, the downloading process always goes through the longest data flow: first from the Internet to the cloud, and then to the smart AP of the user.

In contrast, our ODR middleware adaptively selects the most efficient data flow for users to avoid performance bottlenecks. Therefore, ODR significantly outperforms the current hybrid approach by addressing the bottlenecks of both (cloud and smart AP-based) approaches while also inheriting their advantages.

Offline downloading outside China. Besides those developing countries (as mentioned in Sect. 5.1), developed countries can also benefit from offline downloading (based) services. For example, URL Droplet [41] and the Amazon Silk web browser [42] take advantage of the cloud to speed up file transfers. The former employs the Dropbox cloud storage service to download and host files for its users; the latter utilizes Amazon's cloud servers to improve web page loading performance for Kindle Fire tablets and smartphones. On the other side, the smart AP-based approach is adopted by the Linksys Smart WiFi Router [43] which is sold in the US.

State-of-the-art downloading techniques. Existing techniques for Internet file downloading mainly include the centralized Web-based (or client–server), the hierarchical CDN (i.e., content delivery network like Akamai, L-3, and ChinaCache), the decentralized P2P, and the latest ICN (i.e., information centric networking).

The Web-based technique is obviously subject to the intrinsic dynamics and heterogeneities of the Internet, particularly the single-point bottleneck of the Web server. By strategically deploying edge servers in numerous locations that are closer to users, the CDN technique effectively optimizes file downloading performance. Nevertheless, being a commercial service, CDN vendors typically only help to deliver files for *content providers* who pay for the service. On the contrary, the business model of offline downloading is the opposite of CDN, because it charges (or sometimes frees) its users, i.e., *content receivers*, for better downloading experiences.

As mentioned in Sect. 5.4, the P2P technique is good at distributing popular files that are each shared by a number of users, but cannot guarantee the data availability or maintain a high speed for the downloads of unpopular files. This is why so many users have resorted to offline downloading for acquiring files that are originally hosted in P2P data swarms. In a word, offline downloading addresses the unstability and uncertainty of P2P under certain scenarios.

ICN, also known as CCN (content centric networking) or NDN (named data networking), is motivated by content receivers' interest in the network to achieve efficient and reliable data distribution [44], regardless of the properties of the original data sources. Specifically, ICN is featured by a number of desired functions, such as (1) in-network storage for caching, (2) decoupling content senders and receivers, (3) disruption tolerance, (4) multi-party communication through replication, (5) mobility and multi-homing, etc. It is easy to find that offline downloading fulfills at least the first three desired functions of ICN *in a real-world setting without breaking the current Internet architecture*. Further, we would like to explore whether and how offline downloading can enable the other functions of ICN.

5.3 System Overview

This section provides an overview of the systems studied in this chapter, including the cloud-based offline downloading system (Xuanfeng) and three popular smart AP systems.

5.3.1 Overview of Xuanfeng

Xuanfeng is a major provider of cloud-based offline downloading service in China, possessing over 30 million users at the moment (including a small portion of overseas users). Its service can be accessed via either a PC client (available from http://xf. qq.com) or a web-based portal (available at http://lixian.qq.com/main.html). The former access method is dominant due to its full-fledged functionality (supporting almost all the common file transfer protocols like HTTP/FTP and BitTorrent/eMule). In terms of business model, Xuanfeng exists as a value-added service of the Tencent company, i.e., any registered Tencent user can access it freely. Baidu CloudDisk [17] and Xunlei [20] are the main competitors of Xuanfeng.[1] The former is also a free service, while the latter charges its users around $1.50 per month.

As depicted in Fig. 5.3, the system architecture of the Xuanfeng cloud mainly consists of three clusters of servers: (1) *pre-downloading servers*, (2) *storage servers*, and (3) *uploading servers*, as well as a database (DB) for maintaining the metadata

---

[1]Note that the configuration and engineering of Xunlei and Baidu CloudDisk may differ from those of Xuanfeng. Hence, their performance bottlenecks may also be different.

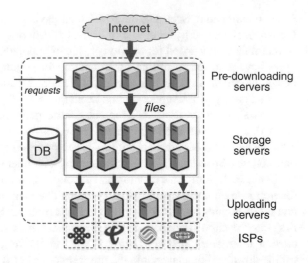

Fig. 5.3 System architecture of the Xuanfeng cloud. (Reprinted with permission from [15].)

information of users and cached files. The total cloud storage space (spread across nearly 500 commodity servers) is nearly 2 PB at the moment, caching around 5 million files. The cached files are replaced in an LRU (least recently used) manner.

Collaborative caching. In the Xuanfeng cloud, all users' requested files are cached in a *collaborative* way. Specifically, every file is identified using the MD5 hash code of its content, which facilitates file-level deduplication across different users. Consequently, the vast majority (89 %) of offline downloading requests can be instantly satisfied with cached files and then no pre-downloading bandwidth cost is incurred. Xuanfeng does not utilize chunk-level deduplication to avoid trading high chunking complexity for low (<1 %) storage space savings. The low storage savings come from the fact that there do exist a few videos sharing a portion of frames/chunks.

When a user-requested file cannot be found in the cloud cache, Xuanfeng assigns a virtual machine (named a *pre-downloader*) to pre-download the file from the Internet. The Internet access bandwidth of a pre-downloader is around 20 Mbps (= 2.5 MBps), equivalent to the high-end, fixed broadband bandwidth in China.

Privileged network path. China has a different Internet topology from Europe and the US. Particularly, China has a simple AS topology with a small number of major ISPs; each ISP has a giant AS built on top of a nationwide backbone network [45]. As a consequence, the performance of cross-ISP data delivery is significantly degraded, a problem which is known as the *ISP barrier* [46, 47]. To accelerate users' fetching processes, Xuanfeng tries to construct *privileged network paths* between the cloud and users by deploying uploading servers within the four major ISPs: Unicom [48], Telecom [49], Mobile [50], and CERNET [51].

To construct a privileged network path, Xuanfeng always attempts to select an uploading server that resides in the same ISP as the fetching user, so that the ISP barrier is avoided. However, privileged path construction may fail in two cases: (1) The fetching user is not within any of the four major ISPs; (2) The fetching user is within one of the four major ISPs (say CERNET) but the uploading servers in CERNET have exhausted their upload bandwidth at that time. In either case, Xuanfeng would select an alternative uploading server that has the shortest network latency from the user.

Once a privileged network path is set up, Xuanfeng sets no limitation on the user's fetching speed, with maximum speeds reaching 50 Mbps (= 6.25 MBps). However, at some "peak" point, all the uploading servers may have exhausted their upload bandwidth. In this case, Xuanfeng temporarily rejects new fetching requests rather than degrade the speeds of active downloads.

5.3.2 Overview of the Smart AP Systems

Though smart APs have only been on the market for around 2 years, they have quickly gained enormous popularity in China. HiWiFi, the first widely available smart AP device released in Mar. 2013 [52], is now striving toward 5 million sales [18]. Despite the late entry into the market (in May 2014), 100,000 MiWiFi devices were sold out in just 59 seconds [16].

As depicted in Fig. 5.4, the system architecture of popular smart APs is essentially made up of three parts: (1) Basic hardware, including CPU, RAM, NIC (network interface card) for xDSL, NIC for WiFi, and the storage device interface(s); (2) The operating system (typically OpenWrt [53]); (3) Shell and the other applications.

Table 5.1 lists the hardware configurations of the three popular smart APs we examine in this study. Among them, MiWiFi has the best configuration in terms of CPU, RAM, storage device, and WiFi data transfer. Accordingly, MiWiFi costs more than $100, while HiWiFi and Newifi each costs around $20.

Fig. 5.4 System architecture of a commerical smart AP. Note that a given smart AP device may not contain all potential storage device interfaces. (Reprinted with permission from [15].)

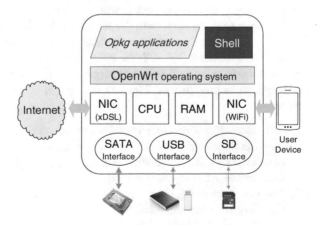

Table 5.1 Hardware configurations of the three popular smart APs studied in this chapter

Smart AP	CPU	RAM	Storage interface (and device)	WiFi protocol
HiWiFi (1S)	MT7620A@580 MHz	128 MB	An SD card interface	IEEE 802.11 b/g/n@2.4 GHz
MiWiFi	Broadcom4709@1 GHz	256 MB	A USB 2.0 interface and an internal 1-TB SATA hard disk drive	IEEE 802.11 b/g/n/ac@2.4/5.0 GHz
Newifi	MT7620A@580 MHz	128 MB	A USB 2.0 interface	IEEE 802.11 b/g/n/ac@2.4/5.0 GHz

(Reprinted with permission from [15].)

All the three popular smart APs utilize OpenWrt, a Linux-based embedded operating system. OpenWrt provides a fully writable filesystem and supports the lightweight Opkg package management system [54], which allows users to install any Opkg application. For instance, the three APs make use of wget and aria2 [55] to support HTTP/FTP and BitTorrent/eMule protocols. Also, a web interface is provided for users to specify offline downloading requests. In our benchmark experiments, we measure and record detailed performance of smart APs with Opkg tools/apps such as BASH, tcpdump, top, iostats, and scp.

5.4 Workload Characteristics

To understand the workload characteristics of offline downloading, we study a large-scale dataset collected from Xuanfeng. We assume that the smart AP-based offline downloading systems have similar workload characteristics to Xuanfeng, since most end users are not familiar with the technical details and cannot differentiate these services. The large-scale dataset contains the complete running logs of Xuanfeng during a whole week (Feb. 22–28, 2015), involving 4,084,417 offline downloading tasks, 783,944 users, and 563,517 unique files. Corresponding to the three stages of offline downloading (refer to Fig. 5.1), the dataset is composed of the following three parts:

1. The trace of user requests (workload trace) records all the offline downloading requests issued by users. For each request, the logs record the user ID, IP address, access bandwidth (if available), request time, file type, file size, link to the original data source, and file transfer protocol;
2. The pre-downloading trace records the performance data of the proxy's pre-downloading user-requested files. It includes the start time, finish time, acquired file size, network traffic consumed, cloud cache hit status, average downloading speed, peak downloading speed, and success or failure for each pre-downloading process;

3. The fetching trace records the performance data of users' fetching processes from the proxy. It contains the user ID, IP address, access bandwidth (if available), start time, finish/pause time, acquired file size, network traffic consumed, average fetching speed, and peak fetching speed for each fetching process.

This section studies the first part of the dataset (i.e., users' offline downloading requests). The second and third parts of the dataset will be examined in Sects. 5.5 and 5.6.

File type. In the workload trace, the majority (75 %) of offline downloading requests are issued for videos; the other 15 % are for software packages. The reason is intuitive: among all the requested files, videos are the largest in size, i.e., the most time and traffic consuming to download, so users are more inclined to issue offline downloading requests for videos. This suggests that offline downloading systems should be mainly optimized for videos.

File size. As shown in Fig. 5.5, the average size of requested files is 390 MB and the maximum size is 4 GB, which is consistent with our observation that most requested files are large videos. Nevertheless, we also find that up to 25 % of requested files are smaller than 8 MB in size, most of which are demo videos, pictures, documents, and small software packages.

File transfer protocol. The majority (87 %) of requested files are hosted in P2P data swarms, including BitTorrent (68 %) and eMule (19 %) swarms. The remaining 13 % are hosted on HTTP or FTP servers. Thus, designers of offline downloading systems should pay special attention to P2P-based file transfer protocols.

Since P2P suffers from several technical shortcomings (e.g., high dynamics and heterogeneities among end user devices and network connections), it is often difficult for users to find peers (including both seeds and leechers) sharing the target files. As a result, the downloading efficacy of P2P can be poor and unpredictable. For this reason, users resort to offline downloading to obtain P2P files over the long run. On the contrary, HTTP and FTP servers are usually stable with more predictable

Fig. 5.5 CDF of requested file size. Min size: 4 B, Median size: 115 MB, Average size: 390 MB, and Max size: 4 GB. (Reprinted with permission from [15].)

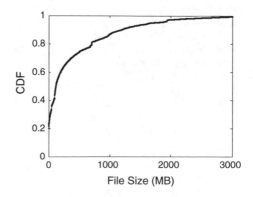

performance, so online downloading is preferred. This explains the dominance of P2P in terms of file transfer protocol.

File popularity. As mentioned in Sect. 5.3.1, Xuanfeng actively maintains a content database where every file is associated with a unique identifier (ID). The ID is the MD5 hash code of the complete file content. Hence, files are considered *identical* as long as they have the same ID. Figure 5.6 (in $log(x)$ vs. $log(y)$ style) and Fig. 5.7 (in $log(x)$ vs. y^c style) indicate that the popularity distribution of requested files is highly skewed, approximately following the well known Zipf model [56] or the SE (stretched exponential) model [57].

Let x denote the popularity ranking of a file, and y denote its popularity (according to the workload trace). Then, we have the following fitting equations:

$$\text{Zipf:}\quad log(y) = -a_1 \times log(x) + b_1,$$

$$\text{SE:}\quad y^c = -a_2 \times log(x) + b_2,$$

where $a_1 = 1.034$, $b_1 = 14.444$, $a_2 = 0.010$, $b_2 = 1.134$, and $c = 0.01$.

Fig. 5.6 Popularity distribution of requested files—Zipf fitting. The average relative error of fitness is 15.3%. (Reprinted with permission from [15].)

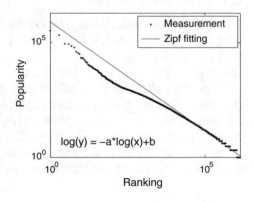

Fig. 5.7 Popularity distribution of requested files—SE fitting. The average relative error of fitness is 13.7%. (Reprinted with permission from [15].)

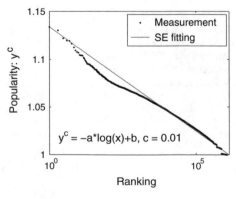

With regard to the average relative error of fitness, SE (13.7%) seems to be a better fit than Zipf (15.3%), especially for those small-ranking (i.e., most popular) files. The reason why SE fits the measurement data better than Zipf can be mainly attributed to the *fetch-at-most-once* effect of P2P video files [58]. It is known that 75% of offline downloading requests are issued for videos and 87% of requested files are hosted in P2P data swarms. That is to say, P2P video files dominate the workload of Xuanfeng. Specifically, a given Xuanfeng user generally fetches a P2P video file for at most once, whereas web pages and other small documents are often fetched repeatedly [56]. Therefore, the access pattern of offline downloaded files deviates from the Zipf access pattern of web objects. The above finding complements the analysis of file popularity in previous studies of offline downloading [22, 25], which simply used the Zipf model to characterize the workload.

5.5 Performance of the Cloud-Based System

This section presents the performance of our representative cloud-based offline downloading system Xuanfeng, including both the pre-downloading and fetching phases. In addition, we analyze the end-to-end performance by combining the two phases.

5.5.1 Pre-downloading Performance

Pre-downloading speed. Figure 5.8 (the upper curve) plots the distribution of pre-downloading speeds in Xuanfeng. The median speed is merely 25 KBps, which

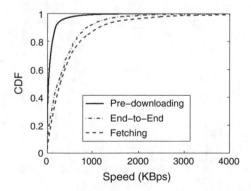

Fig. 5.8 CDF of pre-downloading and fetching speeds in Xuanfeng. As for the pre-downloading speed (excluding the cache hit cases), Min: 0 KBps, Median: 25 KBps, Average: 69 KBps, and Max: 2.37 MBps (≈20 Mbps). As for the fetching speed, Min: 0 KBps, Median: 287 KBps, Average: 504 KBps, and Max: 6.1 MBps (≈50 Mbps). As for the end-to-end speed, Min: 0 KBps, Median: 233 KBps, Average: 380 KBps, and Max: 6.1 MBps (≈50 Mbps). (Reprinted with permission from [15].)

indicates that half of the pre-downloading processes are quite slow. The average speed (69 KBps) is higher than the median speed, but is still far from satisfactory—keep in mind that, as mentioned in Sect. 5.3.1, the access bandwidth of a pre-downloader is around 20 Mbps (= 2.5 MBps). 21 % of the pre-downloading processes even have a speed close to 0 KBps, which is mostly caused by pre-downloading failures.

Pre-downloading delay. Figure 5.9 (the lower curve) plots the distribution of the pre-downloading delay in Xuanfeng (excluding the cache hit cases where the pre-downloading delay is zero). The average delay is as high as 370 min, which is much longer than the length of a common movie (100–120 min). Obviously, such long delay is unfit for continuous video streaming [59, 60]. Also, the average delay is much longer than the median delay (82 min), indicating that the pre-downloading delay of many requested files is extremely long.

Failure ratio. A *pre-downloading failure* occurs when the service gives up the pre-downloading attempt and notifies the requesting user of the failure. It is hard to theoretically define a failure if we allow the pre-downloading process to take infinite time. However, practical systems have to timeout the pre-downloading process if the expected completion time is not reasonable. In practice, Xuanfeng raises a pre-downloading failure for a requested file when *the corresponding pre-downloading progress stagnates for an hour*. This timeout rule is supported by our following observation in Xuanfeng: if the pre-downloading progress of a requested file stagnates for an hour, then this file can hardly be successfully pre-downloaded even if the timeout threshold is set to be one week.

The overall pre-downloading failure ratio of Xuanfeng is 8.7 %. Note that if a user-requested file is already cached in the cloud storage pool, the pre-downloading is immediately successful. On the other hand, if we do not take the cache hit cases into account (i.e., we assume that the cloud storage pool does not exist), the overall

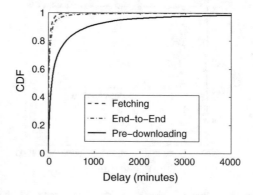

Fig. 5.9 CDF of pre-downloading, fetching, and end-to-end delay in Xuanfeng. As for the pre-downloading delay (excluding the cache hit cases), Min: 0 min, Median: 82 min, Average: 370 min, and Max: 10071 min. As for the fetching delay, Min: 0 min, Median: 7 min, Average: 27 min, and Max: 9724 min. As for the end-to-end delay, Min: 0 min, Median: 10 min, Average: 68 min, and Max: 19553 min. (Reprinted with permission from [15].)

Fig. 5.10 Request
popularity *versus*
Pre-downloading failure
ratio. Request popularity:
[0, 7) → unpopular files,
[7, 84] → popular files, and
(84, MAX] → highly
popular files. (Reprinted
with permission from [15].)

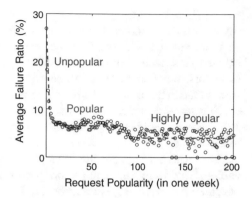

pre-downloading failure ratio will increase to 16.4 %. This confirms the importance
of the massive cloud storage pool as well as the collaborative caching mechanism
(refer to Sect. 5.3.1) in mitigating pre-downloading failures.

More importantly, we discover that the pre-downloading failure ratio correlates
with the popularity of requested files, as shown in the scatter plot of Fig. 5.10. For
the purposes of this discussion, we define a file to be *unpopular* if it was downloaded
less than 7 times per week. *Popular* files are downloaded 7–84 times per week, while
highly popular files are downloaded greater than 84 times per week. Given these
definitions, we find that 93.2 % of files are unpopular while only 0.84 % of files are
highly popular. However, only 36 % of offline downloading requests are issued for
the 93.2 % unpopular files, while 39 % of requests are issued for the 0.84 % highly
popular files.

Network traffic cost. As discussed in Sect. 5.4, only 13 % of requested files are
hosted in HTTP or FTP servers, while 87 % are hosted in P2P data swarms. For
HTTP and FTP, the pre-downloading traffic is slightly (typically 7–10 %) larger
than the file size; the overhead mainly comes from HTTP, FTP, TCP, and IP packet
headers. For P2P, its "tit-for-tat" policy [61] (i.e., a peer that downloads data from
others must upload data to others at the same time) causes the pre-downloading traffic
to be considerably (50–150 %) larger than the file size. In the Xuanfeng system, we
observe that the overall pre-downloading traffic is 196 % of the total file size. That
is to say, the overhead traffic is comparable to the file size.

5.5.2   Fetching Performance

Fetching speed. Figure 5.8 (the lower curve) shows the distribution of users' fetching speeds from the cloud. Owing to the privileged network paths constructed by
Xuanfeng (refer to Sect. 5.3.1), the median and average fetching speeds are as high
as 287 and 504 KBps. Given that the median and average pre-downloading speeds are

merely 25 and 69 KBps, Xuanfeng greatly improves *perceived* downloading speeds (by 7–11 times in terms of median and average speeds) for China's Internet users.

When videos are fetched from the proxy, Xuanfeng supports two different modes: (a) *view as download* and (b) *view after download*. According to Xuanfeng users' behaviors, most users tend to choose the former mode over the latter. Therefore, to facilitate users' real-time video playback in a continuous manner, a *bandwidth bottleneck* is recognized when the fetching speed falls below 125 KBps. The 125 KBps threshold corresponds with the typical 1 Mbps playback rate of large (HD) videos [62, 63].

Specifically, a high portion (28 %) of fetching speeds are below 125 KBps. To explore why Xuanfeng exhibits poor performance during these fetching processes, we carefully examine the corresponding logs in the fetching trace, and find that the bandwidth bottleneck is mainly caused by three issues: (1) cross-ISP data delivery, (2) low user-side access bandwidth, and (3) lack of cloud-side upload bandwidth.

In detail, 9.6 % of fetching processes are limited by the ISP barrier. For these fetching processes, the users' IP addresses do not belong to any of the four ISPs supported by Xuanfeng. Besides, around 10.8 % of fetching processes are limited by low user-side access bandwidth[2] (<125 KBps). Additionally, there are 1.5 % of fetching requests rejected by the cloud due to lack of upload bandwidth (refer to Sect. 5.3.1). These rejected requests explain why the minimum observed fetching speed is 0 KBps. Finally, the remaining unmentioned portion (= 28 % − 9.6 % − 10.8 % − 1.5 % = 6.1 %) are owing to unknown reasons we have not figured out yet, possibly because of the network dynamics or system bugs.

Fetching delay. Figure 5.9 (the upper curve) shows the distribution of users' fetching delay. As a consequence of most users' high fetching speeds, the median fetching delay is as low as 7 min and the average fetching delay is merely 27 min. Given that the median and average pre-downloading delay is as high as 82 and 370 min, Xuanfeng has significantly shortened *perceived* downloading delay (by 12–14 times in terms of median and average fetching delay) for China's Internet users.

In summary, we find the first key performance bottleneck of offline downloading:

- *The cloud-based approach performs poorly once there is a bandwidth bottleneck in the privileged network path between the cloud and the user. This bottleneck is mainly caused by cross-ISP data delivery, low user-side access bandwidth, or lack of cloud-side upload bandwidth.*

Shortage of cloud bandwidth. In order to support high-speed fetching from the cloud to users' devices, Xuanfeng has purchased a total of 30 Gbps of upload bandwidth from the four major ISPs in China. In the 7th day of the measurement week, the peak cloud-side upload bandwidth burden exceeded 30 Gbps, as demonstrated in Fig. 5.11. Consequently, a small portion (1.5 %) of fetching requests were rejected by Xuanfeng. As the user base continues to grow, Xuanfeng will have to reject more fetching requests, which unfortunately harms the user experience.

---

[2]Some users of Xuanfeng did not report their access bandwidth. For these users, we use the peak fetching speed recorded in the fetching trace to approximate their access bandwidth.

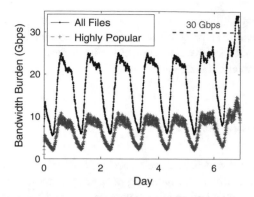

Fig. 5.11 Cloud-side upload bandwidth burden of Xuanfeng in the measurement week (including those rejected fetching requests). The time interval is 5 min. Note that for the 1.5 % of fetching requests rejected by Xuanfeng in the 7th day, their incurred cloud-side upload bandwidth burden (which did not really happen) is estimated by approximately taking their average fetching speed as 504 KBps (i.e., the average speed of all the real fetching processes in Xuanfeng, refer to Fig. 5.8). (Reprinted with permission from [15].)

On the other hand, if we look deeply into the usage of cloud bandwidth, we find that *the current cloud-side upload bandwidth burden is not all necessary.* We calculate the cloud-side bandwidth used for delivering (uploading) highly popular files based on the fetching trace, plotted as the lower, blue curve in Fig. 5.11. We can see that, on average, nearly 40 % of the cloud bandwidth is spent delivering highly popular files. The reason is that a small percentage (0.84 %) of highly popular files account for a large part (39 %) of all downloads, as discussed in Sect. 5.5.1.

In fact, because the majority (87 %) of requested files are hosted in P2P data swarms, many highly popular files can be directly downloaded by users with as good or greater performance than what the cloud provides [64, 65]. This is because P2P data sharing among end users can achieve the so-called "*bandwidth multiplier effect*" [65]. Specifically, by appropriately allocating a certain portion of cloud bandwidth (S_i) to a P2P data swarm i to seed the content, the Xuanfeng system can attain a higher aggregate content distribution bandwidth (D_i) by letting P2P users exchange data and distribute content among themselves. The ratio $\frac{D_i}{S_i}$ is referred to as the bandwidth multiplier for P2P data swarm i. The above observation and analysis lead to the second key performance bottleneck of offline downloading:

- *The cloud-based approach is threatened by running out of upload bandwidth due to unnecessarily sending highly popular files. As the user base continues to grow, the cloud will have to reject more (>1.5 %) fetching requests.*

User-side network overhead. Xuanfeng minimizes the user-side network overhead, as its users only download requested files from the cloud and do not upload data to others. On average, a user's downloading traffic usage is slightly (7–10 %) larger than the file size. This is especially useful for mobile P2P users with limited data plans or traffic caps. As mentioned in Sect. 5.5.1, for an average P2P user to download a file from the corresponding data swarm, the total traffic usage is 196 % of the total file size. Therefore, by resorting to Xuanfeng rather than the original data swarm, an average P2P user could achieve considerable traffic usage saving which is comparable to 86–89 % of the total file size.

5.5.3 End-to-End Performance

Finally, we analyze the *end-to-end speed and delay* of offline downloading in Xuanfeng. For a complete offline downloading process, the end-to-end delay is the sum of pre-downloading delay and fetching delay, and the end-to-end speed is the size of the requested file divided by the end-to-end delay.

As illustrated in Fig. 5.9, the CDF curve of end-to-end delay falls between the CDF curves of pre-downloading delay and fetching delay, which is within our expectation. More importantly, the distribution of end-to-end delay looks much closer to the distribution of fetching delay. This is because the vast majority (89 %) of offline downloading requests can be instantly satisfied by the cloud cache and thus the corresponding pre-downloading delay is almost zero (refer to Sect. 5.3.1). Similarly, Fig. 5.8 indicates that the CDF curve of end-to-end speed falls between the CDF curves of pre-downloading speed and fetching speed, and the distribution of end-to-end speed is much closer to the distribution of fetching speed.

From the above observations, we conclude that even from an end-to-end perspective, the offline downloading service provided by Xuanfeng can effectively improve the *perceived experiences* for its users.

5.6 Performance of the Smart APs

Now that we understand the dynamics and performance characteristics of Xuanfeng, we move on to examining smart AP-based offline downloading. In this section, we report our benchmark methodology and the performance of the three most popular smart APs in China: HiWiFi, MiWiFi, and Newifi.

5.6.1 Methodology

To comprehensively measure the performance of the three popular smart APs (during Mar. 1–22, 2015), we randomly sample 1000 real offline downloading requests[3] issued by Unicom users in the workload trace of Xuanfeng (refer to Sect. 5.4). These

---

[3]Each selected request record should contain the user's access bandwidth information so that we can approximate the user's real network connection characteristics during our benchmarks.

sampled requests (which we refer to as the sampled workload) are restricted to Unicom users because our benchmark experiments are conducted by replaying the sampled workload with smart APs on Unicom network connections. On the other hand, the data sources of these sampled requests are located across various ISPs in China. For every request record, we ignore its user ID, IP address, and request time (since these factors cannot be reproduced in our benchmarks), but reuse the user's access bandwidth, as well as the file type, file size, link to the original data source, and file transfer protocol.

To replay the sampled workload using the three smart APs, we utilize three independent residential ADSL links provided by the Unicom ISP, each of which was used exclusively by one smart AP, as depicted in Fig. 5.12. Each link has 20 Mbps (= 2.5 MBps) of Internet access bandwidth. When replaying an individual offline downloading request, we restrict the smart AP's pre-downloading speed within the recorded user access bandwidth, so as to approximate the real network connection status. We sequentially replay around 333 requests (request $i + 1$ is replayed after request i completes or fails) on each smart AP and record the performance data.

HiWiFi uses an embedded 8-GB SD card (Max Write/Read Speed: 15 MBps/30 MBps) as the storage device. The SD card can only be formatted as FAT (otherwise, HiWiFi does not work). Newifi uses an external 8-GB USB flash drive (Max Write/Read Speed: 10 MBps/20 MBps) via a USB 2.0 interface. The USB flash drive is formatted as NTFS. Since both HiWiFi and Newifi have a small storage capacity, we remove requested files from the storage device after they are completely downloaded or the corresponding pre-downloading task failures (refer to Sect. 5.5.1). At the same time, the performance data is aggregated into a storage server. MiWiFi uses its internal 1-TB SATA hard disk drive (5400 RPM, Max Write/Read Speed: 30 MBps/70 MBps). This hard disk drive has been formatted as EXT4 by the manufacturer, and it cannot be reformatted to any other filesystem.

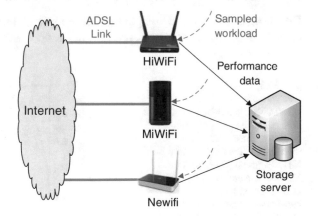

Fig. 5.12 Our benchmark environment. For each smart AP, its embedded/connected storage device is not plotted to make the figure tidy. (Reprinted with permission from [15].)

5.6.2 Benchmark Results

Since smart APs are located in the same LAN (local area network) as users, the performance of the fetching phase is seldom an issue except when multiple user devices are fetching from a smart AP at the same time. Specifically, a user can fetch from a smart AP by directly dumping from the AP's storage device or through a wired/WiFi LAN connection. Even the lowest WiFi fetching speed lies in 8–12 MBps, which is higher than the maximum fetching speed (i.e., 6.1 MBps) of Xuanfeng users. As a consequence, below we focus on the performance of the pre-downloading phase.

Pre-downloading failure ratio. The overall pre-downloading failure ratio of smart APs is 16.8%, which is higher than that of Xuanfeng (8.7%). More importantly, for unpopular files the pre-downloading failure ratio of smart APs is as high as 42%, significantly higher than that of Xuanfeng (13%). Note that according to the workload trace of Xuanfeng, 36% of offline downloading requests are issued for unpopular files. With these results, we discover the third key performance bottleneck of offline downloading:

- *Although smart APs are immune to the two bottlenecks of the cloud-based approach described in Sect. 5.5, they frequently fail in pre-downloading unpopular files. In contrast, the cloud-based approach performs much better at downloading unpopular files since it benefits from the massive geo-distributed cloud storage pool.*

Further, we delve into the details of the pre-downloading failures of smart APs. Among the 168 (= 1000 × 16.8%) failures, the vast majority (145, 86%) were caused by insufficient seeds in a P2P data swarm. This explains why the pre-downloading failure ratio of unpopular files is especially high. Besides, a non-negligible part (17, 10%) were ascribed to poor HTTP/FTP connections, i.e., the server at the other end failed to maintain a persistent/resumable download. The remainder (6, 4%) might be the result of system bugs in HiWiFi, MiWiFi, and Newifi.

Pre-downloading speed and delay. As shown in Figs. 5.13 and 5.14, the pre-downloading speeds of smart APs are just a bit lower than those of Xuanfeng's

Fig. 5.13 CDF of smart APs' pre-downloading speeds. Min: 0 KBps; Median: 27 KBps; Average: 64 KBps; Max: 2.37 MBps (≈20 Mbps) for HiWiFi and MiWiFi, and 0.93 MBps for Newifi. As a comparison, the CDF of cloud-based pre-downloading speeds is also plotted. (Reprinted with permission from [15].)

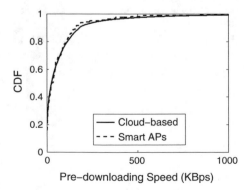

Fig. 5.14 CDF of smart APs' pre-downloading delay. Min: 0 min; Median: 77 min; Average: 402 min; Max: 8297 min. As a comparison, the CDF of cloud-based pre-downloading delay is also plotted. (Reprinted with permission from [15].)

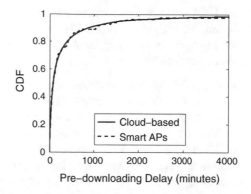

pre-downloaders, and thus the pre-downloading delay of smart APs seems a bit longer than that of Xuanfeng. This is because smart APs work in a similar way as the pre-downloaders (i.e., they also download files using HTTP, FTP, and P2P protocols; refer to Sect. 5.3.1), although their access bandwidths are generally lower than 20 Mbps (or 2.5 MBps, i.e., a pre-downloader's access bandwidth).

However, one detail in Figs. 5.13 and 5.14 is worth discussing: the median pre-downloading speed of smart APs (27 KBps) is *higher* than that of Xuanfeng (25 KBps), but the average pre-downloading speed of smart APs (64 KBps) is *lower* than that of Xuanfeng (69 KBps). Accordingly, the median pre-downloading delay of smart APs (77 min) is *shorter* than that of Xuanfeng (82 min), but the average pre-downloading delay of smart APs (402 min) is *longer* than that of Xuanfeng (370 min). To demystify this counterintuitive phenomenon, we examine the pre-downloading performance data of every task in the sampled workload and its original performance data in the pre-downloading trace. Surprisingly, we uncover the fourth key performance bottleneck of offline downloading:

- *A smart AP's pre-downloading speed can be restricted by its hardware and/or filesystem, since some types of storage devices and filesystems do not fit the pattern of frequent, small data writes during the pre-downloading process.*

In particular, among all the experimented storage devices, USB flash drive is the slowest. When Newifi uses the USB flash drive (in the NTFS format) as its storage device, the max pre-downloading speed is merely 0.93 MBps, much lower than that of HiWiFi and MiWiFi (2.37 MBps). This finding is basically consistent with Sundaresan et al.'s study results on broadband Internet performance in 2011, which also indicate that a user's home network equipment (including the home router of course, though smart APs did not exist in 2011) can significantly affect downloading performance [66].

To comprehensively understand the influence of hardware and filesystem on Newifi's pre-downloading speed, we replay the top-10 popular requests in the sampled workload on Newifi while setting no restriction on its pre-downloading speed (so the maximum speed should be nearly 2.37 MBps). We conducted replays with the USB flash drive formatted as FAT, NTFS, and EXT4, respectively, as well as with the USB flash drive replaced by a USB hard disk drive (5400 RPM, Max Write/Read Speed: 10 MBps/25 MBps). The resulting maximum pre-downloading speeds, as well as the corresponding iowait ratios, are listed in Table 5.2. We make three observations as follows:

- The NTFS filesystem severely harms Newifi's maximum pre-downloading speed, no matter whether the storage device is a USB flash drive or a USB hard disk drive. This is mainly attributed to the incompatibility between NTFS and Newifi's OpenWrt operating system (refer to Sect. 5.3.2) which utilizes the EXT4 filesystem.
- When Newifi uses a USB flash drive as its storage device, FAT and EXT4 filesystems also appear to have degraded its maximum pre-downloading speed. The major reason should be the unsuitability of the USB flash drive on handling frequent, small data writes during pre-downloading. This is reflected by the high iowait ratios (66.3 and 55 %) as shown in Table 5.2. Besides, we observe that the receiver-side TCP sliding window (the typical size is 14608 bytes) is almost full in most of the time during the pre-downloading process.
- When Newifi uses a USB hard disk drive, its maximum pre-downloading speed is considerably enhanced (compared with using a USB flash drive) even when the hard disk drive is formatted as NTFS. No matter which filesystem is used, the iowait ratio is relatively low.

Based on the above observations, we suggest that Newifi-like smart APs upgrade their storage devices and/or change their default filesystems to more performant variants, so as to release the full potential of offline downloading. Currently, because Newifi only has a USB 2.0 interface (refer to Table 5.1), using a USB hard disk drive coupled with the EXT4 filesystem seems to be the best fit. On the other hand, if Newifi upgrades its storage interface to USB 3.0 in the future, using a USB 3.0 flash drive formatted as EXT4 might be a more cost-effective choice, given that a USB flash drive is usually much smaller and cheaper than a USB hard disk drive.

Table 5.2 Max pre-downloading speeds and the corresponding iowait ratios for HiWiFi, MiWiFi, and Newifi, with different storage devices and filesystems

Max pre-downloading speed (MBps)	FAT	NTFS	EXT4
HiWiFi + SD card	2.37	–	–
MiWiFi + SATA hard disk drive	–	–	2.37
Newifi + USB flash drive	**2.12**	**0.93**	**2.13**
Newifi + USB hard disk drive	2.37	**1.13**	2.37
iowait ratio	FAT (%)	NTFS (%)	EXT4 (%)
HiWiFi + SD card	42.1	–	–
MiWiFi + SATA hard disk drive	–	–	29.7
Newifi + USB flash drive	**66.3**	15.1	**55**
Newifi + USB hard disk drive	42	9.8	17.4

(Reprinted with permission from [15].)

5.7 The ODR Middleware

Motivated by the study in Sects. 5.5 and 5.6, we design and implement a proof-of-concept middleware called ODR (Offline Downloading Redirector) to help users get rid of performance bottlenecks. We evaluate the performance of ODR using real-world workloads.

5.7.1 Design and Implementation

ODR is presented as a public web service to users available at http://odr.thucloud. com. It is implemented as a middleware independent of any specific cloud-based offline downloading system or smart AP, and thus can be deployed on any dedicated servers or virtual machines. ODR takes users' offline downloading requests, and adaptively decides in which way the requested files should be downloaded to achieve the best expected downloading experience.

Specifically, when a user wants to download a file from the Internet, she first accesses the web service of ODR (by opening the front web page) and inputs the HTTP/FTP/P2P link to the original data source. In addition, ODR asks for other auxiliary information including the user's IP address, access bandwidth, smart AP type, storage device and filesystem type.[4] All the aforementioned information is straightforward for common users, except the access bandwidth. Fortunately, as the majority of China's Internet users have installed PC-assistant software such as Tencent PC Manager [67], Baidu Guard [68], and 360 Security Guard [69]. With simple instructions, ODR is able to guide users how to obtain the approximate value of access bandwidth with the PC-assistant software.

On receiving an offline downloading request, ODR firstly queries the content database to obtain the latest popularity statistics of the requested file. We use the Xuanfeng database in our implementation, while keep in mind that the performance of ODR would be further enhanced if it is able to use multiple cloud services (e.g., Xuanfeng + Xunlei + Baidu CloudDisk) at once. ODR calculates the decisions based on the popularity of the file and the auxiliary information provided by the user. The decision is then returned to users via the front web page of the ODR service.

Figure 5.15 plots the state transition diagram of ODR's decision making process, which involves a series of conditions and branches as follows.

Handling highly popular files. First and foremost, users are concerned with the downloading success of a requested file. As the downloading failure ratio is tightly related with the popularity (refer to Sects. 5.5.1 and 5.6.2), ODR needs to examine whether the requested file is highly popular. If yes, the ODR is likely to be successful

---

[4]ODR maintains a web cookie at the user side (if her web browser permits), so that the user does not need to repeatedly input the auxiliary information every time.

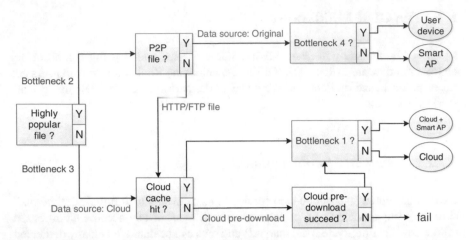

Fig. 5.15 Workflow state transition diagram of ODR. "Y": Yes; "N": No. Bottleneck 1, Bottleneck 2, Bottleneck 3 and Bottleneck 4 denote the four performance bottlenecks of offline downloading mentioned in our key results (refer to Sect. 5.1). (Reprinted with permission from [15].)

at downloading the file, and therefore we can make efforts to mitigate the cloud-side upload bandwidth burden (addressing Bottleneck 2 in Fig. 5.15).

To deal with Bottleneck 2, if the highly popular file is hosted in a P2P data swarm, ODR suggests the user to directly download the file from its original data source (i.e., the abundant peers sharing the file). On the contrary, if the highly popular file is hosted in an HTTP/FTP server, ODR would suggest the user to fall back on the cloud, so as to avoid making the HTTP/FTP server a bottleneck.

Further, to minimize the expected (pre-)downloading time, ODR considers the user-side access bandwidth, as well as the smart AP's storage device and filesystem type (addressing Bottleneck 4 in Fig. 5.15). For example, when the user-side access bandwidth reaches 20 Mbps (= 2.5 MBps), if the smart AP uses a USB flash drive as its storage device or its storage device is formatted as NTFS, ODR would suggest the user to directly download the file using her local device (given that it is usually inconvenient for the user to change the storage device and filesystem of a smart AP during pre-downloading). On the other hand, when the user-side access bandwidth is below 0.93 MBps (refer to Table 5.2), ODR would suggest the user to utilize their smart AP.

Handling less popular files. When a requested file is not highly popular, the success of downloading is our primary concern (addressing Bottleneck 3 in Fig. 5.15). To this end, ODR leverages the cloud storage pool to minimize the failure ratio of (pre-)downloading. Specifically, the downloading falls into the following two cases:

- *Case 1*: If the requested file is already cached in the cloud, ODR should further detect whether there is a bandwidth bottleneck between the cloud and the user by analyzing the user-side access bandwidth and ISP information[5] (addressing Bottleneck 1 in Fig. 5.15). If the user-side access bandwidth is low (<1 Mbps = 125 KBps) or the user is located in a different ISP other than the four ISPs supported by the cloud, ODR would suggest the user to leverage both the cloud and their smart AP to mitigate the impediments of Bottleneck 1 ("Cloud + Smart AP" in Fig. 5.15, i.e., the file should be first pre-downloaded by the smart AP from the cloud, and then fetched by the user from the smart AP). Otherwise, ODR suggests the user to fetch from the cloud.

- *Case 2*: If the requested file is not cached in the cloud, ODR suggests the user to first use the cloud for pre-downloading. After the file is successfully pre-downloaded by the cloud, the user will be notified, and then she can ask ODR again for further suggestions (either directly fetching from the cloud, or from the cloud to a smart AP and then to her local device). If the cloud fails to download the file, the user will be notified of a pre-downloading failure.

Note that ODR never delivers file contents by itself, which makes its operation lightweight in terms of bandwidth and traffic consumption. For our implementation, we rent a low-end virtual machine from Aliyun.com (a major cloud service provider in China) to host the entire ODR service. This virtual machine has a public IP address and 1 Mbps (= 125 KBps) of Internet access bandwidth. The monthly operation cost of ODR is merely $20.

Limitation. By proposing the ODR middleware, our major goal is to demonstrate the potential benefits for a hybrid approach that can effectively address the limitations of the two existing conventional approaches while inheriting their respective advantages. Therefore, the above design and implementation of ODR is basically a *coarse-grained* solution to optimize the offline downloading performance and overhead, where the optimization granularity is a whole offline downloading request/task.

ODR can further benefit from more fine-grained alternative optimization solutions at the chunk, TCP data flow, or sub-stream levels. For instance, a more dynamic solution proposed by Huang et al. [70] (i.e., a buffer-based adaptive bit rate selection algorithm for video streaming) can be used instead of the current hard coded decision procedure of ODR. Moreover, a simple solution (called "mobile phone content pre-staging" [71]) that has been proposed in the past is to simply defer downloads to later times when the download bandwidth is better if the users are not particularly time sensitive. In addition, there are even standards efforts like Low Extra Delay Background Transport (LEDBAT, IETF RFC 6817 [72]) that seeks to utilize the available bandwidth on an end-to-end path while limiting the resulting penalty of delay increase on that path. ODR can learn from LEDBAT to further mitigate the cloud-side upload bandwidth burden.

---

[5]The user's ISP information is obtained based on her IP address with the help of the APNIC service (http://www.apnic.net), a major service provider for IP address collecting/resolving in Asia Pacific.

5.7.2 Performance Evaluation

To evaluate the performance of ODR, we replay the sampled workload (refer to Sect. 5.6.1) using the deployed ODR middleware during Mar. 23–Apr. 13, 2015. The environment is similar to that in Fig. 5.12. For each smart AP, we use a common laptop (with Quad-core Intel i5 CPU @ 1.70 GHz, 4-GB RAM, and 7200-RPM 500-GB hard disk drive) as the user device. Figure 5.16 shows the overall performance results of ODR, compared with the performances of Xuanfeng and the three popular smart APs.

First, the percentage of impeded fetching processes (Bottleneck 1) is reduced from 28 to 9 %. The remainder (9 %) is mostly due to the intrinsic dynamics of the Internet. In detail, Fig. 5.17 shows the fetching speed distribution using ODR. Compared with the fetching speed distribution of Xuanfeng, the median fetching speed is enhanced from 287 to 368 KBps. Limited by our benchmark environment, the max fetching speed using ODR is 20 Mbps (= 2.5 MBps), which is lower than that in Xuanfeng (i.e., 50 Mbps = 6.25 MBps). This is why the average fetching speed using ODR (509 KBps) is comparable to that of Xuanfeng (504 KBps).

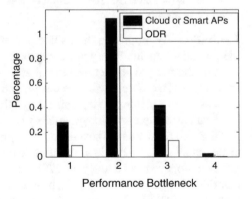

Fig. 5.16 Benchmark performance of ODR, compared with Cloud (i.e., the cloud-based approach) or Smart APs (i.e., the smart AP-based approach). Note that the Y-label of Bottleneck 2 is defined as $\frac{\text{Peak cloud bandwidth burden}}{\text{Purchased cloud bandwidth (30 Gbps)}}$. (Reprinted with permission from [15].)

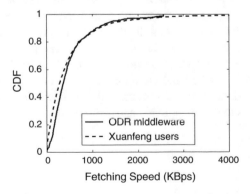

Fig. 5.17 CDF of fetching speeds using ODR. Min: 0 KBps; Median: 368 KBps; Average: 509 KBps; Max: 2.37 MBps ($\approx$20 Mbps). As a comparison, the CDF of cloud-based fetching speeds is also plotted. (Reprinted with permission from [15].)

With regard to Bottleneck 2, the cloud-side upload bandwidth burden under the sampled workload is reduced by 35 %, which is attributable to the fact that the cloud no longer needs to deliver highly popular P2P files. If Xuanfeng had integrated ODR, its peak upload bandwidth burden could decrease from 34 Gbps (refer to Fig. 5.11) to around 22 Gbps, and thus Xuanfeng would not need to reject any fetching request, given their current workload.

Further, the percentage of smart APs' failures in pre-downloading unpopular files (Bottleneck 3) is reduced from 42 to 13 %. In addition, Bottleneck 4 (caused by unsuitable storage devices or filesystems) is almost completely avoided with the use of ODR.

In a nutshell, the integration of ODR into offline downloading services results in a marked reduction of performance bottlenecks, as well as considerable improvement on the quality of service.

Limitation. We acknowledge that ODR occasionally makes incorrect redirection decisions due to the inherent dynamics of Internet that may degrade performance. Fortunately, the percentage of such decisions is negligible (<1 %) in our evaluation. Thus, we believe that the performance of ODR is acceptable in practice, especially given the significant advantages of the system.

5.8 Conclusion

In recent years, the Internet has gained enormous penetration all over the world. However, basic Internet services, like downloading (large) files, remains an issue in most developing countries as a consequence of low-quality network connections. To improve users' downloading experiences, offline downloading services have been proposed and widely deployed in China.

The idea of offline downloading is mainly embodied in two different types of approaches: (1) the cloud-based approach and (2) the smart AP-based approach. Unfortunately, the two approaches are confusing to end users since they offer different strengths and weaknesses (the so-called "selection dilemma"). Our study addresses this dilemma with in-depth analysis of a large-scale cloud-based offline downloading system, as well as comprehensive benchmark experiments of three popular smart APs. Our study shows that the two approaches are subject to distinct performance bottlenecks, while also being complementary to each other. Driven by the study, we build an ODR middleware to help users achieve the best expected performance.

In the future, we envision that offline downloading will become a widely used technology for enhancing the Internet experiences of users across both the developing world and the developed world. For example, people start to build a variety of useful Internet services on top of cloud-based offline downloading systems, such as cloud-based media converters (e.g., Cloud Transcoder [73]) and cloud-accelerated web browsers (e.g., QQ mobile web browser, UCWeb browser, and Amazon Silk web browser). Our study of offline downloading provides solid experiences and valuable heuristics for the developers of similar and relevant services.

References

1. Chetty, M., Sundaresan, S., Muckaden, S., Feamster, N., Calandro, E.: Measuring broadband performance in South Africa. In: Proceedings of the 4th ACM Symposium on Computing for Development (DEV), p. 1 (2013)
2. Fahad, A., Chen, Z., Shen, K., Bigham, J., Fahad, A.: An evaluation of web acceleration techniques for the developing world. In: Proceedings of the 6th USENIX/ACM Workshop on Networked Systems for Developing Regions (NSDR) (2012)
3. Grover, S., Park, M.S., Sundaresan, S., Burnett, S., Kim, H., Ravi, B., Feamster, N.: Peeking behind the NAT: an empirical study of home networks. In: Proceedings of the 13th ACM Internet Measurement Conference (IMC), pp. 377–390 (2013)
4. Johnson, D., Belding, E., Mudenda, C.: Kwaabana: file sharing for rural networks. In: Proceedings of the 4th ACM Symposium on Computing for Development (DEV), p. 4 (2013)
5. Zaki, Y., Chen, J., Pötsch, T., Ahmad, T., Subramanian, L.: Dissecting web latency in Ghana. In: Proceedings of the 14th ACM Internet Measurement Conference (IMC), pp. 241–248 (2014)
6. Zheleva, M., Schmitt, P., Vigil, M., Belding, E.: The increased bandwidth fallacy: performance and usage in Rural Zambia. In: Proceedings of the 4th ACM Symposium on Computing for Development (DEV), p. 2 (2013)
7. FCC raises broadband definition to 25Mbps, Chairman mocks ISPs. http://www.extremetech.com/mobile/198583-fcc-raises-broadband-definition-to-25mbps-chairman-mocks-isps
8. Key ICT indicators for developed and developing countries and the world (totals and penetration rates). http://www.itu.int/en/ITU-D/Statistics/Documents/statistics/2014/ITU_Key_2005-2014_ICT_data.xls
9. Bischof, Z.S., Bustamante, F.E., Stanojevic, R.: Need, want, can afford C broadband markets and the behavior of users. In: Proceedings of the 14th ACM Internet Measurement Conference (IMC), pp. 73–86 (2014)
10. Delay-tolerant networking (DTN) Wiki Page. http://en.wikipedia.org/wiki/Delay-tolerant_networking
11. Isaacman, S., Martonosi, M.: Low-infrastructure methods to improve internet access for mobile users in emerging regions. In: Proceedings of the 20th International World Wide Web Conference (WWW), pp. 473–482 (2011)
12. China's Broadband Penetration Is Increasingly Lagging Behind Developed Nations, Says MIIT's Research Head. http://techcrunch.com/2013/03/21/china-broadband-laggin
13. Statistics of China Internet Users. http://www.internetlivestats.com/internet-users/china
14. The State of Broadband 2014—A Report by the Broadband Commission. http://www.broadbandcommission.org/documents/reports/bb-annualreport2014.pdf
15. Li, Z., Wilson, C., Xu, T., Liu, Y., Lu, Z., Wang, Y.: Offline downloading in China: a comparative study. In: Proceedings of the 15th ACM Internet Measurement Conference (IMC), pp. 473–486 (2015)
16. 100,000 MiWiFi smart AP devices are sold out in just 59 seconds. http://bbs.xiaomi.cn/thread-9658495-1-1.html
17. Baidu CloudDisk offline downloading system. http://pan.baidu.com
18. HiWiFi smart AP is striving towards 5,000,000 sales. http://www.pcpop.com/doc/1/1002/1002782.shtml
19. Xuanfeng offline downloading system. http://xf.qq.com
20. Xunlei offline downloading system. http://lixian.xunlei.com
21. Ao, N., Xu, Y., Chen, C., Guo, Y.: Offline downloading: a non-traditional cloud-accelerated and peer-assisted content distribution service. In: Proceedings of the IEEE International Conference on Cyber-Enabled Distributed Computing and Knowledge Discovery (CyberC), pp. 81–88 (2012)
22. Huang, Y., Li, Z., Liu, G., Dai, Y.: Cloud download: using cloud utilities to achieve high-quality content distribution for unpopular videos. In: Proceedings of the 19th ACM International Conference on Multimedia (ACM-MM), pp. 213–222 (2011)

23. Offline Downloading: the Baidu Wikipedia page. http://baike.baidu.com/view/2718066.htm
24. Offline (movie) Downloading for MiWiFi. http://www.mi.com/miwifi/movie-download
25. Zhou, Y., Fu, Z., Chiu, D.M., Huang, Y.: An adaptive cloud downloading service. IEEE Trans. Multimed. (TMM) **15**(4), 802–810 (2013)
26. HiWiFi smart AP. http://www.hiwifi.com
27. MiWiFi smart AP. http://www.miwifi.com
28. Newifi smart AP. http://www.newifi.com
29. A Collection of the Best Offline Downloading Tools. http://jingyan.baidu.com/article/636f38bb295e9bd6b84610e9.html
30. How to Offline Download? Which is the Best Offline Downloading Tool? http://jingyan.baidu.com/article/a65957f4fe63c424e67f9b92.html
31. An Evaluation Report of HiWiFi. http://news.mydrivers.com/1/279/279305_all.htm
32. An Evaluation Report of MiWiFi. http://www.geekpark.net/read/view/195133
33. An Evaluation Report of NewiFi. http://www.itbear.com.cn/n112446c93.aspx
34. A Comparison of Nine Smart APs. http://net.zol.com.cn/478/4788494.html
35. HiWiFi vs. Newifi: A Benchmark Test. http://test.smzdm.com/pingce/p/20574
36. Three Faults of HiWiFi. http://digi.tech.qq.com/a/20131112/002037.htm
37. Chen, G., Li, Z.: Peer-to-Peer Network: Structure, Application and Design. Tsinghua University Press (2007)
38. HiWiFi APPs. http://bbs.hiwifi.com/thread-22663-1-1.html
39. MiWiFi: System Options. http://www.mi.com/miwifi#op
40. Offline Downloading with Newifi and Xunlei. http://jingyan.baidu.com/article/3d69c5517049e1f0cf02d7a4.html
41. URL Droplet offline downloading system. http://www.urldroplet.com
42. Amazon Silk web browser. http://amazonsilk.wordpress.com
43. Linksys Smart WiFi Router. http://www.linksys.com/en-us/smartwifi
44. Ahlgren, B., Dannewitz, C., Imbrenda, C., Kutscher, D., Ohlman, B.: A survey of information-centric networking. IEEE Commun. **50**(7), 26–36 (2012)
45. Tian, Y., Dey, R., Liu, Y., Ross, K.: Topology mapping and geolocating for China's internet. IEEE Trans. Parallel Distrib. Syst. (TPDS) **24**(9), 1908–1917 (2013)
46. Choffnes, D., Bustamante, F.E.: Taming the torrent: a practical approach to reducing cross-ISP traffic in peer-to-peer systems. ACM SIGCOMM Comput. Commun. Rev. (CCR) **38**(4), 363–374 (2008)
47. Xie, H., Yang, R., Krishnamurthy, A., Liu, Y.G., Silberschatz, A.: P4P: provider portal for applications. ACM SIGCOMM Comput. Commun. Rev. (CCR) **38**(4), 351–362 (2008)
48. China-Unicom ISP. http://www.chinaunicom.com.cn
49. China-Telecom ISP. http://www.chinatelecom.com.cn
50. China-Mobile ISP. http://www.10086.cn
51. CERNET (China Education and Research Network) ISP. http://www.cernet.edu.cn
52. HiWiFi Introduction and History. http://www.hiwifi.com/about
53. OpenWrt operating system. http://openwrt.org
54. Opkg (Open PacKaGe Management) web site. http://code.google.com/p/opkg
55. aria2: The next generation download utility. http://aria2.sourceforge.net
56. Breslau, L., Cao, P., Fan, L., Phillips, G., Shenker, S.: Web caching and zipf-like distributions: evidence and implications. In: Proceedings of the 18th IEEE International Conference on Computer Communications (INFOCOM), pp. 126–134 (1999)
57. Guo, L., Tan, E., Chen, S., Xiao, Z., Zhang, X.: The stretched exponential distribution of internet media access patterns. In: Proceedings of the 27th ACM Symposium on Principles of Distributed Computing (PODC), pp. 283–294 (2008)
58. Gummadi, K.P., Dunn, R.J., Saroiu, S., Gribble, S.D., Levy, H.M., Zahorjan, J.: Measurement, modeling, and analysis of a peer-to-peer file-sharing workload. ACM SIGOPS Oper. Syst. Rev. (OSR) **37**(5), 314–329 (2003)
59. Ganjam, A., Jiang, J., Liu, X., Sekar, V., Siddiqi, F., Stoica, I., Zhan, J., Zhang, H.: C3: Internet-scale control plane for video quality optimization. In: Proceedings of the 12th USENIX Symposium on Networked Systems Design and Implementation (NSDI), pp. 131–144 (2015)

60. Li, Z., Cao, J., Chen, G.: Continustreaming: achieving high playback continuity of gossip-based peer-to-peer streaming. In: Proceedings of the 22nd IEEE International Parallel and Distributed Processing Symposium (IPDPS), pp. 1–12 (2008)
61. Cohen, B.: Incentives build robustness in bittorrent. In: Proceedings of the 1st Workshop on Economics of Peer-to-Peer Systems, pp. 68–72 (2003)
62. Huang, T.Y., Handigol, N., Heller, B., McKeown, N., Johari, R.: Confused, timid, and unstable: picking a video streaming rate is hard. In: Proceedings of the 12th ACM Internet Measurement Conference (IMC), pp. 225–238 (2012)
63. Krishnan, S., Sitaraman, R.: Video stream quality impacts viewer behavior: inferring causality using quasi-experimental designs. IEEE/ACM Trans. Netw. (TON) 21(6), 2001–2014 (2013)
64. Li, Z., Huang, Y., Liu, G., Wang, F., Liu, Y., Zhang, Z.L., Dai, Y.: Challenges, designs, and performances of large-scale open-P2SP content distribution. IEEE Trans. Parallel Distrib. Syst. (TPDS) 24(11), 2181–2191 (2013)
65. Li, Z., Zhang, T., Huang, Y., Zhang, Z.L., Dai, Y.: Maximizing the bandwidth multiplier effect for hybrid cloud-P2P content distribution. In: Proceedings of the 20th IEEE/ACM International Workshop on Quality of Service (IWQoS), pp. 1–9 (2012)
66. Sundaresan, S., De Donato, W., Feamster, N., Teixeira, R., Crawford, S., Pescapè, A.: Broadband internet performance: a view from the gateway. ACM SIGCOMM Comput. Commun. Rev. (CCR) 41(4), 134–145 (2011)
67. Tencent PC Manager. http://guanjia.qq.com
68. Baidu Guard. http://anquan.baidu.com/weishi
69. 360 Security Guard. http://www.360.cn/weishi
70. Huang, T.Y., Johari, R., McKeown, N., Trunnell, M., Watson, M.: A buffer-based approach to rate adaptation: evidence from a large video streaming service. In: Proceedings of the 2014 ACM Conference on Communication Architectures, Protocols and Applications (SIGCOMM), pp. 187–198 (2014)
71. Finamore, A., Mellia, M., Gilani, Z., Papagiannaki, K., Erramilli, V., Grunenberger, Y.: Is there a case for mobile phone content pre-staging? In: Proceedings of the 9th ACM Conference on Emerging Networking EXperiments and Technologies (CoNEXT), pp. 321–326 (2013)
72. Low Extra Delay Background Transport (LEDBAT), IETF RFC 6817. http://datatracker.ietf.org/doc/rfc6817
73. Li, Z., Huang, Y., Liu, G., Wang, F., Zhang, Z.L., Dai, Y.: Cloud transcoder: bridging the format and resolution gap between internet videos and mobile devices. In: Proceedings of the 22nd SIGMM Workshop on Network and Operating System Support for Digital Audio and Video (NOSSDAV), pp. 33–38 (2012)

Part IV
Cloud-Assisted P2P Content Distribution

Chapter 6
Cloud Tracking or Open-P2SP

Abstract Content distribution on today's Internet operates primarily in two modes: *server-based* and *peer-to-peer* (P2P). To leverage the advantages of both modes while circumventing their key limitations, a third mode: *peer-to-server/peer* (P2SP) has emerged in recent years. Although P2SP can provide efficient hybrid server-P2P content distribution, P2SP generally works in a *closed* manner by only utilizing its private owned servers to accelerate its private organized peer swarms. Consequently, P2SP still has its limitations in both content abundance and server bandwidth. To this end, the fourth mode (to be called a generalized mode of P2SP) has appeared as "*cloud tracking*" or "*open-P2SP*," which integrates various third-party servers, contents, and data transfer protocols all over the Internet into a large, open, and federated P2SP platform. In this chapter, based on a large-scale commercial open-P2SP system named QQXuanfeng, we investigate the key challenging problems, practical designs, and real-world performances of open-P2SP. This white box study of open-P2SP provides solid experiences and helpful heuristics for designing similar systems.

6.1 Introduction

P2SP. Content distribution on today's Internet operates primarily in two modes: (a) *server-based* and (b) *peer-to-peer* (P2P). Both modes have their unique characteristics and accompanying disadvantages. To leverage the advantages of both modes while circumventing their key limitations, a third mode: (c) *peer-to-server/peer* (P2SP) (e.g., [1–7]) has emerged in recent years. As depicted in Fig. 6.1c, P2SP usually utilizes a *private owned cloud* (or server cluster) as well as a number of peer swarms for content distribution. A peer swarm starts by obtaining a content seed from the cloud, and subsequently, peers within the swarm can exchange data among themselves via a *private designed P2P protocol*. Compared to the server-based mode, P2SP incurs far lower infrastructure and network bandwidth costs. Meanwhile, P2SP enhances the working efficiency of P2P by providing extra server bandwidth to those peer swarms who do not have adequate download bandwidth among them.

© Springer Science+Business Media Singapore 2016
Z. Li et al., *Content Distribution for Mobile Internet: A Cloud-based Approach*,
DOI 10.1007/978-981-10-1463-5_6

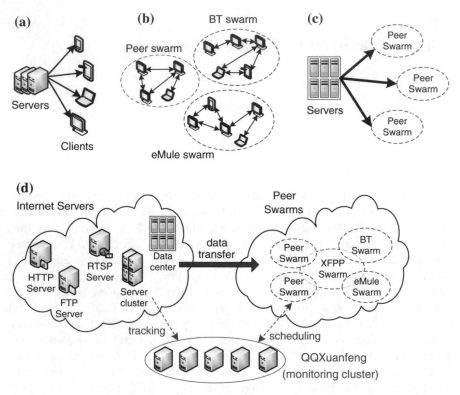

Fig. 6.1 General evolution of Internet content distribution modes: **a** Server-based, **b** P2P, **c** P2SP, and **d** Cloud Tracking or Open-P2SP. XFPP (Xuanfeng P2P Protocol) is a special P2P protocol designed for QQXuanfeng clients. There should be numerous XFPP swarms, BT (BitTorrent) swarms, eMule swarms, etc., while we only draw one swarm for each kind. (Reprinted with permission from [8].)

Although P2SP can provide efficient hybrid server-P2P content distribution with moderate server bandwidth, P2SP generally works in a *closed* manner by only utilizing its private owned servers to accelerate its private organized peer swarms. Consequently, P2SP still has its limitations in both *content abundance* and *server bandwidth*. First, for copyright and storage reasons, a P2SP system only provides a small subset of Internet contents, so its users often have to resort to other web servers, P2P/P2SP systems for contents—a quite inconvenient process. Second, due to the high dynamics of peers, it is quite possible that the server bandwidth of a P2SP system cannot satisfy its users' requirements when the user scale increases suddenly and dramatically [6].

Cloud Tracking or Open-P2SP. To this end, the fourth mode (or says a generalized mode of P2SP) has appeared as (d) *"cloud tracking"* or *"open-P2SP"* (e.g., Xunlei, QQXuanfeng, FlashGet, and Orbit [9]), which integrates various third-party servers, contents, and data transfer protocols all over the Internet into a large, open and federated P2SP platform as shown in Fig. 6.1d. The advantages of open-P2SP are mainly fourfold:

- First, open-P2SP continuously tracks and indexes ubiquitous *downloadable contents* in third-party servers all over the Internet so as to allow end users to search and quickly find contents, and meanwhile enables peer nodes that are interested in the same content to find each other and form an *open and larger* peer swarm. *Downloadable contents* mainly refer to videos, audios, documents, softwares, and so forth.
- Second, open-P2SP dynamically directs peer swarms—especially those that do not have adequate download bandwidth among them—to retrieve data from appropriate third-party servers for download acceleration. Since there are usually a huge number (typically millions) of servers involved in an open-P2SP system, it is resilient to small-scale/localized upsurge of user requirements.
- Third, by intelligently scheduling peers' data requests to appropriate third-party servers, open-P2SP also facilitates load-balancing among the involved servers while avoiding overloading a specific server.
- Finally, building an open-P2SP system does not require enormous storage servers (for storing contents) or upload bandwidth (for uploading data to peers), but merely requires a light-weight monitoring cluster (see Fig. 6.1d) for tracking servers and scheduling peer swarms. For instance, we have implemented such a monitoring cluster (named QQXuanfeng[1]) by using only 53 commodity servers. QQXuanfeng tracks over one million servers and serves around 5 million peers every day.

Challenges of open-P2SP. Despite the above advantages, an open-P2SP system involves far more complicated problems than a conventional P2SP system. The major problem of designing a conventional P2SP system is handling the peer dynamics and properly allocating server bandwidth to peer swarms, while designing an open-P2SP system (e.g., QQXuanfeng) should further deal with the following key challenges:

- *Handling server and content dynamics.* As for conventional P2SP, servers and their affiliated contents are usually stable and controllable so that its designers can focus on handling the inevitable peer dynamics. However, open-P2SP involves various third-party servers and contents with unpredictable dynamics—the involved servers never notify QQXuanfeng of their join, leave or content change.
- *Limited utilization of server bandwidth.* A conventional P2SP system can fully utilize its server bandwidth but an open-P2SP system cannot. The *extra bandwidth* burden posed on an involved server by QQXuanfeng should be within a certain limit; otherwise, the *original service* offered by the server may be interfered. Still worse, QQXuanfeng has no knowledge of the *original bandwidth* of a server spent in its original service, which further complicates such limited utilization.
- *Differentiated acceleration of peer swarms.* Due to the limited utilization of server bandwidth, QQXuanfeng can hardly accelerate all its peer swarms to possess high download bandwidth. Thereby, the only choice of QQXuanfeng is to design proper differentiated acceleration strategies according to the specific requirements of different peer swarms.

---

[1]In the remainder of this chapter, we also use QQXuanfeng as the name of the corresponding open-P2SP system when the context is clear.

- *Bringing extra benefit to server providers.* Even if the extra bandwidth burden directed by QQXuanfeng is always restricted within a proper limit, server providers may still be reluctant to support open-P2SP if they cannot obtain extra benefit from extra bandwidth contribution.

Solutions of QQXuanfeng. Each above-mentioned problem is highly challenging as to a large-scale real-world open-P2SP system. As a matter of fact, in the past several years (since the birth of QQXuanfeng) we have (tried hard but) never figured out a *perfect* solution to any problem. Instead, our methodology is to find a *moderate and practical* solution to each problem based on comprehensive measurements. Specifically, our proposed solutions are briefly described as follows:

- To handle server and content dynamics, we build a *content crawler* and a *content validator*. The *content crawler* continuously crawls content links (URLs) by traversing on third-party servers and receiving user reported novel links. Meanwhile, the *content validator* constantly validates the user reported invalid links by checking them on the Internet.
- Sampling measurements indicate that the *original bandwidth utilization* (*OBU*) of an involved server usually stays below 60 %. Thus as to each server, the *extra bandwidth utilization* (*EBU*) directed by QQXuanfeng had better be controlled within 40 % (= 1 − 60 %). Specifically, QQXuanfeng periodically collects users' reports to calculate the *EBU* of each involved server. If the *EBU* of a server S exceeds 40 %, QQXuanfeng will notify a part of the users served by S to stop their data download from S.
- Although every user of QQXuanfeng hopes to achieve his best user experience, through comprehensive measurements we discover that a user usually has his *basic expectation* for the download rate. Therefore, peer swarms are classified into three categories according to their real-time download rates and data supply-demand conditions: (a) *hungry swarms*, (b) *potentially hungry swarms,* and (c) *high-demand swarms*. Different categories of peer swarms correspond to differentiated acceleration strategies so that each user can have a download rate at least above his basic expectation.
- For a server provider, the two most important benefit metrics are its *page view* (*PV*) [10] and *paid-to-click* (*PTC*) [11]. At present, we are fostering benefit collaborations between QQXuanfeng and server providers from both perspectives of *PV* and *PTC*, in order to encourage more server providers to support QQXuanfeng.

Over the past several years (from the first client version released in 2007 to the 3.9 client version released in 2012), QQXuanfeng has gained over 120 million accumulated users and supports most mainstream data transfer protocols like HTTP, FTP, RTSP, BitTorrent, eMule, and so forth. Currently, it schedules around five million peers to retrieve data in petabytes from over one million servers per day. The average download rate of a peer is enhanced from 57 to 158 KBps, where 45 % of the download rate is obtained from third-party servers. Meanwhile, the extra bandwidth utilization of the involved servers is generally limited within 40 %, so their original services are not obviously interfered. To our knowledge, this chapter is the first white-box study of open-P2SP, which provides solid experiences and helpful heuristics to the designers of similar systems.

Roadmap. The remainder of this chapter is organized as follows. Section 6.2 reviews the related work. Section 6.3 overviews the system design. Section 6.4 describes the challenging problems and corresponding solutions. Section 6.5 evaluates the real-world performance of QQXuanfeng. Finally we conclude the chapter in Sect. 6.6.

6.2 Related Work

In recent years there have been considerable researches on P2SP, such as P2SP streaming [6], P2SP storage [5], hybrid CDN-P2P [1, 7], and so forth.

P2SP streaming. Wu et al. refocused on the important role of servers in P2P video streaming [6]. Through measurements of a popular P2P live TV system called UUSee, they found that the total available bandwidth of the 150 dedicated streaming servers could not meet the increasing demand of download bandwidth from hundreds of TV channels (a TV channel can be seen as a peer swarm), although the total upload bandwidth of peers also increased with download demand. So they proposed an allocation algorithm of server bandwidth named Ration, which proactively predicts the minimum server bandwidth demand of each channel from historical information and thus assigns appropriate server bandwidth to each TV channel.

P2SP storage. Based on a popular P2SP storage system called Rayfile, Sun et al. discussed the tradeoff among file availability, download performance and server resource costs (including both bandwidth and storage cost) in P2SP cooperative storage [5]. In order to save the critical server bandwidth cost, they concluded three conditions in which peers are allowed to obtain data from servers: (1) No online peer owns the requested file; (2) A special block of the requested file is missed in all online peers; (3) The average download rate of the users inside a peer swarm is lower than 10 KBps. When a user uploads a file to the system, the servers make sure only one copy exists so as to save server storage cost.

Hybrid CDN-P2P. Content distribution network (CDN) like Akamai and Lime-light is the most common facility that optimizes the performance of Internet content distribution by strategically deploying edge servers at multiple locations. CDN is traditionally used to accelerate server-based content distribution, but Yin et al. developed a hybrid CDN-P2P video streaming system on top of ChinaCache (the largest CDN in China) to incorporate the strengths on both sides: the quality control and reliability of CDN and the inherent scalability of P2P [7]. They proposed a mechanism for dynamic resource scaling that guarantees adequate quality-of-service to end users, so as to address several shortcomings of common P2P streaming such as high buffering requirement and low streaming quality. Besides, based on the novel Akamai NetSession interface [1], Haeberlen et al. designed a method for providing reliable accounting of client interactions in hybrid CDN-P2P systems [12].

Xunlei open-P2SP system. Xunlei is the biggest open-P2SP system in China (and perhaps in the world also). Unfortunately, till now there has been no official publication on its technical designs or system performances, but some preliminary measurements have been revealed in [13–15] via a black box method. Xunlei takes an *aggressive* data scheduling strategy which often makes nearly full use of server bandwidth to achieve high user experiences. This is a major cause of complaints of Xunlei by various server providers who have accused it of interfering with their original services. And this is one of the reasons that its IPO (initial public offerings) process has been rather difficult [16]. In contrast, QQXuanfeng adopts a *more conservative* data scheduling strategy which strives for a proper tradeoff between user experience and server bandwidth burden.

6.3   QQXuanfeng System Overview

6.3.1   System Architecture and Index Structure

As depicted in Fig. 6.2, the QQXuanfeng system architecture consists of four major building blocks: (1) *Content Index DB*, (2) *Content Crawler*, (3) *Content Validator* and (4) *Data Scheduler*, utilizing 53 commodity servers in total. All these servers run the Enterprise Suse Linux v10.1 and gcc v4.1. The user of QQXuanfeng needs to install its client software (of about 12.5 MB) which simultaneously supports the HTTP, FTP, RTSP, BitTorrent, eMule, and XFPP data transfer protocols (see Fig. 6.3). When installing the client, the user can choose whether to add a QQXuanfeng plugin into his web browser. If the plugin is added, the QQXuanfeng client will automatically take over the user's download task issued from the web browser.

Lying at the center of the system, the *Content Index DB* stores the index information of the downloadable contents detected by the *Content Crawler*. The Content Index DB employs MySQL v5.1 as its database management system. The index information includes the *(content) link, server IP address, name, size, chunk size, type, MD4 hash code, SHA1 hash code, 3-chunk hash code,* and *chunk hash code*

Fig. 6.2 System architecture of QQXuanfeng. (Reprinted with permission from [8].)

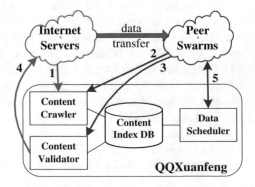

Fig. 6.3 Software architecture of the QQXuanfeng client. In the Chunk Cache, *grey chunks* have been obtained while *white chunks* have not. (Reprinted with permission from [8].)

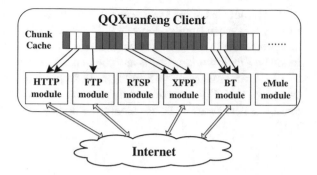

list of every indexed file. The *chunk size* should be a power of 2 bytes—typically between 32 KB and 16 MB. For an indexed file f, the 128-bit *MD4 hash code* is used for eMule data transfer because the eMule protocol employs an MD4 hash code for *content identification*. Similarly, the 160-bit *SHA1 hash code* is used for BitTorrent data transfer. Both the MD4 hash code and the SHA1 hash code are calculated (by the content publisher) from the whole content of f, but the 160-bit *3-chunk hash code* is calculated from only three chunks of f: the first chunk (C_1), the middle chunk ($C_{\lceil n/2 \rceil}$) and the last chunk (C_n) (n is the total number of chunks in f). Specifically, the *3-chunk hash code* $= SHA1(MD4(C_1) \mid MD4(C_{\lceil n/2 \rceil}) \mid MD4(C_n))$, where '$\mid$' means XOR operation. Finally, the *chunk hash code list* contains the MD4 hash code of every chunk.

Why is the *3-chunk hash code* necessary? When the Content Crawler discovers a novel eMule link, it can directly extract the MD4 hash code from the eMule link as the content identification. When it discovers a novel BitTorrent link, it first downloads the .torrent file (of several KBytes) from the BitTorrent link and then extracts the SHA1 hash code from the .torrent file as the content identification. However, when the Content Crawler discovers a novel HTTP/FTP/RTSP link, there is no hash code contained in the link and it is usually impractical for the Content Crawler to download the whole linked file (often up to hundreds of MBytes or several GBytes) in order to calculate the content identification. Instead, the Content Crawler only downloads the three special chunks (first, middle and last chunks) of the linked file to calculate the 3-chunk hash code as the content identification, and thus the resulting download traffic is affordable and the hash conflict probability is extremely low. Besides, the 3-chunk hash code is also used by XFPP (the Xuanfeng P2P Protocol), a special P2P protocol designed for QQXuanfeng clients. With any kind of hash code, the Content Index DB can find other corresponding hash codes and a variety of links that point to the same content (i.e., the *mapping* operation).

The *Content Crawler* crawls content links by traversing on third-party servers (see Arrow 1 in Fig. 6.2) and receiving user reported novel links (see Arrow 2 in Fig. 6.2). Meanwhile, the *Content Validator* validates the user reported invalid links (see Arrow 3 in Fig. 6.2) by checking them on the Internet (see Arrow 4 in Fig. 6.2). With the help of Content Crawler and Content Validator, QQXuanfeng continuously discovers novel links and discards invalid links. The detailed working principles will be presented in Sect. 6.4.1.

The basic roles of the *Data Scheduler* are threefold: (1) maintaining a peer list for every peer swarm (thus acting as a P2P tracker), (2) telling each user which servers and peers contain his interested content, and (3) periodically collecting users' reports to analyze their working status and calculate the extra bandwidth utilization of each involved server (see Arrow 5 in Fig. 6.2). In particular, the Data Scheduler handles two problems: (1) limited utilization of server bandwidth and (2) differentiated acceleration of peer swarms. Their specific solutions will be elaborated in Sects. 6.4.2 and 6.4.3.

6.3.2   A Typical User's Request Processing

Figure 6.4 plots the concrete steps about how a typical user's request is processed. First, the user inputs a link (or via the QQXuanfeng web browser plugin) to the client (see Arrow 1 in Fig. 6.4). The user can also input several keywords and then the client will return a list of related links for a possible choice. If the input link is an HTTP/FTP/RTSP link, the client first downloads the three special chunks of the linked file to calculate the 3-chunk hash code, and then sends the 3-chunk hash code to the Data Scheduler (see Arrow 2 in Fig. 6.4). Likewise, if the link is a BitTorrent link, the client first downloads the .torrent file to extract the SHA1 hash code and then sends the SHA1 hash code. Besides, if the link is an eMule link, the client directly extracts the MD4 hash code from the eMule link and then sends the MD4 hash code.

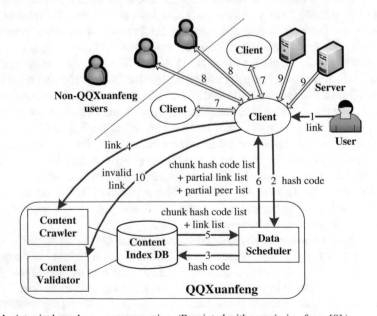

Fig. 6.4 A typical user's request processing. (Reprinted with permission from [8].)

The Data Scheduler inputs the hash code to the Content Index DB to find other corresponding hash codes and existing links that point to the same content (see Arrow 3 in Fig. 6.4). If the hash code is novel to the Content Index DB, the Data Scheduler will notify the client to send the input link to the Content Crawler for further processing (see Arrow 4 in Fig. 6.4). Otherwise, the Content Index DB *maps* the hash code to a chunk hash code list and a (server) link list (see Arrow 5 in Fig. 6.4).

After getting the chunk hash code list and the (server) link list, the Data Scheduler returns the chunk hash code list, a part of the link list (i.e., the partial link list) and a part of the corresponding peer list (i.e., the partial peer list) to the client (see Arrow 6 in Fig. 6.4). Then the client first attempts to set up data connections with the listed peers (see Arrow 7 in Fig. 6.4). Note that the client may also exchange data with non-QQXuanfeng users who are not monitored by QQXuanfeng (see Arrow 8 in Fig. 6.4). The client maintains a chunk map and sends the chunk map to its connected peers in every minute if the chunk map is updated. If the total P2P data transfer rate is below the user's basic expectation, the client will further set up data connections with the listed servers (see Arrow 9 in Fig. 6.4).

The QQXuanfeng client adopts a simple chunk scheduling strategy: at any time it only assigns one chunk for one data connection to retrieve. When the assigned chunk is obtained, the corresponding data connection will be assigned to retrieve another chunk. On the other hand, if the assigned chunk (say C_i) cannot be obtained in a timeout period (generally proportional to the chunk size and no less than 10 seconds) the corresponding data connection will be terminated. Furthermore, if a data connection to a server (link) is terminated for the above reason, the client will report this (possible) *dead link* (regarding to chunk C_i)[2] to the Content Validator (see Arrow 10 in Fig. 6.4). Once a chunk C_i is obtained from a link, the client validates it by using the chunk hash code list. If the client finds an *inconsistent link* (that distributes an inconsistent chunk C_i) it will report this (possible) inconsistent link to the Content Validator (see Arrow 10 in Fig. 6.4). The chunk retrieving priority depends on the user's requirement: if the user chooses the view-as-download mode, the chunks are retrieved in their playback order; otherwise, the chunks are retrieved in the rarest-first manner.

6.4 Challenging Problems and Solutions

6.4.1 Handling Server and Content Dynamics

To handle server and content dynamics, we build the Content Crawler and Content Validator. The Content Crawler continuously crawls content links by BFS (breadth-first search) traversing on third-party servers and meanwhile receiving user reported novel links. The BFS traversing uses a *link queue* as its data structure. Various *file*

---

[2]There are two kinds of invalid links: (a) *dead links,* and (b) *inconsistent links*. Dead means the link is inaccessible while inconsistent means the linked file has been changed.

links (e.g., links to videos, audios, documents and softwares) and *non-file links* (e.g., links to web pages) are collected by the Content Crawler. To avoid crawling loop links, recently visited links are cached to check whether these links have been revisited. Repeated links are discarded. Then, (possible) novel file links are directly put into the Content Index DB for further processing like *file link filtering* and merging into corresponding indexes. Novel non-file links are inserted into the queue for subsequent processing.

Servers may join in or leave from the Internet for various reasons and meanwhile their affiliated contents are constantly emerging, updating and expiring. However, the corresponding links of these contents are often left invariable, thus turning into *invalid links* (including *dead links* and *inconsistent links*) scattered all over the Internet. The negative effects of invalid links are at least threefold: (1) incurring unnecessary storage burden to the Content Index DB, (2) bringing unnecessary network burden to the users who try to connect the linked servers, and (3) degrading the scheduling performance of the Data Scheduler when it assigns some invalid links to a peer swarm for download acceleration. To this end, the Content Validator constantly validates the user reported invalid links by checking them on the Internet:

- On receiving a dead link l (regarding to chunk C_i) reported by a user, the Content Validator attempts to download C_i from l. If C_i cannot be downloaded, l is judged to be a dead link and is then removed from the Content Index DB. Otherwise, the Content Validator simply tells the reporting user that he has misreported a dead link.
- On receiving an inconsistent link l (regarding to chunk C_i) reported by a user, the Content Validator first downloads C_i from l and computes the latest MD4 hash code of C_i. If the latest MD4 hash code is the same as the existing MD4 hash code of C_i contained in the chunk hash code list, the Content Validator simply tells the reporting user that he has misreported an inconsistent link. Otherwise, l is judged to be an inconsistent link and the Content Validator continues to download the whole linked file, updates or adds the corresponding index information in the Content Index DB, and notifies the reporting user to restart his download task.

To check the practical performances of the Content Crawler and the Content Validator, we measure the numbers of involved links, novel links, dead links, and inconsistent links in 20 days in Dec. 2011 in Fig. 6.5. The major observation is that the ratios of novel links, dead links and inconsistent links (over the involved links) are quite stable around 27%, 3.3% and 0.6%, respectively. Although the ratio of inconsistent links (0.6%) is much smaller than that of dead links (3.3%), the negative effect brought by inconsistent links is much larger—for a dead link QQXuanfeng only needs to discard it in the Content Index DB, while for an inconsistent link QQXuanfeng needs to download the whole linked file and notify the reporting user to restart his download task.

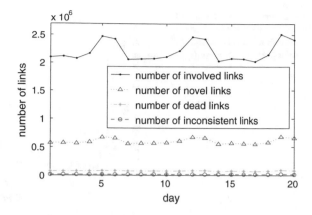

Fig. 6.5 Numbers of involved links, novel links, dead links, and inconsistent links in 20 days. (Reprinted with permission from [8].)

6.4.2 Limited Utilization of Server Bandwidth

Presently, QQXuanfeng tracks over one million servers every day. By intelligently directing peer swarms to retrieve data from appropriate servers, QQXuanfeng achieves limited and balanced utilization of the server bandwidth, so that the original services offered by the involved servers are not interfered. As to each server S, by collecting and analyzing users' reports, QQXuanfeng can get its *approximate maximum bandwidth* and its *extra traffic volume* directed by QQXuanfeng. Due to the high dynamics of the Internet, getting the accurate maximum bandwidth of a server is extremely difficult; instead, we adopt a simple *approximate estimation method* as follows. When the Content Crawler discovers a novel server S, in the subsequent day the Data Scheduler does not limit the server bandwidth utilization of S but directs as many clients to retrieve data from S as possible. Then the peak upload bandwidth of S during this day is approximately taken as its maximum bandwidth. Besides, even the real maximum bandwidth of S can be changed by its administrator, so the abovementioned estimation method is periodically performed to update the maximum bandwidth information of S (the update period is usually set as one month).

The worst thing is that QQXuanfeng cannot obtain the *original traffic volume* of a server consumed to support its original service. To get a basic understanding, we obtain the original traffic information of a sample of servers (named friendly servers) via manual approaches, that is, by directly obtaining the original traffic information of 619 friendly servers (including both file download servers and video streaming servers) from their administrators. Figure 6.6 plots the average *original bandwidth utilization (OBU)* of these friendly servers in 24 h, starting from 0:00, GTM+8, on Dec. 15, 2011. The curve illustrates an obvious diurnal pattern that accords with people's regular pattern of accessing Internet. The *OBU* of these servers usually stays below **60 %** and the whole average utilization is merely 22 %. Furthermore, the measurements done by Heller et al. [17] on 292 servers hosting an e-commerce application and a production Google data center have also revealed low bandwidth utilization of servers (less than 25 % in average), which is basically consistent with our findings.

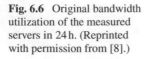

Fig. 6.6 Original bandwidth utilization of the measured servers in 24 h. (Reprinted with permission from [8].)

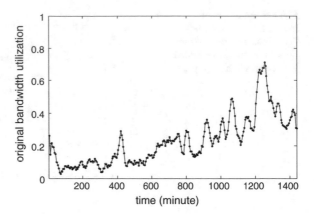

Therefore, as to each involved server, the *extra bandwidth utilization* (*EBU*) directed by QQXuanfeng had better be controlled within **40 %** (= 1− **60 %**). The Data Scheduler periodically collects users' reports to calculate the *EBU* of each server (the period is 5 min). If the *EBU* of a server *S* exceeds 40%, the Data Scheduler notifies a part of the users served by *S* to stop their data download from *S*. For example, suppose the current *EBU* of *S* is 50% and *S* is uploading data to 100 users. Then the Data Scheduler notifies 20 users (20 = 100 × $\frac{50\%-40\%}{50\%}$) who have the highest download rates among the 100 users to stop their data download from *S*.

Besides, the Data Scheduler also *shuffles* the server link list to balance the load among involved servers. As to a file f, the Data Scheduler holds a link list of f, denoted as l_f which is returned by the Content Index DB (see Arrow 5 in Fig. 6.4). Whenever the Data Scheduler decides to allocate a partial link list containing n server links to a user, the Data Scheduler first *shuffles* l_f and then allocates the first n server links in l_f to the user (see Arrow 6 in Fig. 6.4). Moreover, the user can ask the Data Scheduler to update his allocated partial link list if his download rate stays below his basic expectation.

6.4.3   Differentiated Acceleration of Peer Swarms

Although every user of QQXuanfeng hopes to achieve his best experience, through comprehensive measurements and analysis we discover that a user has his *basic expectation* (d_{basic} = 30 KBps) for download rate. Thus, our heuristic is to provide differentiated acceleration of peer swarms. Specifically, peer swarms are classified into three categories according to their real-time download rates and data supply-demand conditions: (a) *hungry swarms*, (b) *potentially hungry swarms,* and (c) *high-demand swarms*. Different categories of peer swarms correspond to differentiated acceleration strategies so that each user can have a download rate at least above his basic expectation.

Table 6.1 *ATD* settings (corresponding to Fig. 6.7)

Leecher scale	<2	2–5	6–10	11–15	16–20	21–30	>30
ATD of 100 KBps (d_{high})	26	19	11	5	4	4	2
ATD of 30 KBps (d_{basic})	6	2	2	1	1	1	1

Reprinted with permission from [8]

Fig. 6.7 Relationship between *ATD* and download rate with various leecher scales. Here leecher scale denotes the number of online leechers inside a peer swarm. (Reprinted with permission from [8].)

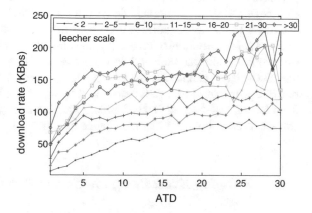

- First, a peer swarm is taken as a *hungry swarm* if the average download rate of its peers is below a common user's basic expectation (d_{basic} = 30 KBps).
- Second, a peer swarm is taken as a *potentially hungry swarm* if the average download rate of its peers exceeds 30 KBps but its *ATD* is quite low. Since *ATD* is an empirical indicator which illustrates the statistically data supply-demand condition of a swarm, low *ATD* often (but not always) implies a *potential* risk of being hungry. Figure 6.7 plots the statistical relationship between *ATD* and download rate with various leecher scales (Fig. 6.7 is obtained from the measurements of one million swarms). Accordingly, the setting of *ATD* varies with the leecher scale, as listed in Table 6.1. Thereby, we use the "ATD of 30 KBps" to recognize potentially hungry swarms.
- Third, a *high-demand swarm* should contain more than ten peers and its file type should be a video type like .rmvb, .mp4, and so on. If a swarm is sharing a video file, its peers may well demand a high download rate (d_{high} = 100 KBps) for continuous playback; and the swarm scale is also demanded to be large enough (typically > 10) so that the invested server bandwidth is cost-effective.[3]

A *hungry swarm* is allocated with a partial link list that contains a certain number (n) of server links to enhance its *ATD* to the "ATD of 30 KBps" (see Table 6.1). For example, if a hungry swarm W_h contains 8 leechers and 6 seed peers sharing a file f and the Data Scheduler holds a link list of f, the Data Scheduler will allocate

---

[3]Inside a swarm, the data exchange between its peers is able to "amplify" the invested server bandwidth, i.e., *the amplification factor* = $\frac{\text{peers' download rate increase}}{\text{invested server bandwidth}}$ > 1. Generally speaking, the larger the swarm scale is, the larger the amplification factor will be.

$n = 2 \times 8 - 6 = 10$ server links to each peer inside W_h for download acceleration. Here "2" is got from Table 6.1: Row 3 and Column 4. Note that different peers inside W_h are usually allocated with different partial link lists because the Data Scheduler always *shuffles* the link list before allocating a partial link list to a peer. Because *ATD* is a statistical indicator rather than an accurate metric, it is possible that some peers still have a download rate below 30 KBps after utilizing the allocated partial link list. Consequently, if the accelerated download rate is still below 30 KBps for a peer p, p will ask the Data Scheduler to update his allocated partial link list.

For a *potentially hungry swarm* W_p, the allocation strategy of server links is alike except that the allocated server links cannot be used to *really* download data (namely, the allocated server links are just taken as contingency data sources). If the download rate of a peer p inside W_p falls below 30 KBps, p is allowed to really download data from his allocated server links. Similarly, a *high-demand swarm* is allocated with sufficient server links in order to enhance its *ATD* to the "ATD of 100 KBps."

6.4.4 Bringing Extra Benefit to Server Providers

QQXuanfeng aims to benefit all the relevant parties: server providers, peer swarms and QQXuanfeng in itself, because any party's resents can hinder or even damage the whole open-P2SP system. Peer swarms get enhanced download rates from QQXuanfeng, but server providers may be reluctant to support QQXuanfeng if they cannot obtain extra benefit from extra bandwidth cost. The two most important benefit metrics of a server provider are its *page view* (*PV*) [10] and *paid-to-click* (*PTC*) [11]. Normally, if an Internet user wants to get a file f from a web site (server provider), he needs to click on several links on multiple pages to get the download link, and thus the *PV* of the web site is added by a certain integer (≥ 1). Meanwhile, the *PTC* of the web site is likely to increase if the user clicks on some advertisements on the web pages. However, QQXuanfeng directly allocates the download link of f to the user (of course this brings convenience to the user), so the server provider gets no *PV* or *PTC* additions and loses his economic benefit.

At present, we are fostering benefit collaborations with server providers from both perspectives of *PV* and *PTC*, in order to encourage more server providers to support QQXuanfeng. Establishing the benefit collaboration scheme involves complicated technical and economic factors, and in fact there exists no commercially mature precedent for us to follow, so our following scheme may be incomprehensible and transitional. On one hand, if a server provider uploads a file f to a peer swarm by the direction of QQXuanfeng, the corresponding *PV* of the server provider will be increased in the web search engine (namely Soso) of QQXuanfeng. Soso is the 4th biggest web search engine in China [18], just lagging behind Baidu, Google China, and Sogou. If a server provider contributes a lot to QQXuanfeng, its corresponding pages or file links will be highly ranked in the search results of Soso, so that the bandwidth contribution of the server provider gets rewarded. On the other hand, QQXuanfeng shares its *PTC* revenue with server providers. QQXuanfeng acquires *PTC* revenue by embedding advertisements into its client software. If a server provider contributes a lot to QQXuanfeng, it will be rewarded by a nontrivial share of our *PTC* revenue.

One thing worth noting is that the above *PV* and *PTC* methods may take different roles for different open-P2SP systems. For example, as for QQXuanfeng, the *PV* method is the dominant because Soso is a mainstream web search engine in China. But as for Xunlei, the *PTC* method is the dominant because the web search engine (namely Gougou) of Xunlei is relatively weak.

6.5 Performance Evaluation

This section evaluates the performance of our QQXuanfeng open-P2SP system via comprehensive real-world measurements, as well as specially operated localized and sampling measurements. First, we measure its acceleration effect on peer swarms and how its acceleration effect behaves as the system scales. Then we measure the bandwidth contribution of the involved servers corresponding to different file sizes and swarm scales. Finally, we measure the extra bandwidth utilization of the involved servers. The major performance metrics are:

1. *Acceleration effect on peer swarms*: represents to what extent the download rates of peers have been increased by QQXuanfeng. This is the kernel performance metric and we extensively evaluate it in three aspects: (a) *download rate distribution*, (b) *acceleration effect brought by QQXuanfeng*, and (c) *acceleration effect as the system scales*.
2. *Bandwidth contribution of servers*: denotes the ratio of the users' download bandwidth obtained from third-party servers.
3. *Extra bandwidth utilization (EBU) of servers*: illustrates the extra bandwidth burden posed on the involved servers by QQXuanfeng.

6.5.1 Acceleration Effect on Peer Swarms

6.5.1.1 Download Rate Distribution

Figure 6.8 depicts the distribution of peers' download rates in one day (Dec. 15, 2011), where "50" denotes the region [40, 50) and "500+" denotes the region [400, +∞). Obviously, three download rate regions: [100K, 150K), [150K, 200K), and [200K, 250K) possess the most peers: $16\% + 15\% + 7\% = 38\%$, and more than half (51.4 %) of the peers have a download rate above 100 KBps (d_{high}). On the other hand, 17.5 % of the peers have a download rate below 30 KBps (d_{basic}). That is to say, more than 1/6 of the peer swarms are still hungry, mainly because QQXuanfeng does not find sufficient servers that provide the corresponding contents—to deal with this case, we

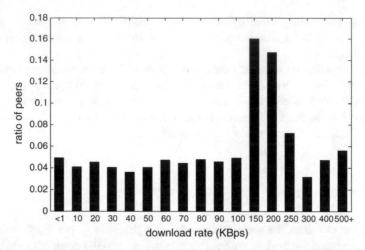

Fig. 6.8 Distribution of peers' download rates in one day. (Reprinted with permission from [8].)

have proposed and implemented a novel *"cloud download"* scheme [19] and have started to implement an ISP-friendly cache mechanism in some cooperative ISPs. Generally speaking, most users have a download rate above their basic expectations and half of the users have a high enough download rate for continuous video playback.

6.5.1.2   Acceleration Effect Brought by QQXuanfeng

For a peer swarm W, to evaluate the acceleration effect on its download rate brought by QQXuanfeng, we need to stop the acceleration support to W to measure the *original* download rate of W. Specifically, stopping the acceleration support to a swarm means that the Data Scheduler does not provide any server link to the peer swarm, and thus the swarm cannot retrieve data from servers. It should be noted that we can only stop the acceleration support to a small number of swarms for a limited period of time to avoid severe degradation in user experience. Therefore, we stop the acceleration support to a random sample of peer swarms (around 1000 swarms in total) for 7 days, and then recover the acceleration support. The acceleration effect on the download rate is plotted in Fig. 6.9, indicating that the average download rate of a peer is enhanced from 57 to 158 KBps (177 % increase). Besides, we record the acceleration effect on the ratio of hungry swarms among the sampling swarms in Fig. 6.10. The ratio of hungry swarms has fallen from 41.6 to 17.2 % (58 % reduction).

6.5.1.3   Acceleration Effect as the System Scales

As time goes on, QQXuanfeng collects more content links from more servers and meanwhile serves more peer swarms. For example, in the year 2010, QQXuanfeng

Fig. 6.9 Acceleration effect of QQXuanfeng on the download rate. (Reprinted with permission from [8].)

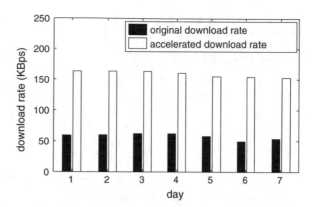

Fig. 6.10 Acceleration effect of QQXuanfeng on the ratio of hungry swarms. (Reprinted with permission from [8].)

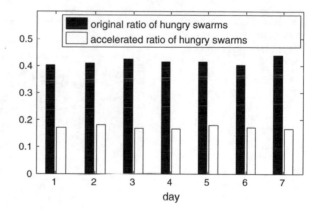

gained around 5 thousand new users and indexed around 0.6 million novel content links per day. To illustrate how the acceleration effect behaves as the system scales, we record the average download rate of all the peers per day in the whole year, as depicted in Fig. 6.11. We can see that the average download rate has been enhanced from 115 to 165 KBps (43.5 % increase). Besides, Fig. 6.12 presents that the ratio of hungry swarms has fallen from around 34 to around 17 % (50 % reduction). During the whole year 2010, our hardware architecture generally worked well without adding or upgrading any machine. In conclusion, the acceleration effect of QQXuanfeng tends to be enhanced as the system scales (and some hardware component may need upgrading accordingly).

6.5.2 Bandwidth Contribution of Servers

A key design target of QQXuanfeng is to let third-party servers contribute their available bandwidth to the peer swarms on demand. In this subsection, we measure the bandwidth contribution (to peer swarms) of the involved servers. Figures 6.13 and

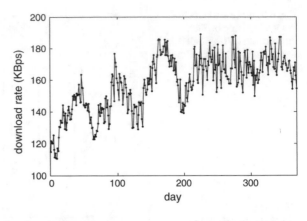

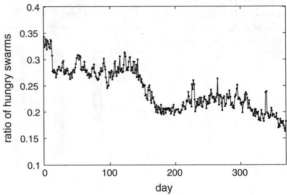

6.14 plot the server bandwidth contribution corresponding to different file sizes and
swarm scales. Generally speaking, when a peer downloads a small file (<100 MB)
or when the peer lies in a small swarm (<20), it mainly relies on server bandwidth;
on the contrary, when a peer downloads a large file (>1 GB) or when the peer lies in
a big swarm (>30), it relies more on its neighboring peers.

The relationship between the server bandwidth contribution and the swarm scale
is straightforward. Now we discuss the impact of file size. Retrieving a small file
directly from a server is convenient and quick, while retrieving a small file from
peers is not cost effective, since the necessary P2P operations (i.e., establishing
and maintaining peer connections) require considerable communication overhead.
Moreover, most peers leave the swarm soon after they finish downloading, so it is
more difficult to find peers that share a small file. In total, up to 45 % of the download
rate of peers is obtained from the involved servers (note that in Fig. 6.13, large files
have significant impact in computing the total server bandwidth contribution).

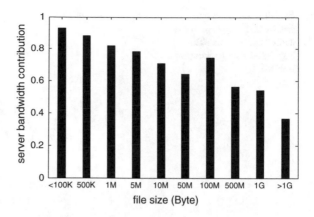

Fig. 6.13 Server bandwidth contribution corresponding to different file sizes. (Reprinted with permission from [8].)

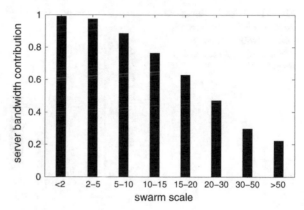

Fig. 6.14 Server bandwidth contribution corresponding to different swarm scales. (Reprinted with permission from [8].)

6.5.3 Extra Bandwidth Utilization of Servers

Another important design target of QQXuanfeng is to facilitate load-balancing among third-party servers so that their original services are not interfered. As depicted in Fig. 6.15, we record the average *extra bandwidth utilization* (*EBU*) of all the involved servers by the direction of QQXuanfeng per 5 min in 24 h starting from 0:00, GTM+8, on Dec. 15, 2011. In each 5-min interval, the average *EBU* is mostly below 40 %. Besides, a "snapshot" distribution of the *EBU* of the involved servers in a 5-min interval is recorded in Fig. 6.16 (where "0.4" denotes the region (0.3, 0.4)). In this 5-min interval, the *EBU* of 88 % involved servers is below 40 %. Because QQXuanfeng periodically (the period is 5 min) collects users' reports to calculate the *EBU* of each involved server and then take measures to restrict the *EBU* of each involved server, it is reasonable that a small portion of the involved servers are temporarily overloaded. In a word, Figs. 6.15 and 6.16 confirm that QQXuanfeng has made limited and balanced utilization of the involved servers.

Fig. 6.15 Average extra
bandwidth utilization of the
involved servers in 24 h.
(Reprinted with permission
from [8].)

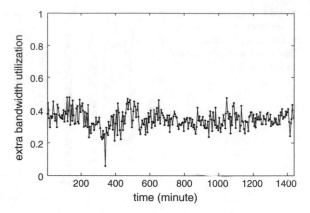

Fig. 6.16 Distribution of the
extra bandwidth utilizations
of the involved servers.
(Reprinted with permission
from [8].)

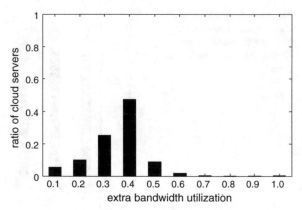

6.6 Conclusion and Future Work

In this chapter, we first review today's three major Internet content distribution modes:
(a) *server-based*, (b) *P2P*, and (c) *P2SP*. Although P2SP can provide efficient hybrid
server-P2P content distribution, it generally works in a closed manner by only utilizing its private owned servers to accelerate its private organized peer swarms.
Consequently, P2SP still has its limitations in both content abundance and server
bandwidth. To this end, the fourth mode (to be called a generalized mode of P2SP)
has appeared as (d) *cloud tracking* or *open-P2SP* which integrates various third-
party servers, contents and data transfer protocols all over the Internet into a large,
open, and federated P2SP platform. Based on a large-scale commercial open-P2SP
system named QQXuanfeng, this chapter investigates the key challenging problems,
practical designs, and real-world performances of open-P2SP.

An important future work is about the setting of system parameters. This chapter
reveals several valuable system parameters via comprehensive measurements, such
as the users' basic expectation of download rate: $d_{basic} = 30$ KBps, the limitation of

extra server bandwidth utilization: $EBU = 40\%$ and so forth. Although the current QQXuanfeng system generally works well with these parameters, it is hard to say these parameters are the best and can well adapt to possible significant changes of underlying network environments or user requirements. It will be interesting and useful to explore how to design some mechanisms to automatically collect and analyze measurements got from servers and peers, and thus dynamically tune the system parameters to match new situations.

In addition, recently there has been a potential trend in integrating open-P2SP service into web browsers to transparently accelerate the common web download (using the HTTP, FTP, or RTSP protocol). To our knowledge, at least three popular web browsers (i.e., Tencent web browser, Sogou web browser, and 360 web browser) have (partially) implemented this service. Undoubtedly, the combination of open-P2SP and web browsers will greatly benefit web users, and their developers may obtain useful heuristics from the design of QQXuanfeng.

References

1. Akamai NetSession interface. http://www.akamai.com/client
2. iKu P2P accelerator. http://c.youku.com/ikuacc
3. Huang, Y., Fu, T.Z., Chiu, D.M., Lui, J., Huang, C.: Challenges, design and analysis of a large-scale P2P-VoD system. ACM SIGCOMM Comput. Commun. Rev. (CCR) 38(4), 375–388 (2008)
4. Li, Z., Zhang, T., Huang, Y., Zhang, Z.L., Dai, Y.: Maximizing the bandwidth multiplier effect for hybrid cloud-P2P content distribution. In: Proceedings of the 20th IEEE/ACM International Workshop on Quality of Service (IWQoS), pp. 1–9 (2012)
5. Sun, Y., Liu, F., Li, B., Li, B., Zhang, X.: FS2You: peer-assisted semi-persistent online storage at a large scale. In: Proceedings of the 28th IEEE International Conference on Computer Communications (INFOCOM), pp. 873–881 (2009)
6. Wu, C., Li, B., Zhao, S.: On dynamic server provisioning in multichannel P2P live streaming. IEEE/ACM Trans. Netw. (TON) 19(5), 1317–1330 (2011)
7. Yin, H., Liu, X., Zhan, T., Sekar, V., Qiu, F., Lin, C., Zhang, H., Li, B.: Design and deployment of a hybrid CDN-P2P system for live video streaming: experiences with LiveSky. In: Proceedings of the 17th ACM International Conference on Multimedia (ACM-MM), pp. 25–34 (2009)
8. Li, Z., Huang, Y., Liu, G., Wang, F., Liu, Y., Zhang, Z.L., Dai, Y.: Challenges, designs and performances of large-scale open-P2SP content distribution. IEEE Trans. Parallel Distrib. Syst. (TPDS) 24(11), 2181–2191 (2013)
9. Orbit downloader. http://www.orbitdownloader.com
10. PV (page view). http://en.wikipedia.org/wiki/Page_view
11. PTC (paid-to-click). http://en.wikipedia.org/wiki/Paid_To_Click
12. Aditya, P., Zhao, M., Lin, Y., Haeberlen, A., Druschel, P., Maggs, B., Wishon, B.: Reliable client accounting for P2P-infrastructure hybrids. In: Proceedings of the 9th USENIX Conference on Networked Systems Design and Implementation (NSDI), pp. 8 (2012)
13. Dhungel, P., Ross, K.W., Steiner, M., Tian, Y., Hei, X.: Xunlei: peer-assisted download acceleration on a massive scale. In: Proceedings of the 13th Passive and Active Measurement Conference (PAM), pp. 231–241. Springer (2012)
14. Zhang, M., John, W., Chen, C.: A Measurement-based study of Xunlei. In: Proceedings of the 10th PAM Student Workshop (2009)

15. Zhang, M., John, W., Chen, C.: Architecture and download behavior of xunlei: a measurement-based study. In: Proceedings of the 2nd IEEE International Conference on Education Technology and Computer (ICETC), vol. 1, pp. 494–498 (2010)
16. Xunlei has delayed its IPO process. http://tech.163.com/11/0728/07/7A1J9GKV000915BF.html
17. Heller, B., Seetharaman, S., Mahadevan, P., Yiakoumis, Y., Sharma, P., Banerjee, S., McKeown, N.: ElasticTree: saving energy in data center networks. In: Proceedings of the 7th USENIX Conference on Networked Systems Design and Implementation (NSDI), pp. 249–264 (2010)
18. A report on China's search engine ranking, Apr 2011. http://search.iresearch.cn/32/20110412/136979.shtml
19. Huang, Y., Li, Z., Liu, G., Dai, Y.: Cloud download: using cloud utilities to achieve high-quality content distribution for unpopular videos. In: Proceedings of the 19th ACM International Conference on Multimedia (ACM-MM), pp. 213–222 (2011)

Chapter 7
Cloud Bandwidth Scheduling

Abstract *Hybrid cloud-P2P* content distribution (CloudP2P) provides a promising alternative to the conventional cloud-based or peer-to-peer (P2P)-based large-scale content distribution. It addresses the potential limitations of these two conventional approaches while inheriting their advantages. A key strength of CloudP2P lies in the so-called *bandwidth multiplier effect*: by appropriately allocating a small portion of cloud (server) bandwidth S_i to a *peer swarm i* (consisting of users interested in the same content) to seed the content, the users in the peer swarm—with an aggregate download bandwidth D_i—can then distribute the content among themselves; we refer to the ratio D_i/S_i as the bandwidth multiplier (for peer swarm i). A major problem in the design of a CloudP2P content distribution system is therefore how to allocate cloud (server) bandwidth to peer swarms so as to maximize the overall bandwidth multiplier effect of the system. In this chapter, using real-world measurements, we identify the key factors that affect the bandwidth multipliers of peer swarms and thus construct a *fine-grained* performance model for addressing the *optimal bandwidth allocation problem* (OBAP). Then we develop a *fast-convergent* iterative algorithm to solve OBAP. Both trace-driven simulations and prototype implementation confirm the efficacy of our solution.

7.1 Introduction

Large-scale content distribution has become increasingly prevalent and contributes to a significant portion of the Internet traffic. Today's large content providers (e.g., YouTube and Netflix) typically employ a *cloud-based* approach which relies on huge data centers for computing and storage and utilizes geographically dispersed CDNs (content distribution networks) to further meet users' demand on content delivery performance. Such an approach requires a massive and costly computing, storage and delivery infrastructure. For instance, YouTube, as a subsidiary of Google, utilizes Google's own massive delivery infrastructure [1], whereas Netflix employs Amazon's cloud services and third-party CDNs such as Akamai and Limelight [5]. In contrast, the *peer-to-peer* (P2P)-based content distribution incurs little infrastructure cost and can scale well with the user base, as it utilizes individual users' machines

© Springer Science+Business Media Singapore 2016   143
Z. Li et al., *Content Distribution for Mobile Internet: A Cloud-based Approach*,
DOI 10.1007/978-981-10-1463-5_7

Fig. 7.1 Hybrid cloud-P2P
content distribution. Inside
each swarm, peers exchange
data with others; meanwhile,
they get data from the cloud.
Different peer swarms share
different contents. (Reprinted
with permission from [11].)

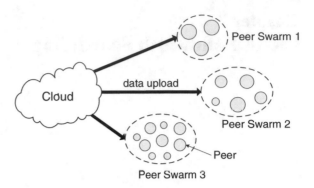

(and their ISPs) for replicating and delivering content to each other. However, P2P
also suffers several technical shortcomings such as end users' high dynamics and
heterogeneity, difficulty to find "seeds" or other peers with the content in which an
end user is interested. As a result, the working efficacy of P2P can be quite poor and
unpredictable.

A third approach—*hybrid cloud-P2P* content distribution (CloudP2P)—has
recently emerged [7–9, 12, 14, 15] as a promising alternative. It addresses the potential limitations of these two conventional approaches while inheriting their advantages. As depicted in Fig. 7.1, CloudP2P comprises of a cloud component as well as
a number of peer swarms. The cloud not only provides content seeds but also assists
end users to find other peers who are interested in the same content. A peer swarm
starts by obtaining a content seed from the cloud, and subsequently, peers within the
swarm can exchange data among themselves. Compared to the purely cloud-based
approach, CloudP2P incurs far lower infrastructure and network bandwidth costs
(especially there is no need for a large-scale CDN infrastructure). Take Youku, the
biggest video sharing site in China, as an example. Since its startup, the cloud bandwidth expense of Youku has consumed more than half of its total income. In the
past two years, Youku has been encouraging its users to install the iKu accelerator
[8], which changes its purely cloud-based content distribution to a hybrid CloudP2P
architecture. Meanwhile, CloudP2P also effectively circumvents the key limitations
of P2P by providing extra cloud bandwidth to those peer swarms who do not work
well for lack of seed peers.

A key strength of CloudP2P lies in the so-called *bandwidth multiplier effect*: by
appropriately allocating a small portion of cloud (server) bandwidth S_i to a *peer
swarm i* (consisting of users interested in the same content) to seed the content,
CloudP2P can attain a higher aggregate content distribution bandwidth (D_i) by letting peers to exchange data and distribute content among themselves. Borrowing a
term from economics, we refer to the ratio D_i/S_i as the *bandwidth multiplier* (for
peer swarm i). A major problem in the design of a CloudP2P content distribution
system is therefore how to allocate cloud (server) bandwidth to peer swarms so
as to maximize the overall bandwidth multiplier effect of the system—the *optimal
bandwidth allocation problem* (OBAP).

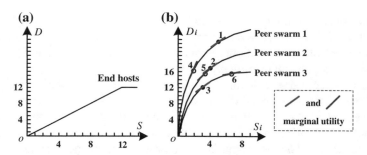

Fig. 7.2 The bandwidth multiplier ($= \frac{D}{S}$) of **a** Cloud and **b** CloudP2P: a simple example. S denotes the invested cloud bandwidth and D denotes the end hosts' aggregate download bandwidth. As to CloudP2P, $S = \sum_i S_i$ and $D = \sum_i D_i$ where i denotes the ith peer swarm. For each peer swarm, its *marginal utility* at a certain point is the partial derivative: $\frac{\partial D_i}{\partial S_i}$. Here we use $\frac{\partial D_i}{\partial S_i}$ rather than $\frac{d D_i}{d S_i}$ because D_i is not fully dependent on S_i. (Reprinted with permission from [11].)

Below we use a simple (artificial) example to illustrate the bandwidth multiplier effect of CloudP2P and argue why in solving OBAP, one must consider the *marginal utility* of cloud bandwidth allocation. As plotted in Fig. 7.2a, in the conventional cloud-based content distribution, the bandwidth multiplier is usually 1.0 because each user typically downloads content directly form the cloud content provider. In the case of CloudP2P, the bandwidth multiplier can be much larger than 1.0, since the data exchange among end host peers can multiply the upload bandwidth of cloud servers. The *achievable* bandwidth multiplier will hinge critically on the bandwidth allocation scheme as well as individual peer swarms. Depending on the specifics of each peer swarm (e.g., its size, the bandwidth available among the peers, etc.), given the same allocated cloud bandwidth, the bandwidth multiplier can vary significantly from one peer swarm to another peer swarm. Figure 7.2b plots three hypothetical bandwidth multiplier curves for three different peer swarms. Suppose the total invested cloud bandwidth is $S = 12$ and the bandwidth allocation scheme corresponds to points $\{1, 2, 3\}$ in Fig. 7.2b, and then the overall bandwidth multiplier for all three peer swarms is $\frac{D}{S} = \frac{\sum_i D_i}{\sum_i S_i} = \frac{23+17+12}{3+4+5} = 4.33$.

Because of the nonlinear nature of the bandwidth multiplier curves, it is clear that we must take into account the *marginal utility* ($\frac{\partial D_i}{\partial S_i}$) of cloud bandwidth allocation in solving the optimal bandwidth allocation problem. The commonly used bandwidth allocation algorithms in commercial systems, however, do not (well) consider the marginal utility of cloud bandwidth allocation, thus leading to suboptimal or even poor bandwidth multiplier effect. For instance, the *free-competitive* strategy simply lets all the end hosts/peer swarms to compete freely for the cloud bandwidth, whereas the *proportional-allocate* scheme allocates cloud bandwidth proportionally to peer swarms according to their size. As a result, an "overfeeding" peer swarm may be allocated with too much cloud bandwidth resulting in low marginal utility, while a "starving" peer swarm may get little cloud bandwidth resulting in high marginal utility. For example, see the other allocation scheme corresponding to points $\{4, 5, 6\}$ in Fig. 7.2b where the cloud bandwidth ($S = 12$) is proportionally allocated into each peer swarm. The overall bandwidth multiplier corresponding to $\{4, 5, 6\}$ is $\frac{16+15+15}{2+3.3+6.7} = 3.83 < 4.33$ (the overall bandwidth multiplier of $\{1, 2, 3\}$). Intuitively, we find larger bandwidth multiplier implies more balanced marginal utilities among peer swarms (which will be formally proved later).

In this chapter, using real-world measurements, we identify the key factors that affect the bandwidth multipliers of peer swarms and thus construct a *fine-grained* performance model for addressing the optimal bandwidth allocation problem (OBAP). This model takes into account the impact of both outer-swarm and intra-swarm bandwidth provisions on a peer swarm and can well match the measurement data. We further prove that the bandwidth multiplier effect is closely related to the marginal utility of cloud bandwidth allocation. To solve OBAP, we develop a *fast-convergent* iterative algorithm by finding the optimal direction and adaptively setting the stepsize in each iteration step. Compared with the commonly used iterative algorithms, our proposed iterative algorithm has provable convergence, faster convergence speed, and ease of use (as to a large-scale highly dynamic CloudP2P system). Our whole solution is named as FIFA which denotes the combination of the **fi**ne-grained performance model (FI) and the **fa**st-convergent iterative algorithm (FA).

We use both large-scale trace-driven simulations and small-scale prototype implementation to evaluate the bandwidth allocation performance of FIFA. Simulation results based on the log trace of around one million peers reveal that the overall bandwidth multiplier of FIFA is 20, 17, and 8 % larger than that of the existing bandwidth allocation algorithms: *free-competitive*, *proportional-allocate*, and *Ration* [14], respectively. Meanwhile, the total control overhead bandwidth of FIFA stays below 15 KBps—even less than a common user's download bandwidth. Small-scale prototype implementation also confirms the efficacy of FIFA.

The remainder of this chapter is organized as follows. Section 7.2 reviews the related work. Through real-world measurements, we construct a fine-grained performance model to address OBAP in Sect. 7.3. Then we propose a fast-convergent iterative algorithm to solve OBAP in Sect. 7.4. After that, the performance of our solution (FIFA) is evaluated in Sects. 7.5 and 7.6. Finally, we conclude this chapter in Sect. 7.7.

7.2 Related Work

The commonly used bandwidth allocation algorithms of CloudP2P generally adopt a coarse-grained performance model by making some ideal or simplified assumptions. For example, most commercial systems use the *free-competitive* algorithm or make some minor changes [7]. Such an algorithm simply allocates a certain amount of cloud bandwidth for all peer swarms to compete freely. Obviously, *free-competitive* benefits those aggressive or selfish peer swarms who might set up numerous TCP/UDP connections to grasp as much cloud bandwidth as possible. To alleviate the drawback of *free-competitive*, some systems (e.g., UUSee) employ the *proportional-allocate* algorithm which proportionally allocates cloud bandwidth to peer swarms based only on their swarm scale. *Proportional-allocate* implies the assumption that the demand of cloud bandwidth is only dependent on the number of peers inside a swarm, which is deviant from reality.

A similar work to FIFA is AntFarm [13], which uses a centralized coordinator to dynamically split seed peers' bandwidth among peer swarms (AntFarm does not consider the outer-swarm cloud bandwidth provision). The practical application of AntFarm may be difficult for two reasons: (1) Accurately splitting a seed peer's bandwidth and allocating it into multiple swarms is quite difficult due to the dynamic nature of end host peers, so it is rarely supported by commercial P2P systems; (2) The coordinator employs a centralized token protocol which strictly controls the behavior of each peer (e.g., neighbor selection and data exchange), which is not quite compatible with the distributed working principle of P2P.

Another similar work is Ration [14], a cloud bandwidth allocation algorithm for P2P live TV streaming. Ration constructs its CloudP2P performance model by using the impact factors S_i and l_i, where S_i denotes the cloud bandwidth allocated to peer swarm i and l_i denotes the number of online leechers inside peer swarm i. Since Ration works in a live TV streaming environment where most viewers devote their bandwidth to downloading and would leave their peer swarm as soon as they finish viewing (that is to say, $s_i \ll l_i$, where s_i is the number of online seed peers inside peer swarm i.), Ration does not (need to) consider the impact of seed peers—the intra-swarm bandwidth provision. In our work, the impact of seed peers is also taken as a key factor and we find it is *nontrivial* for modeling a large-scale CloudP2P file-sharing system. Given that a P2P file-sharing system usually accommodates much more dynamics and heterogeneity than a P2P live streaming system, our proposed performance model should be more fine-grained and general.

To solve the optimal bandwidth allocation problem, AntFarm employs the "hill-climbing" iterative algorithm (HC) while Ration employs the "water-filling" iterative algorithm (WF) [4]. Both HC and WF are commonly used iterative algorithms to solve optimization problems; however, we find their convergence speeds might be quite slow on handling a large number of highly dynamic peer swarms, mainly because they *have to* use a very short stepsize to make their iteration progress converge. We note that Ration had realized the problem of WF and thus proposed an incremental version of WF to increase its convergence speed, but the incremental version only alleviates rather than resolves its problem. By finding the optimal direction and adaptively setting the stepsize in each iteration step, our proposed fast-convergent iterative algorithm (FA) has provable convergence, faster convergence speed and ease of use.

7.3 Fine-Grained Performance Model

7.3.1 Key Impact Factors

A number of factors may affect the bandwidth multiplier of a peer swarm, such as the *allocated cloud bandwidth, number of leechers, number of seeders,*[1] *available bandwidth of each peer, connection topology among peers,* and *distribution of unique data blocks.* Obviously, it is impossible to take all these factors into account, and considering too many detailed/trivial factors will bring the bandwidth allocation algorithm unbearable communication/computation overhead. Instead, our methodology is to find out the key impact factors that influence the bandwidth multiplier of a peer swarm.

To find the key impact factors, we utilize the real-world measurements from QQXuanfeng, a large-scale CloudP2P file-sharing system [10]. We track 1457 peer swarms in one day (involving around one million peers), record their respective working parameters: D_i, S_i, s_i and l_i per five minutes, and then analyze the relationships between these parameters. The meanings of these parameters are listed as follows:

- D_i: the aggregate download bandwidth of the peers inside (peer) swarm i.

- S_i: the cloud bandwidth allocated to swarm i. S_i denotes the outer-swarm bandwidth provision to swarm i.

- s_i: the number of online seeders in swarm i. s_i denotes the intra-swarm bandwidth provision to swarm i.

- l_i: the number of online leechers in swarm i. l_i denotes how many peers are the bandwidth consumers that benefit from S_i and s_i. (Note that a leecher also uploads data to others.)

As depicted in Fig. 7.3, we discover *approximate* exponential relationship between $\frac{D_i}{l_i}$ and $\frac{S_i}{l_i}$, which is further confirmed by the corresponding *log-log* curve in Fig. 7.5. Thus, as to a typical peer swarm i:

$$\frac{D_i}{l_i} \propto (\frac{S_i}{l_i})^{\alpha_i}, \quad 0 < \alpha_i < 1;$$

on the other hand, from Figs. 7.4 and 7.6 we find that the exponential relationship also *approximately* holds between $\frac{D_i}{l_i}$ and $\frac{l_i}{s_i}$, except that the exponent is negative:

$$\frac{D_i}{l_i} \propto (\frac{l_i}{s_i})^{-\beta_i}, \quad \beta_i > 0.$$

The above-mentioned exponential relationships basically comply with our intuitive experiences obtained from Fig. 7.2—when a peer swarm is allocated with too

---

[1]Here a seeder has the same meaning with a seed peer.

Fig. 7.3 Relationships between $\frac{D_i}{l_i}$ and $\frac{S_i}{l_i}$, as to a typical peer swarm i. (Reprinted with permission from [11].)

Fig. 7.4 Relationships between $\frac{D_i}{l_i}$ and $\frac{l_i}{s_i}$, as to a typical peer swarm i. (Reprinted with permission from [11].)

Fig. 7.5 Relationships between $log(\frac{D_i}{l_i})$ and $log(\frac{S_i}{l_i})$. (Reprinted with permission from [11].)

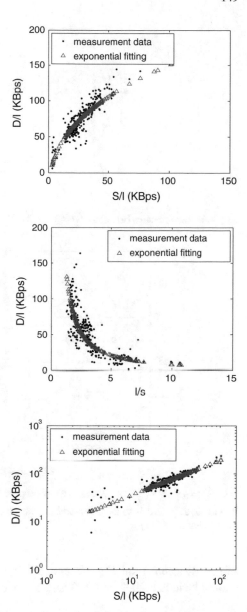

much cloud bandwidth or contains too many seeders, the marginal utility for increasing its aggregate download bandwidth will become trivial. Now that the above exponential relationships are merely *approximate*, we still have a problem whether we should use $\frac{S_i}{l_i}$, $\frac{l_i}{s_i}$, both or even more parameters to well model $\frac{D_i}{l_i}$. To this end, we use $\frac{S_i}{l_i}$, $\frac{l_i}{s_i}$ and both, respectively, to model $\frac{D_i}{l_i}$, where the corresponding constant parameters (α_i, f_i), (β_i, f_i) and (α_i, β_i, f_i) are computed based on the one-day measurements

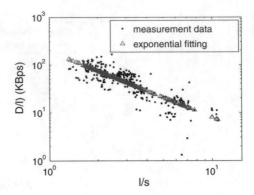

Fig. 7.6 Relationships between $log(\frac{D_i}{l_i})$ and $log(\frac{l_i}{s_i})$. (Reprinted with permission from [11].)

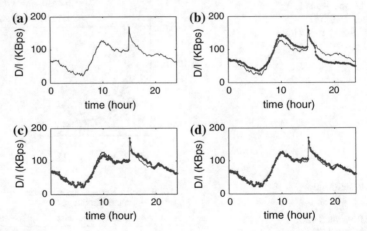

Fig. 7.7 Modeling $\frac{D_i}{l_i}$ using **b** $\frac{l_i}{s_i}$ (i.e., $\frac{D_i}{l_i} = (\frac{l_i}{s_i})^{-\beta_i} \cdot f_i$), **c** $\frac{S_i}{l_i}$ (i.e., $\frac{D_i}{l_i} = (\frac{S_i}{l_i})^{\alpha_i} \cdot f_i$) and **d** both (i.e., $\frac{D_i}{l_i} = (\frac{S_i}{l_i})^{\alpha_i} \cdot (\frac{l_i}{s_i})^{-\beta_i} \cdot f_i$), as to a typical peer swarm. Clearly, the key impact factors should include both $\frac{S_i}{l_i}$ and $\frac{l_i}{s_i}$ so that the model can match the **a** measurement data well. (Reprinted with permission from [11].)

of peer swarm i. From Fig. 7.7 and Table 7.1 we confirm that the key impact factors should include both $\frac{S_i}{l_i}$ and $\frac{l_i}{s_i}$. Therefore, we get the following equation:

$$\frac{D_i}{l_i} = (\frac{S_i}{l_i})^{\alpha_i} \cdot (\frac{l_i}{s_i})^{-\beta_i} \cdot f_i, \qquad (7.1)$$

where $0 < \alpha_i < 1$, $\beta_i > 0$ and $f_i > 0$. Then the aggregate[2] download bandwidth of peer swarm i is:

$$D_i = S_i^{\alpha_i} \cdot l_i^{1-\alpha_i-\beta_i} \cdot s_i^{\beta_i} \cdot f_i. \qquad (7.2)$$

---

[2]If $s_i = 0$, we just let $\frac{l_i}{s_i} = 1$ so that $(\frac{l_i}{s_i})^{-\beta_i}$ is ignored.

Table 7.1 Relative errors of the three models applied to all the 1457 peer swarms, compared with their measurements data

Model	Avg (relative error)	Min	Max
(b) only using $\frac{l_i}{s_i}$	0.1391	0.006	0.9036
(c) only using $\frac{S_i}{l_i}$	0.0738	0	0.2366
(d) using both $\frac{S_i}{l_i}$ and $\frac{l_i}{s_i}$	0.0308	0	0.0972

(Reprinted with permission from [11].)

Since S_i is the only decision variable that we can schedule, we also write D_i as $D_i(S_i)$. Finally, the bandwidth multiplier of peer swarm i is:

$$\frac{D_i}{S_i} = S_i^{\alpha_i - 1} \cdot l_i^{1 - \alpha_i - \beta_i} \cdot s_i^{\beta_i} \cdot f_i. \tag{7.3}$$

To compute the constant parameters α_i, β_i, and f_i, we first transform Eq. (7.1) into its logarithmic form:

$$\log \frac{D_i}{l_i} = \log \frac{S_i}{l_i} \cdot \alpha_i - \log \frac{l_i}{s_i} \cdot \beta_i + \log f_i, \tag{7.4}$$

so that α_i, β_i and f_i can be computed by using the measurements of D_i, l_i, S_i, and s_i, via the classical linear regression method. One thing to note is that the above-mentioned constant parameters (α_i, β_i and f_i) can only be taken as constant during a certain period (typically one day or several hours), so they need to be periodically updated using the latest measurements.

7.3.2 OBAP and Its Optimal Solution

Till now, the optimal bandwidth allocation problem (OBAP) of CloudP2P can be formalized as follows:

OBAP

Maximize the overall bandwidth multiplier ($\frac{D}{S}$)

subject to the following conditions:

$$\begin{cases} D = \sum_{i=1}^{m} D_i, \text{ where } m \text{ is the number of swarms;} \\ S = \sum_{i=1}^{m} S_i, \text{ where } S \text{ is taken as a constant during} \\ \text{an allocation period;} \\ S_i \geq 0, \quad \forall i \in \{1, 2, \ldots, m\}; \\ D_i = S_i^{\alpha_i} \cdot l_i^{1 - \alpha_i - \beta_i} \cdot s_i^{\beta_i} \cdot f_i, \quad \forall i \in \{1, 2, \ldots, m\}; \end{cases}$$

with decision variables $S_1, S_2, \ldots, S_m$.

We can see that OBAP is a constrained nonlinear optimization problem [3]. Given that S is taken as a constant during an allocation period, maximizing $\frac{D}{S}$ is equal to maximizing D. When the optimal solution of OBAP exists, suppose the optimal solution is $\mathbf{S}^* = (S_1^*, S_2^*, \ldots, S_m^*)^3$ and the corresponding aggregate download bandwidth of each swarm is $(D_1^*, D_2^*, \ldots, D_m^*)$. Thus, according to the optimality condition of constrained nonlinear optimization [3], we have:

$$\sum_{i=1}^{m} \frac{\partial D_i(S_i^*)}{\partial S_i}(S_i - S_i^*) \leq 0, \quad \forall S_i \geq 0 \text{ with } \sum_{i=1}^{m} S_i = S. \quad (7.5)$$

Then fixing an arbitrary i and letting j be any other index, we construct a feasible solution $\mathbf{S}'$ to the constraints as:

$$S_i' = 0, S_j' = S_i^* + S_j^*, S_k' = S_k^*, \quad \forall k \neq i, j.$$

Applying $\mathbf{S}'$ to Eq. (7.5), we get:

$$(\frac{\partial D_j(S_j^*)}{\partial S_j} - \frac{\partial D_i(S_i^*)}{\partial S_i}) \cdot S_i^* \leq 0, \quad \forall i, j \ (i \neq j).$$

If $S_i^* = 0$, peer swarm i gets no cloud bandwidth and thus we do not need to consider such a swarm for cloud bandwidth allocation. Consequently, we have $\forall i \in \{1, 2, \ldots, m\}, S_i^* > 0$, and then

$$\frac{\partial D_j(S_j^*)}{\partial S_j} \leq \frac{\partial D_i(S_i^*)}{\partial S_i}, \quad \forall i, j \ (i \neq j). \quad (7.6)$$

Therefore, the optimal solution $\mathbf{S}^*$ has the following form:

$$\frac{\partial D_j(S_1^*)}{\partial S_1} = \frac{\partial D_2(S_2^*)}{\partial S_2} = \cdots = \frac{\partial D_m(S_m^*)}{\partial S_m}, \quad (7.7)$$

which means the *marginal utility* of the cloud bandwidth allocated to each peer swarm should be equal in the optimal solution (if it exists). In practice, there is an exceptional case in which a peer swarm i cannot be adjusted to its ideal status (i.e., the marginal utility of the cloud bandwidth allocated to peer swarm i is equal to that of the other swarms), and this exceptional case will cause OBAP to have no optimal solution in the form of Eq. (7.7). As illustrated in Fig. 7.8, for some reasons peer swarm i has an upper bound of its aggregate download bandwidth ("Maximum D_i"), which prevents the bandwidth allocation algorithm from adjusting peer swarm i to its ideal status. In this situation, we just allocate the least cloud bandwidth to improve its aggregate download bandwidth to "Maximum D_i" so that the relative

---

[3]The **bold** font is used to represent a vector. It is possible that OBAP has no optimal solution within its constrained set.

Fig. 7.8 An exceptional case in which the peer swarm cannot be adjusted to its ideal status. (Reprinted with permission from [11].)

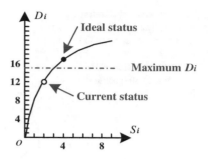

deviation of marginal utility among all the peer swarms can be as little as possible. In conclusion, we have the following theorem:

Theorem 7.1 *For CloudP2P content distribution, the maximum bandwidth multiplier implies that the marginal utility of the cloud bandwidth allocated to each peer swarm should be equal. In practice, we want the relative deviation of marginal utility among all the peer swarms to be as little as possible, i.e., larger bandwidth multiplier implies more balanced marginal utilities among peer swarms.*

7.4 Fast-Convergent Iterative Algorithm

In last section we have formulated the optimal bandwidth allocation problem (OBAP) into a constrained nonlinear optimization problem. The optimal solution of such a problem is typically obtained via iterative operations in multiple steps until the algorithm converges [3]. Therefore, the convergence property of the iterative algorithm is critical in solving OBAP.

The convergence property of an iterative algorithm mainly depends on two aspects: *iteration direction* and *iteration stepsize*. For a d-dimension[4] constrained nonlinear optimization problem, all its feasible solutions compose a d-dimension *iteration space* $\mathbb{S}^d$. Suppose the iterative algorithm starts at an arbitrary point $\mathbf{P}^{(0)} = (P_1^{(0)}, P_2^{(0)}, \ldots, P_d^{(0)}) \in \mathbb{S}^d$. Then in each subsequent iteration step, the algorithm must determine an *iteration direction* and an *iteration stepsize* to go further to a new point $\mathbf{P}^{(k)} = (P_1^{(k)}, P_2^{(k)}, \ldots, P_d^{(k)}) \in \mathbb{S}^d$ so that $\mathbf{P}^{(k)}$ is closer to the optimal point $\mathbf{P}^*$ than $\mathbf{P}^{(k-1)}$, as shown in Fig. 7.9. Specifically, the iteration process can be formalized as:

$$\mathbf{P}^{(k+1)} = \mathbf{P}^{(k)} + t^{(k)}(\overline{\mathbf{P}}^{(k)} - \mathbf{P}^{(k)}),$$

$$\text{until} \quad |(\mathbf{P}^{(k+1)}) - f(\mathbf{P}^{(k)})| < \epsilon. \tag{7.8}$$

---

[4]d-dimension means the optimization problem deals with d decision variables in total. As to OBAP, d is the total number of peer swarms.

Fig. 7.9 A demo iteration process. The *equal-effect surface* is the set of all the points **P** that have the same performance value $f(\mathbf{P})$. (Reprinted with permission from [11].)

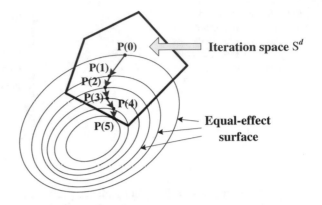

where $f(.)$ is the performance function, ϵ is a very small constant, $(\overline{\mathbf{P}}^{(k)} - \mathbf{P}^{(k)})$ is the iteration direction, and $t^{(k)}$ is the iteration stepsize in the kth step. The task of our fast-convergent iterative algorithm (FA) is to determine appropriate $\overline{\mathbf{P}}^{(k)}$ and $t^{(k)}$ in the kth step so that the iteration process can be as fast as possible.

Iteration direction. For a nonlinear optimization problem, usually it is impossible to directly find the ultimate direction $\mathbf{P}^* - \mathbf{P}^{(0)}$ (or $\mathbf{P}^* - \mathbf{P}^{(k)}$ for a certain k) because this is basically as difficult as to directly find $\mathbf{P}^*$. Instead, FA utilizes the *conditional gradient method* [3] to determine the iteration direction in each step. For a function $f(\mathbf{P})$, it is well known that $f(\mathbf{P}^{(k+1)})$ can be approximated via the Taylor expansion:

$$f(\mathbf{P}^{(k+1)}) = f(\mathbf{P}^{(k)}) + \nabla f(\mathbf{P}^{(k)})(\mathbf{P}^{(k+1)} - \mathbf{P}^{(k)})^T +$$
$$\frac{1}{2}(\mathbf{P}^{(k+1)} - \mathbf{P}^{(k)})\nabla^2 f(\mathbf{P}^{(k)})(\mathbf{P}^{(k+1)} - \mathbf{P}^{(k)})^T + \cdots . \tag{7.9}$$

where $\nabla f(\mathbf{X}) = (\frac{\partial f(\mathbf{X})}{\partial X_1}, \frac{\partial f(\mathbf{X})}{\partial X_2}, \ldots, \frac{\partial f(\mathbf{X})}{\partial X_d})$. The conditional gradient method uses the first-order Taylor expansion to approximate $f(\mathbf{P}^{(k+1)})$:

$$f(\mathbf{P}^{(k+1)}) \approx f(\mathbf{P}^{(k)}) + \nabla f(\mathbf{P}^{(k)})(\mathbf{P}^{(k+1)} - \mathbf{P}^{(k)})^T . \tag{7.10}$$

As to the OBAP problem, the dimension (d) is just the number of peer swarms (m), so that $\mathbf{P}^{(k)} = \mathbf{S}^{(k)}$, $f(\mathbf{P}^{(k)}) = f(\mathbf{S}^{(k)}) = \frac{D^{(k)}}{S} = \frac{\sum_{i=1}^m D_i(S_i)}{S}$ and $D_i(S_i) = S_i^{\alpha_i} \cdot l_i^{1-\alpha_i-\beta_i} \cdot s_i^{\beta_i} \cdot f_i$. Then we have:

$$f(\mathbf{S}^{(k+1)}) \approx f(\mathbf{S}^{(k)}) + \nabla f(\mathbf{S}^{(k)})(\mathbf{S}^{(k+1)} - \mathbf{S}^{(k)})^T . \tag{7.11}$$

Since our goal is to maximize $f(\mathbf{S})$ on condition that $\sum_{i=1}^m S_i = S$ and $S_i \geq 0, \forall i \in \{1, 2, \ldots, m\}$, we need to (greedily) maximize $f(\mathbf{S}^{(k+1)})$ in Eq. (7.11) in the kth iteration step. Thus, we must find the specific $\mathbf{S}$ that satisfies the following problem:

> **Maximize** $\nabla f(\mathbf{S}^{(k)})(\mathbf{S} - \mathbf{S}^{(k)})^T$
>
> **subject to** $\sum_{i=1}^{m} S_i = S$ and $S_i \geq 0, \forall i \in \{1, 2, \ldots, m\}$.

By expanding $\mathbf{S}$, $\mathbf{S}^{(k)}$, and $\nabla f(\mathbf{S}^{(k)})$, we transform the above problem into

> **Maximize** $\sum_{i=1}^{m} \frac{\partial D_i(S_i^{(k)})}{\partial S_i}(S_i - S_i^{(k)})$
>
> **subject to** $\sum_{i=1}^{m} S_i = S$ and $S_i \geq 0, \forall i \in \{1, 2, \ldots, m\}$.

It is not difficult to find that the above problem is a linear optimization problem and the optimal solution $\overline{\mathbf{S}}^{(k)}$ is:

$$\overline{S}_j^{(k)} = S, \text{ for the } j = \arg\max_{i \in \{1,2,\ldots,m\}} \frac{\partial D_i(S_i^{(k)})}{\partial S_i};$$

$$\text{and } \overline{S}_i^{(k)} = 0, \forall i \in \{1, 2, \ldots, j-1, j+1, \ldots, m\}. \tag{7.12}$$

So we get the optimal iteration direction in the kth step:

$$\mathbf{d}^{(k)} = \overline{\mathbf{S}}^{(k)} - \mathbf{S}^{(k)}. \tag{7.13}$$

Iteration stepsize. Till now we have got that the kth step of our FA iterative algorithm proceeds as:

$$\mathbf{S}^{(k+1)} = \mathbf{S}^{(k)} + t^{(k)}\mathbf{d}^{(k)},$$

where $\mathbf{d}^{(k)}$ is determined in Eqs. (7.12) and (7.13). Ideally, the stepsize $t^{(k)}$ should satisfy the following conditions:

> **Maximize** $f(\mathbf{S}^{(k)} + t^{(k)}\mathbf{d}^{(k)})$
>
> **subject to** $\mathbf{S}^{(k)} + t^{(k)}\mathbf{d}^{(k)}$ is a feasible solution.

Unfortunately, the above problem is still a nonlinear optimization problem and thus it is impossible to directly obtain its optimal solution. Instead, we utilize the *Armijo rule* [2] to adaptively set the iteration stepsize $t^{(k)}$, in order to guarantee that $f(\mathbf{S}^{(k+1)})$ is at least larger than $f(\mathbf{S}^{(k)})$ by a bound:

$$f(\mathbf{S}^{(k)} + \tau^j\mathbf{d}^{(k)}) - f(\mathbf{S}^{(k)}) \geq |\sigma\tau^j\nabla f(\mathbf{S}^{(k)})\mathbf{d}^{(k)^T}|, \tag{7.14}$$

where the two constant parameters $\tau, \sigma \in (0, 1)$, and j is tried successively as 0, 1, 2, ..., until the above inequality is satisfied for a certain j (which is $j^{(k)}$). As a result, we get the adaptive iteration stepsize in the kth step for FIFA:

$$t^{(k)} = \tau^{j^{(k)}} \tag{7.15}$$

Summary of FA. The fast-convergent iterative algorithm (FA) efficiently solves OBAP by finding the optimal direction and adaptively setting the stepsize in each iteration step. First, the convergence of FA is provable due to its combinatory use of the *conditional gradient method* and the *Armijo rule* (refer to Proposition 2.2.1 in [3]). Second, FA is easy to use because all the related parameters, τ and σ, can be easily configured. For example, we simply configure $\tau = 0.5$ and $\sigma = 0.01$ for FA, and then it is well applicable to all the simulation/implementation scenarios in Sects. 7.5 and 7.6. Finally, although the accurate convergence speed of FA cannot be theoretically proved, FA exhibits nearly linear convergence speed in our performance evaluation (refer to Sect. 7.5.3). That is to say, for a CloudP2P system consisting of m peer swarms, FA converges in nearly $\Theta(m)$ steps.

Comparisons of WF, HC and FA. The water-filling algorithm (WF) is a classical iterative algorithm in solving constrained nonlinear optimization problems (e.g., [14]) for its simplicity and intuitive explanation. In each iterative step, WF only finds *two* components of $\mathbf{S}^{(k)}$, i.e., $S_h^{(k)}$ and $S_l^{(k)}$ satisfying the following conditions: $h = \arg\max_{i \in \{1,2,\ldots,m\}} \frac{\partial D_i(S_i^{(k)})}{\partial S_i}$ and $l = \arg\min_{i \in \{1,2,\ldots,m\}} \frac{\partial D_i(S_i^{(k)})}{\partial S_i}$. Then WF moves a constant portion δ from $S_l^{(k)}$ to $S_h^{(k)}$: $S_h^{(k)} \leftarrow S_h^{(k)} + \delta$ and $S_l^{(k)} \leftarrow S_l^{(k)} - \delta$. This movement looks like filling some water from one cup to the other. In other words, the iteration direction and iteration stepsize of WF are set as follows: $\mathbf{d}^{(k)} = (d_1^{(k)}, d_2^{(k)}, \ldots, d_m^{(k)})$, where $d_h = 1$, $d_l = -1$, $d_i = 0$, $\forall i \neq h, l$; and $t^{(k)} = \delta$.

Obviously, WF uses a restricted iteration direction (only in two dimensions among the total m dimensions) and a fixed iteration stepsize (δ). The fundamental problem of WF lies in the setting of δ. If δ is set too big, WF will not converge; if δ is set too small, WF will converge slowly. Still worse, on handling a large number of highly dynamic peer swarms, setting an *appropriate* (i.e., neither too big nor too small) iteration stepsize (δ) for WF becomes extremely difficult. Consequently, the only practical choice is to set an extremely small δ resulting in a huge number of iteration steps and slow convergence speed. On the contrary, the iteration stepsize of FA is adaptively set so the number of iteration steps depends on the number of peer swarms. Figure 7.10 is a comparison of the iterative operations of WF and FA when there are only two peer swarms: $S_1 = 0.15$ and $S_2 = 0.85$ (the total cloud bandwidth is normalized as $S = 1$). Additionally, the restricted iteration direction further slows down the iteration process of WF because WF always walks only in two dimensions among the total m dimensions. On the contrary, the iteration direction of FA can be in all dimensions. Figure 7.11 illustrates a demo comparison when there are three peer swarms.

The hill-climbing algorithm (HC) always sets all the components of $\mathbf{S}^{(0)}$ to zero and stores the total cloud bandwidth S in a repository (R) at the starting point. Then in each iteration step, HC just finds *one* component of $\mathbf{S}^{(k)}$, i.e., $S_h^{(k)}$ which satisfies the following condition: $h = \arg\max_{i \in \{1,2,\ldots,m\}} \frac{\partial D_i(S_i^{(k)})}{\partial S_i}$. Then HC moves a constant portion δ from the repository to $S_h^{(k)}$: $S_h^{(k)} \leftarrow S_h^{(k)} + \delta$ and $R \leftarrow R - \delta$. This movement looks like climbing the hill with each step in the steepest dimension. It is easy to see

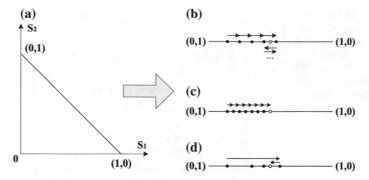

Fig. 7.10 A comparison of the iterative operations of WF and FA when there are only two peer swarms. **a** The iteration space is a line. **b** WF does not converge for the stepsize is too big. **c** WF converges in 7 steps for the stepsize is small enough. **d** FA converges in 2 steps. (Reprinted with permission from [11].)

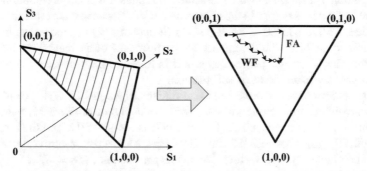

Fig. 7.11 A comparison of the iterative operations of WF and FA when there are three peer swarms. WF always walks only in two dimensions while FA can walk in all the m dimensions. (Reprinted with permission from [11].)

that HC can be taken as a special case of WF which only walks in one dimension among the total m dimensions. Consequently, the number of iteration steps of HC is usually as about several (4–5) times as that of WF when the same stepsize (δ) is used.

7.5 Trace-Driven Simulations

7.5.1 Trace Dataset

Our trace dataset is got from QQXuanfeng, a large-scale CloudP2P file-sharing system. Every online peer reports its *peer status* in a UDP packet to the Bandwidth Scheduler (a centralized server) per 5 min, so the cloud bandwidth allocation period

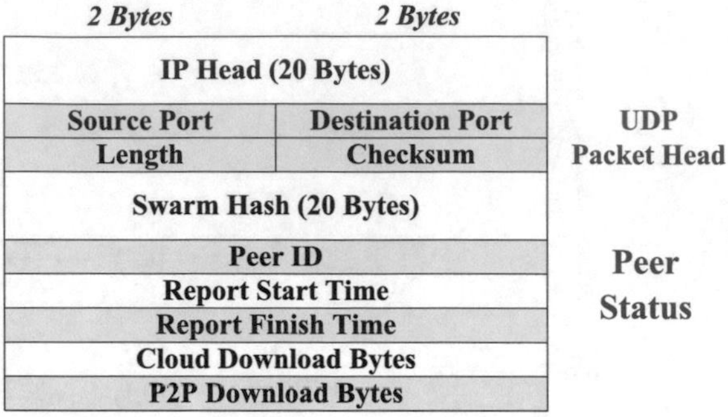

Fig. 7.12 Structure of the peer status report. A seeder's status report does not have the fields of Cloud Download Bytes and P2P Download Bytes. (Reprinted with permission from [11].)

2 Bytes	*2 Bytes*	
IP Head (20 Bytes)		
Source Port	Destination Port	**UDP**
Length	Checksum	**Packet Head**
Swarm Hash (20 Bytes)		
Peer ID		**Peer**
Report Start Time		**Status**
Report Finish Time		
Cloud Download Bytes		
P2P Download Bytes		

is also set as 5 min. The *peer status* report is structured as in Fig. 7.12. During each allocation period, the Bandwidth Scheduler aggregates peer status reports into the corresponding *swarm status* which indicates the status information (including S_i, s_i, l_i, and D_i) of a peer swarm i in the allocation period. Because the peer status reports are carried in UDP packets, a small portion (less than 1 %) of reports might be lost in transmission, which would influence the performance of the bandwidth allocation algorithm. Therefore, if a peer status report is found to be lost, we simply take its previous peer status report as its substitution.

The simulations are performed on a one-day trace (August 17, 2011) of 1457 peer swarms involving around one million peers. As depicted in Fig. 7.13, the number of simultaneously online leechers (l) varies between 4 and 50 K and the total cloud bandwidth (S) varies between 0.2 and 2.25 GBps. As to a peer swarm i, the required constant parameters (α_i, β_i, f_i) for modeling its performance $(D_i = S_i^{\alpha_i} \cdot l_i^{1-\alpha_i-\beta_i} \cdot s_i^{\beta_i} \cdot f_i)$ are computed based on its one-day swarm statuses (including 288 swarm statuses in total, where $288 = \frac{24\,h}{5\,min}$). After obtaining the performance model for each peer swarm, we simulate the *free-competitive*, *proportional-allocate*, *Ration*, and *FIFA*

Fig. 7.13 Evolution of l, s and S over time. (Reprinted with permission from [11].)

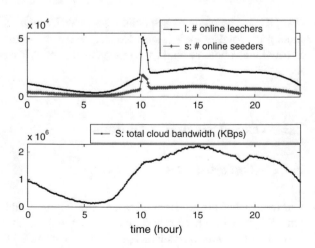

allocation algorithms to reallocate the cloud bandwidth into each peer swarm during each allocation period, and meanwhile observe their *bandwidth multiplier*, *marginal utility*, and so on.

7.5.2 Metrics

- *Bandwidth multiplier* is defined as $\frac{D}{S}$, where D denotes the end hosts' aggregate download bandwidth and S denotes the invested cloud bandwidth. Large bandwidth multiplier means the cloud bandwidth is efficiently used to accelerate the P2P data transfer among end hosts.
- *Marginal utility* is defined as $\mu_i = \frac{\partial D_i}{\partial S_i}$ for a peer swarm i. In **Theorem 7.1** we have proved that for CloudP2P content distribution, (ideally) the maximum overall bandwidth multiplier implies that the marginal utility of the cloud bandwidth allocated to each peer swarm should be equal. In practice, we want the *relative deviation of marginal utility* ($dev_\mu = \frac{\sum_{i=1}^{m}|\mu_i - \bar{\mu}|}{m \cdot \bar{\mu}}$) among all the peer swarms to be as little as possible.
- *Convergence speed* is denoted by the number of iteration steps for an iterative algorithm (FA, WF or HC) to solve OBAP. Besides, we also care about the ease of use of an iterative algorithm.
- *Control overhead* is denoted by the extra communication cost brought by a bandwidth allocation algorithm, because the allocation algorithm usually needs to collect extra status information from end host peers.

7.5.3 Simulation Results

Bandwidth multiplier. Figure 7.14 depicts the evolution of the bandwidth multiplier for each allocation algorithm in one day, starting from 0:00 am (GTM+8). We can see that the bandwidth multiplier of *proportional-allocate* is generally close to that of *free-competitive*. On the other hand, *FIFA* and *Ration* obviously outperform free-competitive, with considerable improvements in average (*FIFA*: 2.20 → 2.64 = 20% increment, and *Ration*: 2.20 → 2.45 = 11% increment). That is to say, the bandwidth multiplier of *FIFA* is 20, 17 and 8% larger than that of *free-competitive*, *proportional-allocate* and *Ration*, respectively.

Marginal utility. Marginal utility provides the microscopic explanation of the bandwidth multiplier—larger bandwidth multiplier implies smaller relative deviation of marginal utility (dev_u). Thus, in Fig. 7.15 we plot the evolution of the relative deviation of marginal utility of all the peer swarms. Clearly, the relative deviation of marginal utility has tight negative correlation with the bandwidth multiplier—*FIFA* has the smallest dev_u and thus its bandwidth multiplier is the biggest.

Fig. 7.14 Evolution of the
bandwidth multiplier in a
whole day. (Reprinted with
permission from [11].)

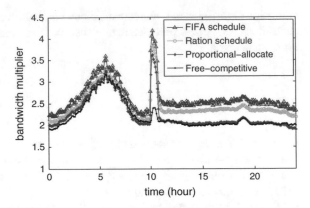

Fig. 7.15 Evolution of the
relative deviation of
marginal utility in a whole
day. (Reprinted with
permission from [11].)

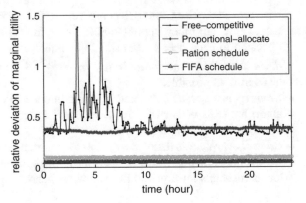

Convergence speed. We theoretically analyzed the convergence property of FA, WF, and HC in Sect. 7.4. In this part, to examine their practical convergence speeds, we utilize the *swarm status* data of different number of peer swarms: 10, 25, ..., 1250, 1457. For FA, we simply use the parameters $\tau = 0.5$ and $\sigma = 0.01$ which are well applicable to all the experimented swarm scales. However, for WF and HC, we made a number of attempts to find an appropriate parameter (stepsize) δ which could make WF and HC converge for all the experimented swarm scales. Finally, we found $\delta = 0.00001$ to be an appropriate parameter and plot the corresponding convergence speeds in Fig. 7.16. We mainly get two findings: (1) FA exhibits nearly linear convergence speed ($\Theta(m)$) as the swarm scale increases, and FA converges faster than WF and HC as to each swarm scale. (2) WF and HC exhibit nearly constant ($\Theta(\frac{1}{\delta})$) convergence speed as the swarm scale increases. The bigger δ is, the faster WF and HC converge, but a bigger δ increases the risk that WF and HC may not converge. If the swarm scale further increases to more than 1457, (very possibly) we need to find a smaller δ to satisfy all the swarm scales. On the contrary, the convergence of FA is not sensitive to its parameters and thus it is easier to use.

Fig. 7.16 Convergence speed of FA ($\tau = 0.5, \sigma = 0.01$), WF and HC ($\delta = 0.00001$). (Reprinted with permission from [11].)

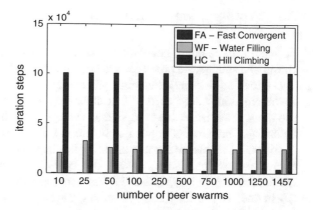

Control overhead. The control overhead of *free-competitive* is zero since it does not collect peers' status information. In Fig. 7.13 we recorded the number of online leechers and online seeders per five minutes in one day, so it is easy to compute the control overhead of *proportional-allocate*, *Ration* and *FIFA*. As to *proportional-allocate*, its peer status report does not have the fields of Cloud Download Bytes and P2P Download Bytes (see Fig. 7.12) and it only collects leechers' status reports. Different from *proportional-allocate*, *FIFA* collects both leechers' and seeders' status reports. Because *Ration* does not consider the impact of seeders, it only collects leechers' status reports. From Fig. 7.13 we figure out that *proportional-allocate* collects 4.52 M leecher status reports without the fields of Cloud Download Bytes and P2P Download Bytes (accounting to $4.52M \times 60\,\mathrm{B} = 271$ MB in total), *Ration* collects 4.52 M leecher status reports (accounting to $4.52M \times 68\,\mathrm{B} = 307$ MB in total), and *FIFA* collects 6.05M peer status reports (accounting to $4.52M \times 68\,\text{Bytes} + 1.53M \times 60\,\mathrm{B} = 399$ MB in total). Averaging the total control overhead into each second, we plot the *control overhead bandwidth* of *FIFA*, *Ration*, and *proportional-allocate* in Fig. 7.17. Obviously, the total control overhead bandwidth of *FIFA* always stays below 15 KBps—even less than a common user's download bandwidth.

Fig. 7.17 Evolution of the control overhead bandwidth. (Reprinted with permission from [11].)

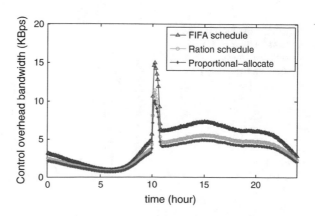

7.6 Prototype Implementation

Besides the trace-driven simulations, we have also implemented the FIFA algorithm
on top of a small-scale prototype system named CoolFish. CoolFish is a CloudP2P
VoD (video-on-demand) streaming system mainly deployed in the CSTNet [6]. With
its "micro cloud" composed of four streaming servers and its P2P organization of
end users, CoolFish is able to support an average video bit rate over 700 Kbps (about
50 % higher than that of popular commercial P2P-VoD systems).

Figure 7.18 plots the number of online leechers (l), online seeders (s), and online
swarms (m) of CoolFish in one day. Obviously, the user scale of CoolFish is much
smaller than that of the QQXuanfeng trace, in particular the average number of peers
($\overline{p}$) in one swarm: for the QQXuanfeng trace, $\overline{p} \approx 1M/1457 = 686$, while for
CoolFish, $\overline{p} = 1327/46 \approx 29$. Since there are much fewer peer swarms working in
CoolFish and a swarm usually possesses much fewer peers, the bandwidth multiplier
of CoolFish is remarkably lower and more unstable than that of QQXuanfeng, as
illustrated in Fig. 7.19. When FIFA is applied, the bandwidth multiplier of QQXuanfeng lies between 2.25 and 4.2 while that of CoolFish lies between 1.0 and 2.1.

Fig. 7.18 Evolution of l, s
and m in CoolFish.
(Reprinted with permission
from [11].)

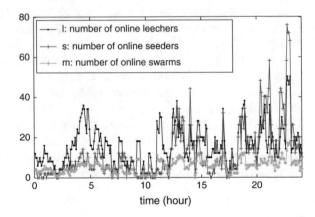

Fig. 7.19 Evolution of the
bandwidth multiplier in
CoolFish. (Reprinted with
permission from [11].)

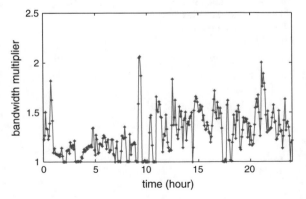

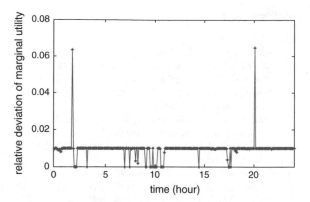

Fig. 7.20 Evolution of the relative deviation of marginal utility in CoolFish. (Reprinted with permission from [11].)

Although the bandwidth multiplier of CoolFish (using FIFA) seems not high, the efficacy of FIFA can still be confirmed from the relative deviation of marginal utility (dev_u stays around 1%, as shown in Fig. 7.20) since we have proved that very low relative deviation of marginal utility is equal to nearly maximum bandwidth multiplier.

7.7 Conclusion and Future Work

As a hybrid approach, CloudP2P inherits the advantages of both cloud and P2P and thus offers a promising alternative in future large-scale content distribution over the Internet. This chapter investigates the optimal bandwidth allocation problem (OBAP) of CloudP2P content distribution so as to maximize its bandwidth multiplier effect. Based on real-world measurements, we build a fine-grained performance model for addressing OBAP. And we prove that the bandwidth multiplier is closely related to the marginal utility of cloud bandwidth allocation. Then we propose a fast-convergent iterative algorithm to solve OBAP. Both trace-driven simulations and prototype implementation confirm the efficacy of our solution.

Still some future work remains. For CloudP2P content distribution, this chapter focuses on the bandwidth multiplier effect and the corresponding microscopic aspect, i.e., marginal utility. In fact, for some special (but important) CloudP2P content distribution scenarios, we should also take *user satisfaction* or *swarm priority* into account. A download rate up to 30 KBps can be satisfactory for a file-sharing user, while a download rate up to 300 KBps may be still unsatisfactory for an HDTV viewer. Therefore, although FIFA has achieved maximum bandwidth multiplier for the whole CloudP2P system, we cannot say FIFA has brought the maximum user satisfaction. The difficulty lies in that we may need to simultaneously consider several metrics: bandwidth multiplier, user satisfaction and so forth, among which there are conflicts in essence. Consequently, special attention must be paid to a proper tradeoff then.

References

1. Adhikari, V., Jain, S., Chen, Y., Zhang, Z.L.: Vivisecting youtube: an active measurement study. In: Proceedings of the 31st IEEE International Conference on Computer Communications (INFOCOM) Mini-conference, pp. 2521–2525 (2012)
2. Armijo, L.: Minimization of functions having lipschitz continuous first partial derivatives. Pac. J. Math. **16**(1), 1–3 (1966)
3. Bertsekas, D.P.: Nonlinear Programming. Athena Scientific Belmont Press (1999)
4. Boyd, S., Vandenberghe, L.: Convex Optimization. Cambridge University Press (2004)
5. Cockroft, A., Hicks, C., Orzell, G.: Lessons Netflix learned from the AWS outage. Netflix Techblog (2011)
6. CSTNet web site. http://www.cstnet.net.cn
7. Huang, Y., Fu, T.Z., Chiu, D.M., Lui, J., Huang, C.: Challenges, design and analysis of a large-scale P2P-VoD system. ACM SIGCOMM Comput. Commun. Rev. (CCR) **38**(4), 375–388 (2008)
8. iKu P2P accelerator. http://c.youku.com/ikuacc
9. iTudou P2P accelerator. http://www.tudou.com/my/soft/speedup.php
10. Li, Z., Huang, Y., Liu, G., Dai, Y.: CloudTracker: accelerating internet content distribution by bridging cloud servers and peer swarms. In: Proceedings of the 19th ACM International Conference on Multimedia (ACM-MM) Doctoral Symposium, vol. 46, p. 49 (2011)
11. Li, Z., Zhang, T., Huang, Y., Zhang, Z.L., Dai, Y.: Maximizing the bandwidth multiplier effect for hybrid cloud-P2P content distribution. In: Proceedings of the 20th IEEE/ACM International Workshop on Quality of Service (IWQoS), pp. 1–9 (2012)
12. Liu, F., Shen, S., Li, B., Li, B., Yin, H., Li, S.: Novasky: cinematic-quality VoD in a P2P storage cloud. In: Proceedings of the 30th IEEE International Conference on Computer Communications (INFOCOM), pp. 936–944 (2011)
13. Peterson, R., Sirer, E.G.: AntFarm: efficient content distribution with managed swarms. In: Proceedings of the 6th USENIX Conference on Networked Systems Design and Implementation (NSDI), pp. 107–122 (2009)
14. Wu, C., Li, B., Zhao, S.: On dynamic server provisioning in multichannel P2P live streaming. IEEE/ACM Trans. Netw. (TON) **19**(5), 1317–1330 (2011)
15. Yin, H., Liu, X., Zhan, T., Sekar, V., Qiu, F., Lin, C., Zhang, H., Li, B.: Design and deployment of a hybrid CDN-P2P system for live video streaming: experiences with livesky. In: Proceedings of the 17th ACM International Conference on Multimedia (ACM-MM), pp. 25–34 (2009)

Part V
Cloud Storage-Oriented Content Distribution

Chapter 8
Toward Network-Level Efficiency for Cloud Storage Services

Abstract Cloud storage services such as Dropbox, Google Drive, and Microsoft OneDrive provide users with a convenient and reliable way to store and share data from anywhere, on any device, and at any time. The cornerstone of these services is the *data synchronization* (sync) operation which *automatically* maps the changes in users' local filesystems to the cloud via a series of network communications in a *timely* manner. If not designed properly, however, the tremendous amount of data sync traffic can potentially cause (financial) pains to both service providers and users. This chapter addresses a simple yet critical question: *Is the current data sync traffic of cloud storage services efficiently used?* We first define a novel metric named *TUE* to quantify the *Traffic Usage Efficiency* of data synchronization. Based on both real-world traces and comprehensive experiments, we study and characterize the *TUE* of six widely used cloud storage services. Our results demonstrate that a considerable portion of the data sync traffic is in a sense wasteful, and can be effectively avoided or significantly reduced via carefully designed data sync mechanisms. Overall, our study of *TUE* of cloud storage services not only provides guidance for service providers to develop more efficient, traffic-economic services, but also helps users pick appropriate services that best fit their needs and budgets.

8.1 Introduction

Cloud storage services such as Dropbox, Google Drive, and Microsoft OneDrive (renamed from SkyDrive since Feb. 2014) provide users with a convenient and reliable way to store and share data from anywhere, on any device, and at any time. The users' data (e.g., documents, photos, and music) stored in cloud storage are *automatically* synchronized across all the designated devices (e.g., PCs, tablets, and smartphones) connected to the cloud in a *timely* manner. With multiplicity of devices—especially mobile devices—that users possess today, such "anywhere, anytime" features significantly simplify data management and consistency maintenance, and thus provide an ideal tool for data sharing and collaboration.

© Springer Science+Business Media Singapore 2016   167
Z. Li et al., *Content Distribution for Mobile Internet: A Cloud-based Approach*,
DOI 10.1007/978-981-10-1463-5_8

Fig. 8.1 Data
synchronization principle.
(Reprinted with permission
from [33].)

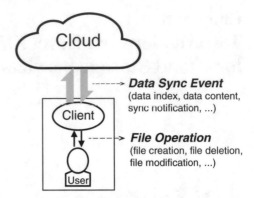

In a few short years, cloud storage services have reached phenomenal levels of success, with the user base growing rapidly. For example, Microsoft OneDrive claims that over 200 million customers have stored more than 14 PB of data using their service [9], while Dropbox has claimed more than 100 million users who store or update *1 billion* files everyday [6]. Despite the late entry into this market (in April 2012), Google Drive obtained 10 million users just in its first 2 months [7].

The key operation of cloud storage services is *data synchronization* (sync) which automatically maps the changes in users' local filesystems to the cloud via a series of network communications. Figure 8.1 demonstrates the general data sync principle. In a cloud storage service, the user usually needs to assign a designated local folder (called a "sync folder") in which every file operation is noticed and synchronized to the cloud by the client software developed by the service provider. Synchronizing a file involves a sequence of data sync events, such as transferring the data index, data content, sync notification, sync status/statistics, and sync acknowledgement. Naturally, each data sync event incurs network traffic. In this chapter, this traffic is referred to as *data sync traffic*.

If not designed properly, the amount of data sync traffic can potentially cause (financial) pains to both providers and users of cloud storage services. From the providers' perspective, the aggregate sync traffic from all users is enormous (given the huge number of files uploaded and modified each day!). This imposes a heavy burden in terms of infrastructure support and monetary costs (e.g., as payments to ISPs or cloud infrastructure providers). To get a quantitative understanding, we analyze a recent large-scale Dropbox trace [11] collected at the ISP level [23]. The analysis reveals: (1) The sync traffic contributes to more than 90 % of the total service traffic. Note that the total service traffic is equivalent to one third of the traffic consumed by YouTube [23]; (2) Data synchronization of a file (sometimes a batch of files) generates 2.8 MB of *inbound* (client to cloud) traffic and 5.18 MB of *outbound* (cloud to client) traffic on average. According to the Amazon S3 pricing policy [1] (Dropbox stores all the data content in S3 and S3 only charges for outbound traffic), the Dropbox traffic would consume nearly $0.05/GB × 5.18 MB × 1 billion

= \$260,000 every day.[1] These costs grow even further when we consider that *all* cloud storage service providers must bear similar costs, not just Dropbox [4].

Data sync traffic can also bring considerable (and unexpected) financial costs to end users, despite that basic cloud storage services are generally free. News media has reported about user complaints of unexpected, additional charges from ISPs, typically from mobile users with limited data usage caps [2, 8]. As a consequence, some users have warned: "*Keep a close eye on your data usage if you have a mobile cloud storage app.*" In addition, some cloud storage applications (e.g., large data backup [3]) are also impaired by the bandwidth constraints between the user clients and the cloud. This limitation is regarded as the "dirty secrets" of cloud storage services [5]. Hence users likewise would also benefit from more efficient sync traffic usage.

This chapter addresses a simple yet critical question: *Is the current data sync traffic of cloud storage services efficiently used?* Our goal is to quantify and optimize the *efficiency* of data sync traffic usage, i.e., the pivotal network-level efficiency for cloud storage services. Without impairing user experience, providers would like to limit data sync traffic as much as possible to reduce operational costs. On the other side, users also desire more efficient traffic usage, which can save money and result in better quality of experience. Although several studies have measured cloud storage services [18, 22, 23, 28, 30, 31, 35, 44], none have addressed the issue of sync traffic efficiency using real-world, large-scale data from multiple cloud storage services.

To answer the question thoroughly, we first define a novel metric named *TUE* to quantify the *Traffic Usage Efficiency* of data synchronization. Borrowing a term similar to *PUE* (i.e., the *Power Usage Effectiveness* $= \frac{\text{Total facility power}}{\text{IT equipment power}}$ [12], a widely adopted metric for evaluating the cloud computing energy efficiency), we define

$$TUE = \frac{\text{Total data sync traffic}}{\text{Data update size}}. \tag{8.1}$$

When a file is updated (e.g., created, modified, or deleted) at the user side, the *data update size* denotes the size of altered bits relative to the cloud-stored file.[2] From the users' point of view, the data update size is an intuitive and natural signifier about how much traffic *should* be consumed. Compared with the absolute value of sync traffic (used in previous studies), *TUE* better reveals the essential traffic harnessing capability of cloud storage services.

In order to gain a practical and in-depth understanding of *TUE*, we collect a real-world user trace and conduct comprehensive benchmark experiments of six widely used cloud storage services, including Google Drive, OneDrive, Dropbox, Box, Ubuntu One, and SugarSync. We examine key *impact factors* and *design choices*

---

[1] We assume that there is no special pricing contract between Dropbox and Amazon S3, so our calculation of the traffic costs may involve potential overestimation.

[2] If data compression is utilized by the cloud storage service, the *data update size* denotes the compressed size of altered bits.

that are common across all of these services. *Impact factors* include file size, file operation, data update size, network environment, hardware configuration, access method, and so on. Here the "access method" refers to PC client software, web browsers, and mobile apps. *Design choices* (of data sync mechanisms) include data sync granularity, data compression level, data deduplication granularity, and sync deferment (for improved batching).

By analyzing these factors and choices, we are able to thoroughly unravel the *TUE* related characteristics, design tradeoffs, and optimization opportunities of these state-of-the-art cloud storage services. The major findings in this chapter and their implications are summarized as follows:

- The majority (77 %) of files in our collected trace are small in size (less than 100 KB). Nearly two-thirds (66 %) of these small files can be logically combined into larger files for *batched data sync* (BDS) in order to reduce sync traffic. However, only Dropbox and Ubuntu One have partially implemented BDS so far.
- The majority (84 %) of files are modified by users at least once. Unfortunately, most of today's cloud storage services are built on top of RESTful infrastructure (e.g., Amazon S3, Microsoft Azure, and OpenStack Swift) that typically only support data access operations at the *full-file* level [15, 24]. For these services, enabling the efficient *incremental data sync* (IDS) mechanism requires an extra mid-layer for transforming MODIFY into GET + PUT + DELETE file operations. Given that file modifications frequently happen, implementing IDS is worthwhile for improved network-level efficiency.
- 52 % of files can be effectively compressed and 18 % of files can be deduplicated. Nevertheless, Google Drive, OneDrive, Box, and SugarSync never compress or deduplicate data. Even for Dropbox and Ubuntu One, the effect of compression and deduplication is largely influenced by the access method.
- Implementing compression and block-level deduplication together is technically challenging. Based on our trace analysis, we suggest providers to implement compression and full-file deduplication because the combination of these two techniques is sufficient to provide efficient usage of sync traffic.
- Frequent modifications to a file often lead to large *TUE*. For instance, for 8.5 % of Dropbox users, more than 10 % of their sync traffic is caused by frequent modifications [35]. Some services deal with this issue by batching file updates using a fixed sync deferment. However, fixed sync deferments are inefficient in some scenarios. We propose an *adaptive sync defer* (ASD) mechanism to overcome this limitation.
- In the presence of frequent file modifications, surprisingly, users with relatively "poor" hardware or Internet access save on sync traffic, because their file updates are naturally batched.

In a nutshell, our research findings demonstrate that for today's cloud storage services, a considerable portion of the data sync traffic is in a sense wasteful, and can be effectively avoided or significantly reduced through carefully designed data sync mechanisms. In other words, there is plenty of space for optimizing the network-level efficiency of these services. Our study of *TUE* provides guidance in two folds:

(1) help service providers develop more efficient, traffic-economic cloud storage services; and (2) help end users select appropriate services that best fit their needs and budgets.

8.2 Related Work

As cloud storage services are becoming more pervasive and changing the way people store and share data, a number of research efforts have been made in academia, including the design and implementation of the service infrastructure [20, 29, 41, 42], integration services with various features and functionalities [21, 26, 27, 32, 34, 35, 40], performance measurement [18, 22, 23, 31, 43], as well as privacy and security issues [19, 25, 30, 37, 39]. While the previous work covers the data sync mechanism as one of the key operations and the resulting traffic usage, none of them tries to understand the *efficiency* of the traffic usage *comprehensively*. Due to the system complexity and implementation difference, one can hardly form a general and unified view of the traffic usage efficiency, not to mention the further improvement.

Our work is different from and complementary to previous studies by quantifying and optimizing traffic usage efficiency, the pivotal network-level efficiency for cloud storage services. Based on the measurements and analysis of six state-of-the-art cloud storage services, we unravel the key impact factors and design choices that may significantly affect the traffic usage efficiency. Most importantly, we provide guidance and implications for both service providers and end users to economize their sync traffic usage.

Dropbox is one of the earliest and most popular cloud storage services, and its data sync mechanism has been studied in depth in [23, 35]. Through an ISP-level large-scale measurement, Drago et al. first uncover the performance bottlenecks of Dropbox due to both the system architecture and the data sync mechanism [23]. They suggest a bundling sync scheme with delayed sync ACK to improve the sync performance of Dropbox. In addition, Li et al. identify a pathological issue that may lead to the "traffic overuse problem" in Dropbox by uploading a large amount of unnecessary (overhead) traffic [35]. They propose an efficient batched sync algorithm (named UDS) to address this issue. Complementary to these studies, our results are not limited to Dropbox. Instead, we unravel the general factors that may significantly affect the data sync traffic. In consequence, our results are more general and applicable for designing network-level efficient cloud storage services, rather than improving one particular service.

Some measurement studies have partially covered the traffic usage of cloud storage services. Hu et al. examine "the good, the bad and the ugly" of four cloud storage services by comparing their traffic usage, delay time, and CPU usage of uploading new files [28]. They observe that the sync traffic usage varies substantially with factors such as file size, data compressibility, and data duplication levels. Drago et al. further compare the system capabilities of five cloud storage services, and find that each service has limitations with regard to data synchronization [22]. Both of these studies confirm the importance of sync traffic usage, and the possibility of further optimizing the sync traffic usage.

In this chapter, we zoom into the problem toward a comprehensive understanding of traffic usage efficiency. Different from the simplified benchmarks used in the above-mentioned studies [22, 28, 35], we consider the diversity of access methods, client locations, hardware configurations, and network conditions to match the real-world usage. Indeed, we discover that these factors lead to different traffic usage patterns, some of which are even not expected. Last but not the least, different from previous studies that never consider mobile usage, one of our focus is the mobile usage of sync traffic—mobile users are those who mostly suffer from traffic overuse.

8.3   Common Design Framework

From the perspective of sync traffic usage, the common design framework of cloud storage services involves a number of *impact factors* and *design choices*, which can be on the client side, server (cloud) side, or network side. The *impact factors* refer to those (*objective*) factors such as the client location, hardware, file size, data update size, network environment, and so on that must be accounted for in the design and usage of cloud storage services. The *design choices* (of data sync mechanisms) refer to those (*subjective*) design decisions which the system designers make, such as the data sync granularity, data compression level, data deduplication granularity, and so forth.

Both the impact factors and design choices may influence the data sync *TUE*. To avoid being trapped by trivial or elusive issues, we select key impact factors and design choices according to the following two rules:

- *Rule 1: The impact factors should be relatively constant or stable, so that our research results can be easily repeated.*
- *Rule 2: The design choices should be measurable and service/implementation independent, so as to make our research methodology widely applicable.*

Following *Rule 1*, we do not study impact factors such as sync delay,[3] cloud server location, etc. For example, we observe that uploading a 1-MB JPEG photo to Google Drive may incur an elusive sync delay varying between several seconds and several minutes (under different network environments). Instead, we choose to study the *sync traffic*, which is almost invariable in all cases. Besides, we observe that the cloud server location serving a given file is not constant. This is because a cloud storage service usually hosts a user's files across multiple geographically dispersed data centers, and it often migrates or copies a file from one cloud server to another. Instead, we record the *bandwidth* and *delay* between the client and the cloud, as they can be reproduced using client-side methods (introduced in Sect. 8.4.2).

---

[3] *sync delay* measures how long the user client synchronizes a file to the cloud.

Table 8.1 Key impact factors and *design choices*

Client side	Client location, client hardware, access method, file size, file operation, data update size, data update rate, *data compression level, sync deferment*
Server side	*Data sync granularity, data deduplication granularity, (data compression level)*[a]
Network side	Sync traffic, bandwidth, latency

Reprinted with permission from [33]

[a]*Note* The server-side data compression level may be different from the client-side data compression level

Following *Rule 2*, we do not consider design choices such as the metadata structures, file segmentation, and replication on the cloud side, because they require specific knowledge of the back-end cloud implementation. For example, the metadata structure (including the list of the user's files, their attributes, and indices to where the files can be found inside the cloud) cannot be extracted from the network communication packets, because almost all the commercial cloud storage services have encrypted their application-layer data in certain (unknown) ways.

In the end, ten key impact factors and four design choices are selected, as listed in Table 8.1. Some of them are self-explanatory or have been explained before. Below we further explain a few:

- *File operation* includes file creation, file deletion, file modification, and frequent file modifications.
- *Data update rate* denotes how often a file operation happens.
- *Sync deferment*. When frequent file modifications happen, some cloud storage services *intentionally* defer the sync process for a certain period of time for batching file updates.
- *Data sync granularity*. A file operation is synchronized to the cloud either in a *full-file* granularity or in an incremental, *chunk-level* granularity. When the former is adopted, the whole updated file is delivered to the cloud; when the latter is adopted, only those file chunks that contain altered bits (relative to the file stored in the cloud) are delivered.
- *Data deduplication granularity* denotes the *unit* at which data fingerprints are computed and compared to avoid delivering duplicate data units to the cloud. The unit can be either a full file or a file block. Note that data deduplication can be performed across different files owned by different users.
- *Bandwidth* is defined as the peak upload rate between the client and the cloud server. We measure it by uploading a large file to the cloud and meanwhile recording the network traffic with the Wireshark network protocol analyzer [16].
- *Latency* is defined as the round trip time (RTT) between the client and the cloud. We measure it by using the standard Ping command.

8.4   Methodology

This section describes our methodology for studying the *TUE* of cloud storage services. First, we introduce a real-world cloud storage trace collected to characterize the key impact factors. Next, we design a variety of benchmark experiments to uncover the key design choices of data sync mechanisms. Last but not the least, we provide an overview of the research results.

8.4.1   Real-World Cloud Storage Trace

Our measurement study takes advantage of a real-world user trace of cloud storage services. It is collected in several universities and companies in the US and China from July 2013 to March 2014, including 153 long-term users with 222,632 files inside their sync folders. Refer to Table 8.2 for the per service statistics. This trace is used to characterize the key impact factors with regard to the six widely used services. It is also used to guide the design of benchmark experiments and enable further macro-level analysis (in particular, the *TUE* related optimization opportunities of cloud storage services).

This cloud storage trace records detailed information of every tracked file in multiple aspects. Table 8.3 lists the concrete file attributes recorded. Figure 8.2 depicts the distributions of original file size and compressed file size corresponding to the trace. We have made this trace publicly available to benefit other researchers. It can be downloaded via the following link:

http://www.greenorbs.org/people/lzh/public/traces.zip.

Table 8.2 Number of users and files recorded in our collected cloud storage trace

	Google Drive	OneDrive	Dropbox	Box	Ubuntu One	SugarSync
Number of users	33	24	55	13	13	15
Number of files	32,677	17,903	106,493	19,995	27,281	18,283

Reprinted with permission from [33]

Table 8.3 File attributes recorded in our collected trace

User name, File name MD5, Original file size
Compressed file size, Creation time, Last modification time
Full-file MD5, 128 KB/256 KB/512 KB/1 MB/2 MB/4 MB/8 MB/16 MB block-level MD5 hash codes

Reprinted with permission from [33]

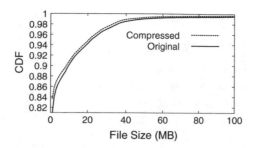

Fig. 8.2 CDF (cumulative distribution function) of (1) original file size and (2) compressed file size, corresponding to our collected trace. For original files, the maximum size is 2.0 GB, the average size is 962 KB, and the median size is 7.5 KB. For compressed files, the maximum size is 1.97 GB, the average size is 732 KB, and the median size is 3.2 KB. Clearly, the tracked files can be effectively compressed on the whole, and the majority of them are small in size. (Reprinted with permission from [33].)

8.4.2 Benchmark Experiments

To obtain an in-depth understanding of *TUE* and the key design choices of data sync mechanisms, we design a variety of benchmarks for performing comprehensive controlled experiments. The benchmarks span multiple commercial cloud storage services, involving diverse client machines locating at distinct locations and network environments.

Cloud storage services. Among today's dozens of commercial cloud storage services, our research focuses on the following six mainstream services: Google Drive, OneDrive, Dropbox, Box, Ubuntu One, and SugarSync, as they are either the most popular (in terms of user base) or the most representative (in terms of data sync mechanism). Other cloud storage services are also briefly discussed when necessary.

Client locations. Since the above cloud storage services are mainly deployed in the US, we select two distinct locations to perform each experiment: MN (i.e., Minnesota, US) and BJ (i.e., Beijing, China). In a *coarse-grained* manner, MN represents a location close to the cloud: the bandwidth is nearly 20 Mbps and the latency ∈ (42, 77) ms, while BJ represents a location remote from the cloud: the bandwidth is nearly 1.6 Mbps the latency ∈ (200, 480) ms.

Controlled bandwidth and latency. To tune the network environment in a *fine-grained* manner, we interpose a pair of packet filters in the communication channel between the client and the cloud in MN. These filters enable fine-grained adjustment of the bandwidth (the maximum possible speed is 20 Mbps) and latency in either direction. Specifically, the packet filters are interposed by using an intermediate proxy that runs the Linux Netfilter/Iptables tool, thus behaving like a common software firewall.

Controlled file operations. We synthetically generate almost all kinds of file operations appearing in the literature. Moreover, these operations are applied upon both

Table 8.4 Hardware information of the experimental client machines

Machine	CPU	Memory (GB)	Disk storage
M1 @ MN	Quad-core Intel i5 @ 1.70 GHz	4	7200 RPM, 500 GB
M2 @ MN	Intel Atom @ 1.00 GHz	1	5400 RPM, 320 GB
M3 @ MN	Quad-core Intel i7 @ 1.90 GHz	4	SSD, 250 GB
M4 @ MN	Dual-core ARM @ 1.50 GHz	1	MicroSD, 16 GB
B1 @ BJ	Quad-core Intel i5 @ 1.70 GHz	4	7200 RPM, 500 GB
B2 @ BJ	Intel Atom @ 1.00 GHz	1	5400 RPM, 250 GB
B3 @ BJ	Quad-core Intel i7 @ 1.90 GHz	4	SSD, 250 GB
B4 @ BJ	Dual-core ARM @ 1.53 GHz	1	MicroSD, 16 GB

Reprinted with permission from [33]

compressed and compressible files. These controlled file operations will be elaborated in Sects. 8.5, 8.6, and 8.7.

Client machine hardware. A total of eight client machines are employed in the experiments: four in MN (i.e., M1, M2, M3, and M4) and four in BJ (i.e., B1, B2, B3, and B4). Their detailed hardware information is listed in Table 8.4. M1/B1 represents a typical client machine at the moment, M2/B2 an outdated machine, M3/B3 an advanced machine with SSD storage, and M4/B4 an Android smartphone. M1–M3 and B1–B3 are installed with Windows 7-SP1 and the Chrome-30.0 web browser.

Benchmark software and access methods. For each cloud storage service, all the experiments regarding M1–M3 and B1–B3 are performed with the latest version (as of Jan. 2014) of the client software on Windows 7. For the M4 and B4 smartphones, we experiment with the latest-version Android apps (as of Jan. 2014). The corresponding sync traffic (i.e., incoming/outgoing packets) are recorded using Wireshark. For the Android smartphones, we route the network traffic through a PC that promiscuously monitors the packets using Wireshark.

Overview of our major findings. Based on the above methodology, we are able to thoroughly unravel the *TUE* relevant characteristics, design tradeoffs, and optimization opportunities of the six mainstream cloud storage services. The detailed research results (from simple to complex) will be presented in the following three sections: simple file operations (Sect. 8.5), compression and deduplication (Sect. 8.6), and frequent file modifications (Sect. 8.7). As an overview and a roadmap of our research results, Table 8.5 summarizes the major findings and their implications.

8.5   Simple File Operations

This section presents our major measurement results, findings, and implications on the *TUE* of simple file operations. For each measurement, we first introduce the

Table 8.5 Our major findings, their implications, and locations of relevant sections

Simple file operations	Implications
Section 8.5.1 (File creation): The majority (77%) of files in our trace are small in size (<100 KB), which may result in poor *TUE*	For providers, nearly two-thirds (66%) of small files can be logically combined into larger files for *batched data sync* (BDS). However, only Dropbox and Ubuntu One have partially implemented BDS so far
Section 8.5.2 (File deletion): Deletion of a file usually incurs negligible sync traffic	For users, no need to worry about the traffic for file deletion
Section 8.5.3 (File modification): The majority (84%) of files are modified by users at least once. Most cloud storage services employ *full-file sync*, while Dropbox and SugarSync utilize *incremental data sync* (IDS) to save traffic for PC clients (but not for mobile or web-based access methods)	Most of today's cloud storage services are built on top of RESTful infrastructure (e.g., Amazon S3, Microsoft Azure, and OpenStack Swift) that only support data access operations at the *full-file* level. *TUE* can be significantly improved by implementing IDS with an extra mid-layer that transforms MODIFY into GET + PUT + DELETE file operations
Compression and deduplication	Implications
Section 8.6.1 (Data compression): 52% of files can be effectively compressed. However, Google Drive, OneDrive, Box, and SugarSync never compress data, while Dropbox is the only one that compresses data for every access method	For providers, data compression is able to reduce 24% of the total sync traffic. For users, PC clients are more likely to support compression versus mobile or web-based access methods
Section 8.6.2 (Data deduplication): Although we observe that 18% of files can be deduplicated, most cloud storage services do not support data deduplication, especially for the web-based access method	For providers, implementing compression and block-level deduplication together is technically challenging. Based on the trace analysis, we suggest providers implement compression and full-file deduplication since the two techniques work together seamlessly
Frequent file modifications	Implications
Section 8.7.1 (Sync deferment): Frequent modifications to a file often lead to large *TUE*. Some services deal with this issue by batching file updates using a fixed sync deferment. However, we find that fixed sync deferments are inefficient in some scenarios	For providers, we demonstrate that an *adaptive sync defer* (ASD) mechanism that dynamically adjusts the sync deferment is superior to fixed sync deferment
Section 8.7.2 (Network and hardware): Suprisingly, we observe that users with relatively low bandwidth, high latency, or slow hardware save on sync traffic, because their file updates are naturally batched together	For users, in the presence of frequent file modifications, today's cloud storage services actually bring good news (in terms of *TUE*) to those users with relatively "poor" hardware or Internet access

Reprinted with permission from [33]

experiment process and results, and then unravel several interesting findings and implications. In this section, we do not mention the client locations, network environments, and hardware configurations, because the *TUE* of simple file operations is independent to these impact factors.

8.5.1   File Creation

[**Experiment 1**]: We first study the simple case of creating a highly compressed file of Z bytes inside the sync folder (we will further study the data compression in detail in Sect. 8.6.1). Thereby, calculating the *TUE* of file creation becomes straightforward (i.e., $TUE = \frac{Total\ sync\ traffic}{Z\ bytes}$). According to Fig. 8.2, most compressed files are small in size (several KBs), and the maximum compressed file size is below 2.0 GB. Therefore, we experiment with $Z \in \{1, 1\ K, 10\ K, 100\ K, 1\ M, 10\ M, 100\ M, 1\ G\}$.

The second goal of **Experiment 1** is to get a quantitative understanding of the *overhead traffic*, as *TUE* heavily depends on the ratio of the overhead traffic over the total sync traffic. Synchronizing a file to the cloud always involves a certain amount of overhead traffic, which arises from TCP/HTTP(S) connection setup and maintenance, metadata delivery, etc. Specifically, the overhead traffic is equal to the total sync traffic excluding the payload traffic for delivering the file content, so in **Experiment 1**, Overhead traffic $\approx$ Total sync traffic $- Z$ bytes.

Table 8.6 lists the results of **Experiment 1** regarding the six concerned cloud storage services. We vary the file size from 1 B to 1 GB, but for brevity only list four typical sizes: 1 B, 1 KB, 1 MB, and 10 MB. The table records the sync traffic generated by the three typical service access methods: PC client, web (browser) based, and mobile app. In general, from Table 8.6 we have the following finding and implication:

- *TUE* for synchronizing a (compressed) file creation mainly depends on the file size. A *small* file results in big *TUE* up to 40,000, while a *big* file incurs small *TUE* approaching 1.0. Therefore, for providers, a number of small files can be logically combined into a *moderate-size* file for *batched data sync* (BDS) to save traffic, in particular the overhead traffic.

This finding poses a key question: *What is a small size and what is a moderate size?* By plotting the *TUE* versus File Size relationship (for PC clients) in Fig. 8.3, we get an intuitive conclusion that a moderate size should be at least 100 KB and had better exceed 1 MB, in order to achieve small *TUE*—at most 1.5 and had better stay below 1.2. Here we only draw the curve for PC clients since the corresponding curves for web-based and mobile apps are similar.

As a consequence, small size is regarded as less than 100 KB, which together with Fig. 8.2 reveals that the majority (77%) of tracked files are small in size (meanwhile, 81% in terms of compressed size). More importantly, by analyzing our collected trace, we find that nearly two-thirds (66%) of these small files can be created in batches and thus can effectively benefit from BDS.

[**Experiment 1'**]: Given that the BDS mechanism can effectively optimize *TUE*, a new question comes out: *Is BDS adopted by the six mainstream cloud storage services?* To get the answer, we first generate 100 (distinct) highly compressed files, and then move all of them into the sync folder in a batch. Each file is 1 KB in size, so $TUE = \frac{Total\ sync\ traffic}{100\ KB}$. If BDS is adopted, the total sync traffic should be around 100 KB and *TUE* should be close to 1.0.

Table 8.6 Sync traffic of a (compressed) file creation

Service	PC client sync traffic (Bytes)				Web-based sync traffic (Bytes)					Mobile app sync traffic (Bytes)				
	1	1 K	1 M	10 M	1	1 K	1 M	10 M		1	1 K	1 M	10 M
Google Drive	9 K	10 K	1.13 M	11.2 M	6 K	7 K	1.06 M	10.6 M	32 K	71 K	1.27 M	11.0 M
OneDrive	19 K	20 K	1.14 M	11.4 M	28 K	31 K	1.11 M	11.7 M	29 K	44 K	1.23 M	10.7 M
Dropbox	38 K	40 K	1.28 M	12.5 M	31 K	37 K	1.09 M	10.6 M	18 K	32 K	1.08 M	10.9 M
Box	55 K	47 K	1.10 M	10.6 M	55 K	58 K	1.10 M	10.5 M	16 K	34 K	1.29 M	10.8 M
Ubuntu One	2 K	3 K	1.11 M	11.2 M	37 K	39 K	1.20 M	11.3 M	20 K	24 K	1.08 M	10.9 M
SugarSync	9 K	19 K	1.17 M	11.4 M	31 K	32 K	1.10 M	10.7 M	31 K	47 K	1.22 M	10.9 M

Reprinted with permission from [33]

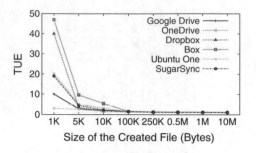

Fig. 8.3 *TUE* versus Size of the created file. (Reprinted with permission from [33].)

Table 8.7 Total traffic for synchronizing 100 compressed file creations

Service	PC client		Web-based		Mobile app	
	Sync traffic	(TUE)	Sync traffic	(TUE)	Sync traffic	(TUE)
Google Drive	1.1 MB	(11)	1.2 MB	(12)	5.6 MB	(56)
OneDrive	1.3 MB	(13)	2.2 MB	(22)	1.9 MB	(19)
Dropbox	**120 KB**	**(1.2)**	600 *KB*	**(6.0)**	**360 KB**	**(3.6)**
Box	1.2 MB	(12)	3.2 MB	(32)	3.2 MB	(32)
Ubuntu One	**140 KB**	**(1.4)**	500 *KB*	**(5.0)**	2.5 MB	(25)
SugarSync	0.9 MB	(9)	4.0 MB	(40)	1.5 MB	(15)

Each file is 1 KB in size. Reprinted with permission from [33]

The results of **Experiment 1'** listed in Table 8.7 reveal that Dropbox and Ubuntu One have adopted BDS for PC clients. Further, it is possible that Dropbox has adopted BDS for web-based and mobile access methods, because the corresponding sync traffic (600 and 360 KB) is within an order of magnitude of the data update size (100 KB). Also, Ubuntu One may have used BDS in its web-based data synchronization, since the sync traffic (500 KB) lies between 600 and 360 KB. On the contrary, Google Drive, OneDrive, Box, and SugarSync have not adopted BDS yet.

8.5.2   File Deletion

[**Experiment 2**]: Each file created in **Experiment 1** is deleted after it is completely synchronized to the cloud, so as to acquire the sync traffic information of a file deletion.

The **Experiment 2** results indicate that deletion of a file usually generates negligible (<100 KB) sync traffic, regardless of the cloud storage service, file size, or access method. The reason is straightforward: when a file f is deleted in the user's local sync folder, the user client just notifies the cloud to change some attributes of f rather than remove the content of f. In fact, such "fake deletion" also facilitates users' data recovery, such as the version rollback of a file. Naturally, we get the following implication:

- Cloud storage service users do not need to worry about the sync traffic when deleting a file.

8.5.3   File Modification and Sync Granularity

[**Experiment 3**]: The analysis of our collected cloud storage trace reveals that the majority (84 %) of files are modified by users at least once. That is to say, file modifications are frequently made by cloud storage users. This subsection studies a simple case of file modification, i.e., modifying a random byte in a compressed file of Z bytes inside the sync folder. In this case, $TUE = \frac{\text{Total sync traffic}}{1 \text{ Byte}}$. Similar as Sect. 8.5.1, we experiment with $Z \in \{1, 1\text{ K}, 10\text{ K}, 100\text{ K}, 1\text{ M}, 10\text{ M}, 100\text{ M}, 1\text{ G}\}$ and plot the sync traffic of four typical sizes: $Z = 1$ K, 10 K, 100 K, and 1 M in Fig. 8.4.

Fig. 8.4 Sync traffic of a random byte modification, corresponding to the three typical service access methods: **a** PC client, **b** Web-based, and **c** Mobile app. By comparing the three subfigures, we discover that only the PC clients of Dropbox and SugarSync utilize the *incremental data sync* (IDS) mechanism for improved network-level efficiency. (Reprinted with permission from [33].)

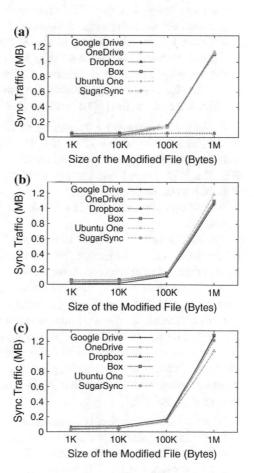

Figure 8.4 shows that today's cloud storage services generally utilize two kinds of data sync granularity: (1) full-file and (2) chunk-level. Accordingly, their data sync mechanisms are classified into *full-file sync* and *incremental sync* as follows:

- **Full-file sync**. Google Drive is an example to use the full-file sync mechanism. When a random byte is modified in a Z-byte compressed file, the resulting sync traffic is almost the same as that of creating a new Z-byte compressed file. In other words, Google Drive deals with each file modification by simply uploading the full content of the modified file to the cloud and then deleting the old file. Consequently, Google Drive is more suitable for hosting media files (like photos, music, and videos) which are rarely modified by users. The full-file sync mechanism is also employed by OneDrive, Box, Ubuntu One, Amazon Cloud Drive, and some popular cloud storage services in China like Kuaipan, Kanbox, Baidu CloudDisk, and 115 CloudDisk.

- **Incremental sync** (or **delta sync**). Dropbox (PC client) is an example to use the incremental data sync (IDS) mechanism. When a random byte modification happens, the resulting sync traffic stays around 50 KB, regardless of the size of the modified file. According to the working principle of the incremental sync algorithm: rsync [14], once a random byte is changed in a file f, in most cases the whole data chunk that contains this byte must be delivered for synchronizing f. Therefore, the sync granularity (i.e., the chunk size C) can be approximately estimated as $C \approx$ Total sync traffic − Overhead traffic.

From the **Experiment 1** results, we understand that the overhead traffic of synchronizing a one-byte file with the Dropbox PC client is nearly 40 KB. Therefore, the data sync granularity of Dropbox PC client is estimated as: $C \approx 50$ KB-40 KB $= 10$ KB. This is further validated by the recommended default chunk size (i.e., from 700 B to 16 KB) in the original rsync implementation [13]. Moreover, we find that SugarSync, IDriveSync, and 360 CloudDisk also utilize the IDS mechanism for their PC clients.

On the contrary, as depicted in Fig. 8.4b, c, web-based apps and mobile apps for all the six services still use the full-file sync mechanism, probably because IDS is hard to implement in JavaScript (for web-based apps) or due to energy concerns (for mobile apps). Specifically, JavaScript is the most widely used script language for the development of web-based apps (including cloud storage apps). Nevertheless, for security concerns, JavaScript is unable to directly invoke file-level system calls/APIs like open, close, read, write, stat, rsync, and gzip [10]. Instead, JavaScript can only access users' local files in an indirect and constrained manner, which is of less efficiency in terms of implementing IDS.

In summary, we have the following finding about simple file modification and the data sync granularity:

- When a file modification is synchronized to the cloud, *TUE* is mostly affected by the data sync granularity which varies significantly among different cloud storage services. Most services simply use full-file sync, but some services (like Dropbox and SugarSync) utilize IDS to achieve improved network-level efficiency for PC clients.

Conflicts between IDS and RESTful infrastructure. Although enabling the IDS mechanism can help service providers reduce the data sync traffic, implementing IDS is not an easy job in practice. Most of today's cloud storage services (e.g., OneDrive, Dropbox, and Ubuntu One) are built on top of RESTful infrastructure (e.g., Amazon S3, Microsoft Azure, and OpenStack Swift). For simplifying both the providers' implementation complexities and the developers' programming complexities, RESTful infrastructure typically only supports data access operations at the *full-file* level, like PUT (upload a new file), GET (download a whole file), DELETE (delete a whole file), and so forth. Note that the PUT, GET, and DELETE operations may have aliases in other RESTful infrastructure.

Thus, enabling IDS usually requires an extra mid-layer for transforming MODIFY into GET + PUT + DELETE file operations in an *efficient* manner (like what Dropbox has done [23, 35]).[4] Since file modifications frequently happen, implementing such a mid-layer is worthwhile for improved network-level efficiency.

8.6 Compression and Deduplication

In a real-world storage system, compression and deduplication are the two most commonly used techniques for saving space and traffic. This section makes a detailed study of cloud storage compression and deduplication, from both the system designers' and users' perspectives.

8.6.1 Data Compression Level

[**Experiment 4**]: To study whether data updates are compressed before they are synchronized to the cloud, we create an X-byte text file inside the sync folder. As a small file is hard to compress, we experiment with $X = 1$ M, 10 M, 100 M, and 1 G. Each text file is filled with random English words. If data compression is actually used, the resulting sync traffic should be much less than the original file size. Furthermore, after each text file is completely synchronized, we download it from the cloud with a PC client, a web browser, and a mobile app, respectively, so as to examine whether the cloud delivers data updates in a compressed form.

As a typical case, the **Experiment 4** results corresponding to a 10-MB text file are listed in Table 8.8. First, in the file upload (UP) phase, among the six mainstream cloud storage services, only Dropbox and Ubuntu One compress data with PC clients and mobile apps. No service ever compresses data with web browsers. Further, we observe that the 10-MB text file can be compressed to nearly 4.5 MB using the highest

---

[4]An alternative to enable IDS is to store every chunk of a file as a separate data object. When a file is modified, the modified chunks are deleted with the new chunks being stored as new objects; also, file metadata has to be updated (as what is used in Cumulus [41]).

Table 8.8 Sync traffic of a 10-MB text file creation

Service	Sync traffic (MB)					
	PC client		Web-based		Mobile app	
	UP	DN	UP	DN	UP	DN
Google Drive	11.3	11.0	10.6	11.7	11.8	10.8
OneDrive	11.4	11.2	11.0	11.0	12.2	10.7
Dropbox	**6.1**	**5.5**	10.6	**5.5**	**8.1**	**5.5**
Box	10.6	11.2	10.5	11.3	10.4	11.1
Ubuntu One	**5.6**	**5.3**	10.9	**5.3**	**8.6**	10.6
SugarSync	11.3	11.5	10.4	10.7	11.6	11.8

UP The user uploads the file to the cloud. *DN* The user downloads the file from the cloud. Reprinted with permission from [33]

level WinZip compression on our desktop. Thus, for Dropbox and Ubuntu One, the compression level with PC clients seems moderate, while the compression level with mobile apps is quite low. The motivation of such a difference is intuitive: to reduce the battery consumption of mobile devices caused by the computation-intensive data compressions.

Next, in the file download (DN) phase, only Dropbox and Ubuntu One compress data with PC clients and web browsers, and the compression level is higher than that in the file upload phase. For mobile apps, only Dropbox compresses data.

By analyzing our collected cloud storage trace, we find that 52 % of files can be *effectively compressed*. Here "effectively compressed" implies that $\frac{\text{Compressed file size}}{\text{Original file size}}$ <90 % when the highest-level WinZip compression is applied. As a result, the total *compression ratio* ($= \frac{\text{Size of data before compression}}{\text{Size of data after compression}}$) regarding all the files recorded in the trace reaches 1.31. In other words, data compression is able to reduce 24 % of the data sync traffic (compared with no compression). These observations lead to the following findings and implications:

- Data compression provides obvious benefits by reducing the sync traffic, but is not supported by every cloud storage service. Google Drive, OneDrive, Box, and SugarSync never compress data, while Dropbox is the only service that compresses data for every access method.
- Web browser typically *does not* compress a file when uploading it to the cloud storage, probably also due to the limitations of JavaScript or other web-based script languages (refer to Sect. 8.5.3). Besides, using a mobile app is usually not as efficient as using a PC client.

Algorithm 1 Iterative Self Duplication Algorithm Reprinted with permission from [33].

1: Set the lower bound: $L = 0$ bytes, and the upper bound: $U = +\infty$ bytes. Guess a deduplication block size: B_1;

2: **Step 1**:
3:   Generate a new compressed file f_1 of B_1 bytes;
4:   Upload f_1 to the cloud. When f_1 is completely synchronized to the cloud, record the total sync traffic: Tr_1;

5: **Step 2**:
6:   Generate another file f_2 by appending f_1 to itself, that is $f_2 = f_1 + f_1$ (the so-called "self duplication");
7:   Upload f_2 to the cloud. When f_2 is completely synchronized to the cloud, record the total sync traffic: Tr_2;

8: **Step 3**:
9: **if** $Tr_2 \ll Tr_1$ **and** Tr_2 is small ($\approx$ tens of KBs) **then**
10:   B_1 is actually the deduplication block size (B);
11:   **exit**;
12: **else** there are two cases
13:   **case 1**: $Tr_2 < 2B_1$ and Tr_2 is not small (implying that $B_1 > B$) **then**
14:   Set B_1 as the upper bound: $U \leftarrow B_1$, and decrease the guessing value of B_1: $B_1 \leftarrow \frac{L+U}{2}$;
15:   **case 2**: $Tr_2 > 2B_1$ (implying that $B_1 < B$) **then**
16:   Set B_1 as the lower bound: $L \leftarrow B_1$, and increase the guessing value of B_1: $B_1 \leftarrow \frac{L+U}{2}$;
17: **goto Step 1**;

8.6.2   Data Deduplication Granularity

[**Experiment 5**]: Data deduplication is another potential method to reduce data sync traffic, with the intuition that users often upload duplicated files with similar content. Inferring the deduplication granularity of a cloud storage service requires some efforts, especially when the deduplication block size B (bytes) is not a power of two (i.e., $B \neq 2^n$, where n is a positive integer).[5] To measure the deduplication granularity, we design and implement Algorithm 1 (named the "Iterative Self Duplication Algorithm"). It infers the deduplication granularity by iteratively duplicating and uploading one or multiple synthetic file(s) and meanwhile analyzing the incurred data sync traffic. It is easy to prove that the iteration procedure can finish in $O(\log(B))$ rounds.

First, we study interfile data deduplication with respect to an identical user account. By applying **Experiment 5** to the six mainstream cloud storage services, we figure out their data deduplication granularity in Table 8.9 (the 2nd column). In

---

[5]The deduplication block size B (bytes) is traditionally a power of two [38], but we still have to thoughtfully consider the exception when $B \neq 2^n$.

Table 8.9 Data deduplication granularity

Service	Same user	Cross users
	PC client and Mobile app	PC client and Mobile app
Google Drive	No	No
OneDrive	No	No
Dropbox	4 MB	No
Box	No	No
Ubuntu One	Full file	Full file
SugarSync	No	No

We do not list the web-based case because the web-based file synchronization typically *does not* apply data deduplication. Reprinted with permission from [33]

this table, "Full file" (only for Ubuntu One) means that data deduplication only happens at the full-file level, "4 MB" (only for Dropbox) indicates that the deduplication block size $B = 4$ MB, and "No" shows that there is no deduplication performed. Note that block-level deduplication naturally implies full-file deduplication, but *not* vice versa.

Second, we study cross-user data deduplication. For each cloud storage service, we first upload a file f to the cloud, and then use another user account to upload f to the cloud again. In this case, the sync traffic should be trivial if full-file deduplication is performed across users. If the cross-user full-file deduplication is confirmed, **Experiment 5** is run again to figure out the accurate cross-user deduplication granularity; otherwise, we can conclude that there is no cross-user data deduplication at all. The results are also shown in Table 8.9 (the 3rd column). Obviously, only Dropbox employs a different cross-user data deduplication granularity from the identical-user case.

From the above measurements, we get the following findings and implications:

- A cloud storage service usually adopts the same data deduplication granularity for PC clients and mobile apps, while the web-based data synchronization typically *does not* apply data deduplication.
- By analyzing our collected trace, we find that cross-user data (block) duplication pervasively exists: even the full-file level *duplication ratio* ($= \frac{\text{Size of duplicate files}}{\text{Size of all files}}$) reaches 18.8%. However, most cloud storage services do not support cross-user deduplication (perhaps for privacy and security concerns) or block-level deduplication at the moment, thus losing considerable opportunities for optimizing *TUE*.

Further, we compare the two types of deduplication granularity to answer a question: *Is the block-level deduplication much better (i.e., has a much larger deduplication ratio) than the full-file deduplication?* Since the computation complexity of block-level deduplication is much higher than that of full-file deduplication, the answer could help decide whether or not the block-level deduplication is worthwhile. Note that when referring to the "file blocks", we are dividing files to blocks *in a simple and natural way*, that is to say, by starting from the head of a file with a fixed block

Fig. 8.5 *Deduplication ratio* (cross-user) versus Block size. Here the deduplication ratio = $\frac{\text{Size of data before deduplication}}{\text{Size of data after deduplication}}$. (Reprinted with permission from [33].)

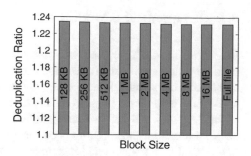

size. So clearly, we are not dividing files to blocks in the best possible manner [17, 38] which is much more complicated and computation intensive.

As our collected trace contains both the full-file hash codes and the block-level (128 KB–16 MB blocks) hash codes of each tracked file (refer to Sect. 8.4.1, Table 8.3), we perform the trace-driven simulation to figure out the (cross-user) deduplication ratio when each deduplication granularity is adopted. The simulation results demonstrate that the block-level deduplication usually exhibits *trivial superiority* to the full-file deduplication, as shown in Fig. 8.5. Therefore, we have the following implication:

- For providers, in terms of deduplication granularity, supporting full-file deduplication is basically sufficient.

Conflicts between compression and block-level deduplication. Although data deduplication can reduce the sync traffic, we notice that it has a potential performance conflict with data compression. Implementing block-level deduplication and compression together is technically challenging.

For cloud storage service providers, though storing and delivering data in its compressed form can effectively save storage space and sync traffic, it may significantly increase the (computation and I/O) complexity of block-level deduplication. Specifically, after a file (f) is delivered to the cloud storage in its compressed form (f'), f' must be first uncompressed to calculate each block's fingerprint, so as to enable block-level deduplication. Then, the uncompressed file must be deleted from disk. Furthermore, the above operations must be re-executed (in part) as long as one block of f is modified. It is basically unwise for a service provider to shift these operations to its user clients, unless the service provider does not care about user experience.

In this subsection, we have known that block-level deduplication exhibits trivial superiority to full-file deduplication. Meanwhile, full-file deduplication is not challenged by data compression, because full-file deduplication can be directly performed on compressed files. Therefore, we suggest that providers implement full-file deduplication and compression since these two techniques work together seamlessly.

8.7   Frequent File Modifications

In addition to backing up and retrieving files, cloud storage services are also widely
used for collaboration, such as collaborative document editing, team project building,
and database hosting. All the above-mentioned advanced functions involve a special
kind of file operations: *frequent modifications* to a file.

In Sects. 8.5 and 8.6, we have studied various simple file operations that are
each performed at once. On the contrary, frequent modifications imply that a file
is modified in a frequent and incremental manner. Thus, they exhibit diverse data
update patterns in terms of data update *size* and *rate*. The large-scale trace collected
by Drago et al. [11] reveals that for 8.5 % of Dropbox users, more than 10 % of their
sync traffic is caused by frequent modifications [35]. Further, frequent modifications
may well incur abundant overhead traffic that far exceeds the amount of useful data
update traffic sent by the user client over time, which is referred to as the *traffic
overuse problem* [35]. Besides, in this section we will elaborate on client locations,
network environments, and hardware configurations, because the *TUE* of frequent
file modifications is largely influenced by these factors.

8.7.1   Sync Deferment

[**Experiment 6**]: To experiment with frequent file modifications, we append X random kilobytes to an empty file inside the sync folder every X seconds, until the total
appended bytes reach a certain size C (typically $C = 1$ MB). This is denoted as the
"X KB/X sec" appending experiment. We use random bytes since they are difficult
to compress, thus preventing file compression from influencing our measurements
of *TUE*.

Our goal is three folds by doing this experiment: (1) We observe and understand
the sync traffic and *TUE* in response to frequent modifications; (2) We aim to discover
whether the cloud storage service has used the *sync deferment* in order to avoid or
mitigate the traffic overuse problem; and (3) If the sync deferment is adopted, we
want to measure how long the sync deferment is.

All the experiments in this section are performed using M1 @ MN (refer to
Table 8.4) with 20 Mbps of bandwidth, and the latency (between M1 and each cloud)
is between 42 and 77 ms. In terms of service access method, we only examine the PC
client, because almost all the frequent modifications are generated from PC clients
in practice.[6] Experiments with other benchmarks will be presented in Sect. 8.7.2.

First, to investigate the impact of frequent file modifications on *TUE*, we examine
the cases for $X \in \{1, 2, \ldots, 19, 20\}$. As depicted in Fig. 8.6, the six mainstream
cloud storage services exhibit diverse and interesting phenomena:

---

[6]The UIs (user interfaces) of web browser and mobile apps for cloud storage services are usually
not fit for performing frequent modifications to a file.

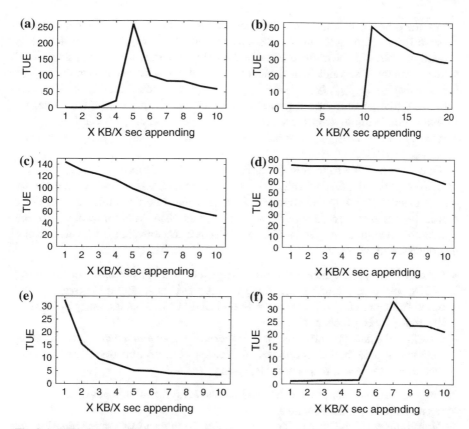

Fig. 8.6 *TUE* of the six cloud storage services in response to controlled frequent file modifications. Note that the subfigures have distinct Y-axes, and the **b** OneDrive subfigure has a different X-axis. **a** Google Drive. **b** OneDrive. **c** Ubuntu One. **d** Box. **e** Dropbox. **f** SugarSync. (Reprinted with permission from [33].)

- Frequent modifications to a file often lead to large *TUE* (the aforementioned "traffic overuse problem"). As for the six mainstream services, the maximum *TUE* can reach 260, 51, 144, 75, 32, and 33, respectively.
- We observe (except in the sync defer cases: Fig. 8.6a, b, f) that *TUE* generally decreases as the modification frequency ($= \frac{1024}{X}$) decreases. The reason is straightforward: though the total data update size is always $C = 1$ MB, a lower data update frequency implies fewer data sync events, and thus the overhead traffic is reduced.

A natural question is: *Why are the maximum* TUE *values of Google Drive (260), OneDrive (51), Ubuntu One (144), and Box (75) much larger than those of Dropbox (32) and SugarSync (33)?* The answer can be found from their data sync granularity (refer to Sect. 8.5.3): Google Drive, OneDrive, Ubuntu One, and Box employ *full-file sync*, while Dropbox and SugarSync employ block-level *incremental sync* which significantly improves the network-level traffic efficiency.

On the other hand, there do exist a few cases (in Fig. 8.6a, b, f) where *TUE* is close to 1.0. According to our observations, (a) Google Drive, (b) OneDrive, and (f) SugarSync deal with the traffic overuse problem by batching file updates using a *fixed* sync deferment: T seconds (which cannot be reconfigured by users). Figure 8.6a, b, f indicate that $T_{GoogleDrive} \in (3, 5)$ s, $T_{SugarSync} \in (4, 6)$ s, and $T_{OneDrive} \in (10, 11)$ s. Moreover, to figure out a more accurate value of T, we further tune X from integers to floats. For example, we experiment with $X = 3.1, 3.2, \ldots, 4.9$ for $T_{GoogleDrive}$, and then find that $T_{GoogleDrive} \approx 4.2$ s. Similarly, we find that $T_{SugarSync} \approx 6$ s and $T_{OneDrive} \approx 10.5$ s.

One may have the following question: *Is it possible that the deferred data synchronization of (a) Google Drive, (b) OneDrive, and (f) SugarSync is triggered by a* byte counter *or an* update counter *rather than the* time threshold *(T)?* In other words, the three concerned services may trigger the data synchronization once the number of uncommitted bytes or updates exceeds a certain value. This question can be addressed in two cases:

- Case 1: If the data synchronization is triggered by a *byte counter*, the resulting *TUE* would be close to 1.0 according to our previous study on the byte-counter based "efficient batched synchronization" (UDS) [35]. This is clearly not true as illustrated by Fig. 8.6a, b, f.
- Case 2: If the data synchronization is triggered by an *update counter*, the resulting *TUE* in Fig. 8.6a, b, f would *linearly* decrease as the modification period (X sec) increases. Obviously, this is not true, either.

Therefore, we conclude that the deferred data synchronization is not triggered by a byte counter or an update counter.

Unfortunately, fixed sync deferments are limited in terms of usage scenarios. As shown in Fig. 8.6a, b, f, the traffic overuse problem still occurs when $X > T$.

To overcome the limitation of fixed sync deferments, we propose an *adaptive sync defer* (ASD) mechanism. ASD adaptively tunes its sync deferment (T_i) to follow the latest (say, the ith) data update. In other words, when data updates happen more frequently, T_i gets shorter; when data updates happen less frequently, T_i gets longer. In either case, T_i tends to be slightly longer than the latest interupdate time, so that frequent modifications can be properly batched for synchronization (without harming user experience). Specifically, T_i can be adapted in such an iterative manner:

$$T_i = \min \left(\frac{T_{i-1}}{2} + \frac{\Delta t_i}{2} + \varepsilon, \ T_{max} \right) \tag{8.2}$$

where Δt_i is the inter-update time between the $(i - 1)$th and the ith data updates, and $\varepsilon \in (0, 1.0)$ is a small constant that guarantees T_i to be slightly longer than Δt_i in a small number of iteration rounds. T_{max} is also a constant representing the upper bound of T_i, as a too large T_i will harm user experience by bringing about intolerably long sync delay.

If Google Drive would utilize ASD on handling the "X KB/X sec" ($X >$ $T_{GoogleDrive}$) appending experiments, the resulting TUE will be close to 1.0 rather than the original 260 ($X = 5$), 100 ($X = 6$), 83 ($X = 7$), and so forth. The situation is similar for OneDrive and SugarSync. More detailed performance evaluation of ASD can be found in our previous work [36].

8.7.2 Impact of Network and Hardware

In this subsection, we first study the impact of network and hardware on TUE, and then explore why they impact TUE.

[Experiment 7, Network environment]: To study the impact of network environment (including both bandwidth and latency) on TUE, we conduct the following two batches of experiments.

The first batch of experiments are performed on B1 @ BJ. It represents a relatively poor network environment: low bandwidth (nearly 1.6 Mbps) and long latency (between 200 and 480 ms) relative to the cloud, because the six mainstream cloud storage services are mainly deployed in US. After repeating **Experiments 1–6** in this network environment, we compare the results with the corresponding results by using M1 @ MN with abundant bandwidth (nearly 20 Mbps) and short latency (between 42 and 77 ms), which represents a good network environment.

The second batch of experiments are performed by using M1 @ MN with controlled bandwidth (between 1.6 and 20 Mbps) and latency (between 40 and 1000 ms), so that we are able to get fine-grained results about how the network environment impacts TUE.

From the two batches of experiments, we mainly get the following findings and implications:

- TUE of a simple file operation is usually not affected by network environment.
- However, in the case of frequent file modifications, a user client with relatively low bandwidth or long latency can save more sync traffic.

Specifically, for the first batch of experiments, we plot the TUE of (a) OneDrive, (b) Box, and (c) Dropbox on handling the "X KB/X sec" appending experiment in Minnesota and Beijing in Fig. 8.7a, b, c, respectively. The situation of Google Drive and SugarSync is similar to Fig. 8.7a, and the situation of Ubuntu One looks like Fig. 8.7b. In each subfigure, the two curves ("@ MN" vs. "@ BJ") clearly illustrate that poor network environment leads to smaller TUE, especially when the modification period (X sec) is short (excluding the sync defer cases).

For the second batch of experiments, as a typical example, we plot the TUE of Dropbox on handling the "1 KB/s" appending experiment with variable bandwidths and latencies in Fig. 8.8a, b, respectively. In Fig. 8.8a, the latency is fixed to around 50 ms and the bandwidth is tuned from 1.6 to 20 Mbps. In Fig. 8.8b, the bandwidth is fixed to around 20 Mbps and the latency is tuned from 40 to 1000 ms. Obviously, higher bandwidth or shorter latency leads to larger TUE.

Fig. 8.7 *TUE* of
a OneDrive, **b** Box, and
c Dropbox on handling the
"*X* KB/*X* sec" appending
experiment, in Minnesota
(MN) and Beijing (BJ),
respectively. (Reprinted with
permission from [33].)

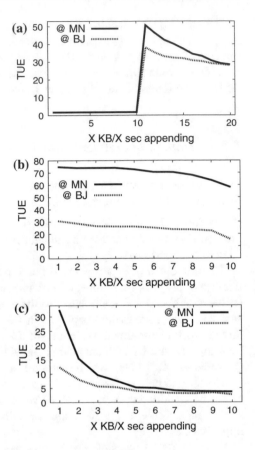

[**Experiment 7', Hardware configuration**]: Next, we examine the impact of hardware configuration on *TUE* by repeating **Experiments 1–6** with distinct client machines: M1 (a typical machine), M2 (an outdated machine), and M3 (an advanced machine). Their detailed hardware information is listed in Table 8.4. All the experiments are performed in Minnesota with abundant bandwidth (nearly 20 Mbps) and short latency (between 42 and 77 ms).

Through the **Experiment 7'** results, we observe that *TUE* of a simple file operation generally has no relation with hardware configuration, but *TUE* of frequent file modifications is actually affected by hardware configuration. As a typical example, in Fig. 8.8c we plot the *TUE* of Dropbox on handling the "*X* KB/*X* sec" appending experiment with M1, M2, and M3. The three curves clearly demonstrate that slower hardware incurs less sync traffic.

Why do network environment and hardware configuration impact *TUE*? To explore the reason why network environment and hardware configuration impact *TUE*, we analyze the communication packets of data synchronization, in particular the TCP data flows. The analysis reveals that in the presence of frequent modifications

Fig. 8.8 *TUE* of Dropbox
on handling the **a** "1 KB/s"
appending experiment with
variable bandwidths,
b "1 KB/s" appending
experiment with variable
latencies, and **c** "X KB/X
sec" appending experiment
with distinct hardware
configurations. (Reprinted
with permission from [33].)

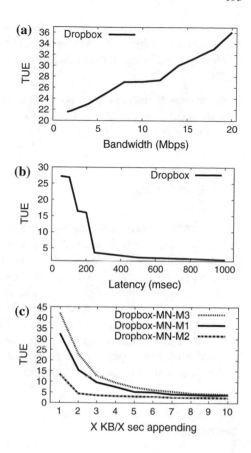

to a file, the user client does *not* always synchronize every file modification to the
cloud *separately*. Instead, the user client often batches multiple file modifications for
data synchronization. Specifically, a new file modification (or a sequence of new file
modifications) is synchronized to the cloud when at least the following two conditions
are both satisfied:

- **Condition 1**: The previous file modification (or the previous batch of file modifications) has been completely synchronized to the cloud.
- **Condition 2**: The client machine has finished calculating the latest metadata of
  the modified file.

As to Condition 1, when the network environment is relatively poor, synchronizing the previous file modification (or the previous batch of file modifications) takes
more time, so the client needs to wait for a longer period of time to synchronize the
new file modification. As to Condition 2, when the client runs on top of slower hardware, calculating the latest metadata (which is computation-intensive) also requires
a longer period of time. Because the failure of either condition will cause the new
file modification (or the sequence of new file modifications) to be naturally batched,

poor network environment or poor hardware increases the probability that a file modification gets batched, and thereby optimizes the *TUE*.

Finally, combining all the findings in this subsection, we get the following implication:

- In the case of frequent file modifications, today's cloud storage services actually bring good news (in terms of *TUE*) to those users with relatively poor hardware or Internet access.

8.8   Conclusion

The tremendous increase in data sync traffic has brought growing pains to today's cloud storage services, in terms of both infrastructure support and monetary costs. Driven by this problem, this chapter quantifies and analyzes the data sync traffic usage efficiency (*TUE*) of six widely used cloud storage services, using a real-world trace and comprehensive experiments. Our results and findings confirm that much of the data sync traffic is unnecessary and can be avoided or mitigated by careful design of data sync mechanisms. In other words, there is enormous space for optimizing the network-level efficiency of existing cloud storage services. We sincerely hope that our work can inspire the cloud storage designers to enhance their system and software, and meanwhile guide the users to pick appropriate services.

References

1. Amazon S3 Pricing Policy. http://aws.amazon.com/s3/#pricing (2014)
2. Bandwidth Costs for Cloud Storage. http://blog.dshr.org/2012/11/bandwidth-costs-for-cloud-storage.html
3. Bandwidth Limitations Are a Concern with Cloud Backup. http://searchdatabackup.techtarget.com/video/Bandwidth-limitations-are-a-concern-with-cloud-backup
4. Cisco Global Cloud Index: Forecast and Methodology, 2012-2017. Trend 3: Remote Data Services and Storage Access Services Growth. http://www.cisco.com/en/US/solutions/collateral/ns341/ns525/ns537/ns705/ns1175/Cloud_Index_White_Paper.html
5. Dirty Secrets: 5 Weaknesses of Cloud Storage Gateways. http://www.nasuni.com/blog/28-dirty_secrets_5_weaknesses_of_cloud_storage
6. Dropbox Is Now The Data Fabric Tying Together Devices For 100M Registered Users Who Save 1B Files A Day. http://techcrunch.com/2012/11/13/dropbox-100-million
7. Google Drive Now Has 10 Million Users: Available on iOS and Chrome OS. http://techcrunch.com/2012/06/28/google-drive-now-has-10-million-users-available-on-ios-and-chrome-os-offline-editing-in-docs
8. Hidden Costs of Cloud Storage. http://www.onlinefilestorage.com/hidden-costs-of-cloud-storage-1756
9. How Fast is SkyDrive (OneDrive) Growing? http://www.liveside.net/2012/10/27/how-fast-is-skydrive-growing
10. JavaScript Tutorials, Refernces, and Documentation. http://developer.mozilla.org/en-US/docs/Web/javascript

11. Large-Scale Dropbox Trace Collected at the ISP Level. http://traces.simpleweb.org/wiki/Dropbox_Traces
12. PUE (Power Usage Effectiveness). http://en.wikipedia.org/wiki/Power_usage_effectiveness
13. A Question About the Default Chunk Size of rsync. http://lists.samba.org/archive/rsync/2001-November/000595.html
14. rsync web site. http://www.samba.org/rsync
15. Why RESTful Design for Cloud is Best. http://www.redhat.com/promo/summit/2010/presentations/cloud/fri/galder-945-why-RESTful/RestfulDesignJBWRH2010.pdf
16. Wireshark Network Protocol Analyzer. http://www.wireshark.org
17. Aggarwal, B., Akella, A., Anand, A., Balachandran, A., Chitnis, P., Muthukrishnan, C., Ramjee, R., Varghese, G.: EndRE: An end-system redundancy elimination service for enterprises. In: Proceedings of the 7th USENIX Conference on Networked Systems Design and Implementation (NSDI), pp. 419–432 (2010)
18. Bergen, A., Coady, Y., McGeer, R.: Client bandwidth: the forgotten metric of online storage providers. In: Proceedings of the 2011 IEEE Pacific Rim Conference on Communications, Computers and Signal Processing (PacRim), pp. 543–548 (2011)
19. Bessani, A., Correia, M., Quaresma, B., André, F., Sousa, P.: DepSky: dependable and secure storage in a cloud-of-clouds. ACM Trans. Storage (TOS) 9(4), 12 (2013)
20. Calder, B., Wang, J., Ogus, A., Nilakantan, N., Skjolsvold, A., McKelvie, S., Xu, Y., Srivastav, S., Wu, J., Simitci, H., et al.: Windows azure storage: a highly available cloud storage service with strong consistency. In: Proceedings of the 23rd ACM Symposium on Operating Systems Principles (SOSP), pp. 143–157 (2011)
21. Chen, Y., Srinivasan, K., Goodson, G., Katz, R.: Design implications for enterprise storage systems via multi-dimensional trace analysis. In: Proceedings of the 23rd ACM Symposium on Operating Systems Principles (SOSP), pp. 43–56 (2011)
22. Drago, I., Bocchi, E., Mellia, M., Slatman, H., Pras, A.: Benchmarking personal cloud storage. In: Proceedings of the 13th ACM Internet Measurement Conference (IMC), pp. 205–212 (2013)
23. Drago, I., Mellia, M., Munafò, M., Sperotto, A., Sadre, R., Pras, A.: Inside dropbox: understanding personal cloud storage services. In: Proceedings of the 12th ACM Internet Measurement Conference (IMC), pp. 481–494 (2012)
24. Fielding, R.: Architectural styles and the design of network-based software architectures. Ph.D. thesis, University of California, Irvine (2000)
25. Halevi, S., Harnik, D., Pinkas, B., Shulman-Peleg, A.: Proofs of ownership in remote storage systems. In: Proceedings of the 18th ACM Conference on Computer and Communications Security (CCS), pp. 491–500 (2011)
26. Harnik, D., Kat, R., Sotnikov, D., Traeger, A., Margalit, O.: To zip or not to zip: effective resource usage for real-time compression. In: Proceedings of the 11th USENIX Conference on File and Storage Technologies (FAST), pp. 229–242 (2013)
27. Harnik, D., Pinkas, B., Shulman-Peleg, A.: Side channels in cloud services: deduplication in cloud storage. IEEE Secur. Priv. 8(6), 40–47 (2010)
28. Hu, W., Yang, T., Matthews, J.: The good, the bad and the ugly of consumer cloud storage. ACM SIGOPS Oper. Syst. Rev. (OSR) 44(3), 110–115 (2010)
29. Huang, Y., Li, Z., Liu, G., Dai, Y.: Cloud download: using cloud utilities to achieve high-quality content distribution for unpopular videos. In: Proceedings of the 19th ACM International Conference on Multimedia (ACM-MM), pp. 213–222 (2011)
30. Kholia, D., Wegrzyn, P.: Looking inside the (Drop) box. In: Proceedings of the 7th USENIX Workshop on Offensive Technologies (WOOT) (2013)
31. Li, A., Yang, X., Kandula, S., Zhang, M.: CloudCmp: comparing public cloud providers. In: Proceedings of the 10th ACM Internet Measurement Conference (IMC), pp. 1–14 (2010)
32. Li, Z., Huang, Y., Liu, G., Wang, F., Zhang, Z.L., Dai, Y.: Cloud transcoder: bridging the format and resolution gap between internet videos and mobile devices. In: Proceedings of the 22nd SIGMM Workshop on Network and Operating Systems Support for Digital Audio and Video (NOSSDAV), pp. 33–38 (2012)

33. Li, Z., Jin, C., Xu, T., Wilson, C., Liu, Y., Cheng, L., Liu, Y., Dai, Y., Zhang, Z.L.: Towards network-level efficiency for cloud storage services. In: Proceedings of the 14th ACM Internet Measurement Conference (IMC), pp. 115–128 (2014)
34. Li, Z., Li, J.: Deficiency of scientific research behind the price war of cloud storage services. Commun. China Comput. Fed. (CCCF) **10**(8), 36–41 (2014)
35. Li, Z., Wilson, C., Jiang, Z., Liu, Y., Zhao, B., Jin, C., Zhang, Z.L., Dai, Y.: Efficient batched synchronization in dropbox-like cloud storage services. In: Proceedings of the 14th ACM/IFIP/USENIX International Middleware Conference (Middleware), pp. 307–327. Springer (2013)
36. Li, Z., Zhang, Z.L., Dai, Y.: Coarse-grained cloud synchronization mechanism design may lead to severe traffic overuse. J. Tsinghua Sci. Technol. (JTST) **18**(3), 286–297 (2013)
37. Mahajan, P., Setty, S., Lee, S., Clement, A., Alvisi, L., Dahlin, M., Walfish, M.: Depot: cloud storage with minimal trust. ACM Trans. Comput. Syst. (TOCS) **29**(4), 12 (2011)
38. Meyer, D., Bolosky, W.: A study of practical deduplication. ACM Trans. Storage (TOS) **7**(4), 14 (2012)
39. Mulazzani, M., Schrittwieser, S., Leithner, M., Huber, M., Weippl, E.: Dark clouds on the horizon: using cloud storage as attack vector and online slack space. In: Proceedings of the 20th USENIX Security Symposium, pp. 65–76 (2011)
40. Shilane, P., Huang, M., Wallace, G., Hsu, W.: WAN-optimized replication of backup datasets using stream-informed delta compression. ACM Trans. Storage (TOS) **8**(4), 13 (2012)
41. Vrable, M., Savage, S., Voelker, G.: Cumulus: filesystem backup to the cloud. ACM Trans. Storage (TOS) **5**(4), 14 (2009)
42. Vrable, M., Savage, S., Voelker, G.: Bluesky: a cloud-backed file system for the enterprise. In: Proceedings of the 10th USENIX Conference on File and Storage Technologies (FAST), p. 19 (2012)
43. Wallace, G., Douglis, F., Qian, H., Shilane, P., Smaldone, S., Chamness, M., Hsu, W.: Characteristics of backup workloads in production systems. In: Proceedings of the 10th USENIX Conference on File and Storage Technologies (FAST), p. 500 (2012)
44. Zhang, Y., Dragga, C., Arpaci-Dusseau, A., Arpaci-Dusseau, R.: ViewBox: Integrating local file systems with cloud storage services. In: Proceedings of the 12th USENIX Conference on File and Storage Technologies (FAST), pp. 119–132 (2014)

Chapter 9
Efficient Batched Synchronization for Cloud Storage Services

Abstract As tools for personal storage, file synchronization and data sharing, cloud storage services such as Dropbox have quickly gained popularity. These services provide users with ubiquitous, reliable data storage that can be automatically synced across multiple devices, and also shared among a group of users. To minimize the network overhead, cloud storage services employ binary diff, data compression, and other mechanisms when transferring updates among users. However, despite these optimizations, we observe that in the presence off *frequent, short updates* to user data, the network traffic generated by cloud storage services often exhibits pathological inefficiencies. Through comprehensive measurements and detailed analysis, we demonstrate that many cloud storage applications generate session maintenance traffic that *far exceeds* the useful update traffic. We refer to this behavior as the *traffic overuse problem*. To address this problem, we propose the *update-batched delayed synchronization* (UDS) mechanism. Acting as a middleware between the user's file storage system and a cloud storage application, UDS batches updates from clients to significantly reduce the overhead caused by session maintenance traffic, while preserving the rapid file synchronization that users expect from cloud storage services. Furthermore, we extend UDS with a backwards compatible Linux kernel modification that further improves the performance of cloud storage applications by reducing the CPU usage.

9.1 Introduction

As tools for personal storage, file synchronization and data sharing, cloud storage services such as Dropbox, Google Drive, and SkyDrive (renamed to OneDrive in 2014) have become extremely popular. These services provide users with ubiquitous, reliable data storage that can be synchronized ("sync'ed") across multiple devices, and also shared among a group of users. Dropbox is arguably the most popular cloud storage service, reportedly hitting more than 100 million users who store or update one billion files per day [4].

Cloud storage services are characterized by two key components: a (front-end) client application that runs on user devices, and a (back-end) storage service that

© Springer Science+Business Media Singapore 2016   197
Z. Li et al., *Content Distribution for Mobile Internet: A Cloud-based Approach*,
DOI 10.1007/978-981-10-1463-5_9

resides within the "cloud," hosting users' files in huge data centers. A user can "drop" files into or directly modify files in a special "sync folder" that is then automatically synchronized with cloud storage by the client application.

Cloud storage applications typically use two algorithms to minimize the amount of network traffic that they generate. First, the client application computes the binary diff of modified files and only sends the altered bits to the cloud. Second, all updates are compressed before they are sent to the cloud. As a simple example, if we append 100 MB of identical characters (e.g., "a") to an existing file in the Dropbox sync folder (thus the binary diff size is 100 MB), the resulting network traffic is merely 40 KB. This amount of traffic is just slightly more than the traffic incurred by appending a single byte "a" (i.e., around 38 KB, including meta-data overhead).

The Traffic Overuse Problem. However, despite these performance optimizations, we observe that the network traffic generated by cloud storage applications exhibits pathological inefficiencies in the presence of *frequent, short updates* to user data. Each time a synced file is modified, the cloud storage application's *update-triggered real-time synchronization* (URS) mechanism is activated. URS computes and compresses the binary diff of the new data, and sends the update to the cloud along with some *session maintenance data*. Unfortunately, when there are frequent, short updates to synced files, the amount of session maintenance traffic *far exceeds* the amount of useful update traffic sent by the client over time. We call this behavior the *traffic overuse problem*. In essence, the traffic overuse problem originates from the *update sensitivity* of URS.

Our investigation into the traffic overuse problem reveals that this issue is pervasive among users. By analyzing data released from a large-scale measurement of Dropbox [17], we discover that for around 8.5 % of users, $\geq 10\,\%$ of their traffic is generated in response to frequent, short updates (refer to Sect. 9.4.1). In addition to Dropbox, we examine seven other popular cloud storage applications across three different operating systems, and discover that their software also exhibits the traffic overuse problem.

As we show in Sect. 9.4, the traffic overuse problem is exacerbated by "power users" who leverage cloud storage in situations it was not designed for. Specifically, cloud storage applications were originally designed for simple use cases like storing music and sharing photos. However, cloud storage applications are now used in place of traditional source control systems (Dropbox markets their Teams service specifically for this purpose [6]). The problem is especially acute in situations where files are shared between multiple users, since frequent, short updates by one user force all users to download updates. Similarly, users now employ cloud storage for even more advanced use cases like setting up databases [1].

Deep Understanding of the Problem. To better understand the traffic overuse problem, we conduct extensive, carefully controlled experiments with the Dropbox application (Sect. 9.3). In our tests, we artificially generate streams of updates to synced files, while varying the size and frequency of updates. Although Dropbox is a closed-source application and its data packets are SSL encrypted, we are able to conduct black-box measurements of its network traffic by capturing packets with Wireshark [10].

By examining the time series of Dropbox's packets, coupled with some analysis of the Dropbox binary, we quantitatively explore the reasons why the ratio of session maintenance traffic to update traffic is poor during frequent, short file updates. In particular, we identify the operating system features that trigger Dropbox's URS mechanism, and isolate the series of steps that the application goes through before it uploads data to the cloud. This knowledge enables us to identify the precise update-frequency intervals and update sizes that lead to the generation of pathological session maintenance traffic. We reinforce these findings by examining traces from real Dropbox users in Sect. 9.4.

UDS: Addressing the Traffic Overuse Problem. Guided by our measurement findings, we develop a solution to the traffic overuse problem called *update-batched delayed synchronization* (UDS) (Sect. 9.5). As depicted in Fig. 9.1, UDS acts as a middleware between the user's file storage system and a cloud storage client application (e.g., Dropbox). UDS is independent of any specific cloud storage service and requires no modifications to proprietary software, which makes UDS simple to deploy. Specifically, UDS instantiates a "SavingBox" folder that replaces the sync folder used by the cloud storage application. UDS detects and batches frequent, short data updates to files in the SavingBox and delays the release of updated files to the cloud storage application. In effect, UDS forces the cloud storage application to batch file updates that would otherwise trigger pathological behavior. In practice, the additional delay caused by batching file updates is very small (around several seconds), meaning that users are unlikely to notice, and the integrity of cloud-replicated files will not be adversely affected.

To evaluate the performance of UDS, we implement a version for Linux. Our prototype uses the inotify kernel API [8] to track changes to files in the SavingBox folder, while using rsync [9] to generate compressed diffs of modified files. Results from our prototype demonstrate that it reduces the overhead of session maintenance traffic to less than 30 %, compared to 620 % overhead in the worst case for Dropbox.

UDS+: Reducing CPU Overhead. Both URS and UDS have a drawback: in the case of frequent data updates, they generate considerable CPU overhead from constantly *re-indexing* the updated file (i.e., splitting the file into chunks, checksumming each chunk, and calculating diffs from previous versions of each chunk). This re-indexing occurs because the inotify kernel API reports *what* file/directory has been modified

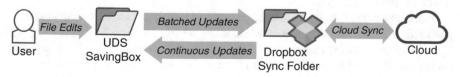

Fig. 9.1 High-level design of the UDS middleware. (Reprinted with permission from [24].)

on disk, but not *how* it has been modified. Thus, rsync (or an equivalent algorithm) must be run over the entire modified file to determine how it has changed.

To address this problem, we modify the Linux inotify API to return the *size* and *location* of file updates. This information is readily available inside the kernel; our modified API simply exposes this information to applications in a backwards compatible manner. We implement an improved version of our system, called UDS+, that leverages the new API (Sect. 9.6). Microbenchmark results demonstrate that UDS+ incurs significantly less CPU overhead than URS and UDS. Our kernel patch is available at http://www.greenorbs.org/people/lzh/public/inotify-patch.html.

Although convincing the Linux kernel community to adopt new APIs is a difficult task, we believe that our extension to inotify is a worthwhile addition to the operating system. Using the strace command, we tracked the system calls made by many commercial cloud storage applications (e.g., Dropbox, UbuntuOne, Team-Drive, SpiderOak, etc.) and confirmed that they all use the inotify API. Thus, there is a large class of applications that would benefit from merging our modified API into the Linux kernel.

9.2   Related Work

As the popularity of cloud storage services has quickly grown, so too have the number of research papers related to these services. Hu et al. performed the first measurement study on cloud storage services, focusing on Dropbox, Mozy, CrashPlan, and Carbonite [21]. Their aim was to gauge the relative upload/download performance of different services, and they find that Dropbox performs best while Mozy performs worst.

Several studies have focused specifically on Dropbox. Drago et al. study the detailed architecture of the Dropbox service and conduct measurements based on ISP-level traces of Dropbox network traffic [17]. The data from this paper is open-source, and we leverage it in Sect. 9.4 to conduct trace-driven simulations of Dropbox behavior. Drago et al. further compare the system capabilities of Dropbox, Google Drive, SkyDrive, Wuala, and Amazon Cloud Drive, and find that each service has its limitations and advantages [16]. A study by Wang et al. reveals that the scalability of Dropbox is limited by their use of Amazon's EC2 hosting service, and they propose novel mechanisms for overcoming these bottlenecks [31]. Dropbox cloud storage deduplication is studied in [18, 20], and some security/privacy issues of Dropbox are discussed in [21, 26].

Amazon's cloud storage infrastructure has also been quantitatively analyzed. Burgen et al. measure the performance of Amazon S3 from a client's perspective [11]. They point out that the perceived performance at the client is primarily dependent on the transfer bandwidth between the client and Amazon S3, rather than the upload bandwidth of the cloud. Consequently, the designers of cloud storage services must pay special attention to the client-side, perceived quality of service.

   Li et al. developed a tool called CloudCmp [23] to comprehensively compare the performances of four major cloud providers: Amazon AWS [22], Microsoft Azure [14], Google AppEngine and Rackspace CloudServers. They find that the performance of cloud storage can vary significantly across providers. Specifically, Amazon S3 is observed to be more suitable for handling large data objects rather than small data objects, which is consistent with our observation in this chapter.

   Based on two large-scale network-attached storage file system traces from a real-world enterprise datacenter, Chen et al. conduct a multi-dimensional analysis of data access patterns at the user, application, file, and directory levels [15]. Based on this analysis, they derive 12 design implications for how storage systems can be specialized for specific data access patterns. Wallace et al. also present a comprehensive characterization of backup workloads in a large production backup system [30]. Our work follows a similar methodology: study the data access patterns of cloud storage users and then leverage the knowledge to optimize these systems for improved performance.

   Finally, there are more works related to Dropbox-like cloud storage services, such as the cloud-backed file systems [28, 29], delta compression [27], real-time compression [19], dependable cloud storage design [12, 25], and economic issues [13].

9.3 Understanding Cloud Storage Services

In this section, we present a brief overview of the data synchronization mechanism of cloud storage services, and perform fine-grained measurements of network usage by cloud storage applications. Although we focus on Dropbox as the most popular service, we demonstrate that our findings generalize to other services as well.

9.3.1 Data Synchronization Mechanism

Figure 9.2 depicts a high-level outline of Dropbox's data sync mechanism. Each instance of the Dropbox client application sends three different types of traffic. *First*, each client maintains a connection to an *index server*. The index server authenticates each user, and stores meta-data about the user's files, including: the list of the user's files, their sizes and attributes, and pointers to where the files can be found on Amazon's S3 storage service. *Second*, file data is stored on Amazon's S3 storage service. The Dropbox client compresses files before storing them in S3, and modifications to synced files are uploaded to S3 as compressed, binary diffs. *Third*, each client maintains a connection to a *beacon server*. Periodically, the Dropbox client sends a message to the user's beacon server to report its online status, as well as receives notifications from the cloud (e.g., a shared file has been modified by another user and should be re-synced).

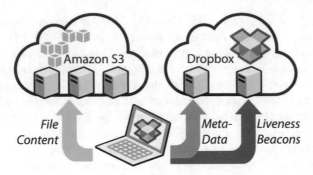

Fig. 9.2 Dropbox data sync mechanism. (Reprinted with permission from [24].)

Relationship between the Disk and the Network. In addition to understanding the network connections made by Dropbox, we also seek to understand what activity on the local file system triggers updates to the Dropbox cloud. To measure the fine-grained behavior of the Dropbox application, we leverage the Dropbox command-line interface (CLI) [2], which is a Python script that enables low-level monitoring of the Dropbox application. Using Dropbox CLI, we can programmatically query the status of the Dropbox application after adding files to or modifying files in the Dropbox Sync folder.

By repeatedly observing the behavior of the Dropbox application in response to file system changes, we are able to discern the inner workings of Dropbox's *update-triggered real-time synchronization* (URS) system. Figure 9.3a depicts the basic operation of URS. First, a change is made on disk within the Dropbox Sync folder, e.g., a new file is created or an existing file is modified. The Dropbox application uses OS-specific APIs to monitor for changes to files and directories of interest. After receiving a change notification, the Dropbox application indexes or re-indexes the affected file(s). Next, the compressed file or binary diff is sent to Amazon S3, and the file meta-data is sent to the Dropbox cloud. This process is labeled as "Sync to the

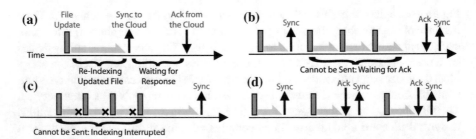

Fig. 9.3 Diagrams showing the low-level behavior of the Dropbox application following a file update. **a** shows the fundamental operations, while **b** and **c** show situations where file updates are batched together. **d** shows the worst-case scenario where no file updates are batched together. (Reprinted with permission from [24].)

Cloud" in Fig. 9.3a. After these changes have been committed in the cloud, the Dropbox cloud responds to the client with an acknowledgment message. In Sect. 9.3.2, we investigate the actual length of time it takes to commit changes to the Dropbox cloud.

Although the process illustrated in Fig. 9.3a appears to be straightforward, there are some hidden conditions that complicate the process. Specifically, not every file update triggers a cloud synchronization: there are two situations where file updates are batched by the Dropbox application before they are sent to the cloud.

The first scenario is depicted in Fig. 9.3b. In this situation, a file is modified numerous times after a cloud sync has begun, but before the acknowledgment is received. URS only initiates one cloud sync at a time, thus file modifications made during the network wait interval get batched until the current sync is complete. After the acknowledgment is received, the batched file changes are immediately synced to the cloud.

The second scenario is shown in Fig. 9.3c. In this situation, a file is modified several times in such rapid succession that URS does not have time to finish indexing the file. Dropbox cannot begin syncing changes to the cloud until after the file is completely indexed, thus these rapid edits prevent the client from sending any network traffic.

The two cases in Fig. 9.3b, c reveal that there are complicated interactions between on-disk activity and the network traffic sent by Dropbox. On one hand, a carefully timed series of file edits can generate only a single network transfer if they occur fast enough to repeatedly interrupt file indexing. On the other hand, a poorly timed series of edits can initiate an enormous number of network transfers if the Dropbox software is not able to batch them. Figure 9.3d depicts this worst-case situation: each file edit (regardless of how trivially small) results in a cloud synchronization. In Sect. 9.4, we demonstrate that this worst-case scenario actually occurs under real-world usage conditions.

9.3.2 Controlled Measurements

Our investigation of the low-level behavior of the Dropbox application reveal complex interactions between file writes on disk and Dropbox's network traffic to the cloud. In this section, we delve deeper into this relationship by performing carefully controlled microbenchmarks of cloud storage applications. In particular, our goal is to quantify the relationship between frequency and size of file updates with the amount of traffic generated by cloud storage applications. As before, we focus on Dropbox, however we also demonstrate that our results generalize to other cloud storage systems as well.

All of our benchmarks are conducted on two test systems located in the United States in 2012. The first is a laptop with a dual-core Intel processor @2.26 GHz, 2 GB of RAM, and a 5400 RPM, 250 GB hard drive disk (HDD). The second is a desktop with a dual-core Intel processor @3.0 GHz, 4 GB of RAM, and a 7200 RPM, 1 TB HDD. We conduct tests on machines with different hard drive rotational speeds because this impacts the time it takes for cloud storage software to index files. Both machines run Ubuntu Linux 12.04, the Linux Dropbox application version 0.7.1 [3], and the Dropbox CLI extension [2]. Both machines are connected to a 4 Mbps Internet connection, which gives Dropbox ample resources for syncing files to the cloud.

File Creation. First, we examine the amount of network traffic generated by Dropbox when new files are created in the Sync folder. Table 9.1 shows the amount of traffic sent to the index server and to Amazon S3 when files of different sizes are placed in the Sync folder on the 5400 RPM machine. We use JPEG files for our tests (except the 1 byte test) because JPEGs are a compressed file format. This prevents the Dropbox application from being able to further compress data updates to the cloud.

Table 9.1 reveals several interesting facets about Dropbox traffic. First, regardless of the size of the created file, the size of the meta-data sent to the index server remains almost constant. Conversely, the amount of data sent to Amazon S3 closely tracks the size of the created file. This result makes sense, since the actual file data (plus some checksumming and HTTP overhead) are stored on S3.

The α column in Table 9.1 reports the ratio of total Dropbox traffic to the size of new file. α close to 1 is ideal, since that indicates that Dropbox has very little overhead beyond the size of the user's file. For small files, α is large because the fixed size of the index server meta-data dwarfs the actual size of the file. For larger files α is more reasonable, since Dropbox's overhead is amortized over the file size.

The last column of Table 9.1 reports the average time taken to complete the cloud synchronization. These tests reveal that, regardless of file size, all cloud synchronizations take at least 4 s on average. This minimum time interval is dictated by Dropbox's cloud infrastructure, and is not a function of hard drive speed, Internet connection speed or RTT. For larger files, the sync delay grows commensurately larger. In these cases, the delay is dominated by the time it takes to upload the file to Amazon S3.

Short File Updates. The next set of experiments examine the behavior of Dropbox in the presence of short updates to an existing file. Each test starts with an empty file in the Dropbox Sync folder, and then periodically we append one random byte to the

Table 9.1 Network traffic generated by adding new files to the Dropbox Sync folder

New file size	Index server traffic (KB)	Amazon S3 traffic	α	Sync delay (s)
1 B	29.8	6.5 KB	38200	4.0
1 KB	31.3	6.8 KB	40.1	4.0
10 KB	31.8	13.9 KB	4.63	4.1
100 KB	32.3	118.7 KB	1.528	4.8
1 MB	35.3	1.2 MB	1.22	9.2
10 MB	35.1	11.5 MB	1.149	54.7
100 MB	38.5	112.6 MB	1.1266	496.3

Reprinted with permission from [24]

file until its size reaches 1 KB. Appending random bytes ensures that it is difficult for Dropbox to compress the binary diff of the file.

Figures 9.4 and 9.5 show the network traffic generated by Dropbox when 1 byte per second is appended on the 5400 and 7200 RPM machines. Although each append is only 1 byte long, and the total file size never exceeds 1 KB, the total traffic sent by Dropbox reaches 1.2 MB on the 5400 RPM machine, and 2 MB on the 7200 RPM machine. The majority of Dropbox's traffic is due to meta-data updates to the index server. As shown in Table 9.1, each index server update is roughly 30 KB in size, which dwarfs the size of our file and each individual update. The traffic sent to Amazon S3 is also significant, despite the small size of our file, while Beacon traffic is negligible. Overall, Figs. 9.4 and 9.5 clearly demonstrate that under certain conditions, the amount of traffic generated by Dropbox can be several orders of magnitude larger than the amount of underlying user data. The faster, 7200 RPM hard drive actually makes the situation worse.

Timing of File Updates. As depicted in Fig. 9.3b, c, the timing of file updates can impact Dropbox's network utilization. To examine the relationship between update timing and network traffic, we now conduct experiments where the time interval between 1 byte file appends in varied from 100 ms to 10 s.

Figures 9.6 and 9.7 display the amount of network traffic generated by Dropbox during each experiment on the 5400 and 7200 RPM machines. The results show a clear trend: faster file updates result in less network traffic. This is due to the mechanisms highlighted in Fig. 9.3b, c, i.e., Dropbox is able to batch updates that occur very quickly. This batching reduces the total number of meta-data updates that are sent to the index sever, and allows multiple appended bytes in the file to

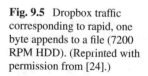

Fig. 9.4 Dropbox traffic corresponding to rapid, one byte appends to a file (5400 RPM HDD). (Reprinted with permission from [24].)

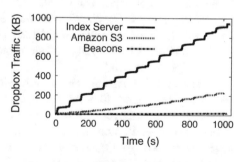

Fig. 9.5 Dropbox traffic corresponding to rapid, one byte appends to a file (7200 RPM HDD). (Reprinted with permission from [24].)

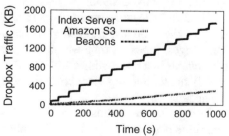

Fig. 9.6 Dropbox traffic as
the time between one byte
appends is varied (5400
RPM HDD). (Reprinted with
permission from [24].)

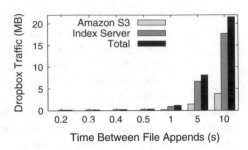

Fig. 9.7 Dropbox traffic as
the time between one byte
appends is varied (7200
RPM HDD). (Reprinted with
permission from [24].)

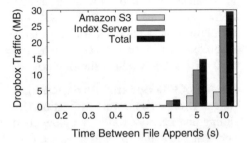

be aggregated into a single binary diff for Amazon S3. Unfortunately, Dropbox is
able to perform less batching as the time interval between appends grows. This is
particularly evident for the 5 and 10 s tests in Figs. 9.6 and 9.7. This case represents
the extreme scenario shown in Fig. 9.3d, where almost every 1 byte update triggers
a full synchronization with the cloud.

Indexing Time of Files. The results in Figs. 9.6 and 9.7 reveal that the timing of
file updates impacts Dropbox's network traffic. However, at this point we do not
know which factor is responsible for lowering network usage: is it the network
waiting interval as in Fig. 9.3b, the interrupted file indexing as in Fig. 9.3c, or some
combination of the two?

To answer this question, we perform microbenchmarks to examine how long it
takes Dropbox to index files. As before, we begin with an empty file and periodically
append one random byte until the file size reaches 1 KB. In these tests, we wait 5 s
in-between appends, since this time is long enough that the indexing operation is
never interrupted. We measure the time Dropbox spends indexing the modified file
by monitoring the Dropbox process using Dropbox CLI.

Figure 9.8 shows the indexing time distribution for Dropbox. The median indexing
time for the 5400 and 7200 RPM drives are ≈400 ms and ≈200 ms, respectively.
The longest indexing time we observed was 960 ms. These results indicates that
file updates that occur within ≈200–400 ms of each other (depending on hard drive
speed) should interrupt Dropbox's indexing process, causing it to restart and batch
the updates together.

Comparing the results from Figs. 9.6 and 9.7 to Fig. 9.8 reveals that indexing
interrupts play a role in reducing Dropbox's network traffic. The amount of traffic

Fig. 9.8 Distribution of
Dropbox file indexing time.
Total file size is 1 KB.
(Reprinted with permission
from [24].)

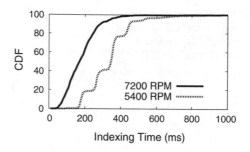

generated by Dropbox steadily rises as the time between file appends increases from
200 to 500 ms. This corresponds to the likelihood of file appends interrupting the
indexing process shown in Fig. 9.8. When the time between appends is 1 s, it is highly
unlikely that sequential appends will interrupt the indexing process (the longest index
we observed took 960 ms). Consequently, the amount of network traffic generated
during the 1 s interval test is more than double the amount generated during the 500
ms test.

Although indexing interrupts are responsible for Dropbox's network traffic patterns at short time scales, they cannot explain the sharp increase in network traffic that
occurs when the time between appends rises from 1 to 5 s. Instead, in these situations
the delimiting factor is the network synchronization delay depicted in Fig. 9.3b. As
shown in Fig. 9.9, one third of Dropbox synchronizations complete in 1–4 s, while
another third complete in 4–7 s. Thus, increasing the time between file appends from
1 to 10 s causes the number of file updates that trigger network synchronization to
rise (i.e., there is little batching of updates).

Long File Updates. So far, all of our results have focused on very short, 1 byte
updates to files. We now seek to measure the behavior of Dropbox when updates
are longer. As before, we begin by looking at the amount of traffic generated by
Dropbox when a file in the Sync folder is modified. In these tests, we append blocks
of randomized data to an initially empty file every second until the total file size
reaches 5 MB. We vary the size of the data blocks between 50 KB and 100 KB, in
increments of 10 KB.

Fig. 9.9 Distribution of
sync delays. Total file size is
1 KB. (Reprinted with
permission from [24].)

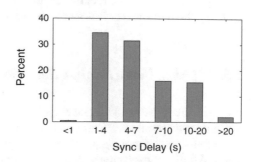

Fig. 9.10 Network traffic as
the speed of file appends is
varied. (Reprinted with
permission from [24].)

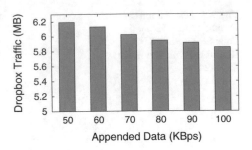

Fig. 9.11 File indexing time
as the total file size is varied.
(Reprinted with permission
from [24].)

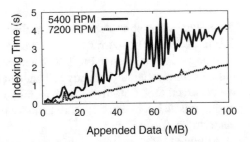

Figure 9.10 shows the results of the experiment for the 5400 RPM test machine.
Unlike the results for the 1 byte append tests, the amount of network traffic generated by Dropbox in these experiments is comparable to the total file size (5 MB).
As the number of kilobytes per second appended to the file increases, the ratio of
network traffic to total file size falls. These results reiterate the point that the Dropbox
application uses network resources more effectively when dealing with larger files.

Figure 9.11 explores the relationship between the size of appended data and the
file indexing time for Dropbox. There is a clear linear relationship between these two
variables: as the size of the appended data increases, so does the indexing time of
the file. This makes intuitive sense, since it takes more time to load larger files from
disk.

Figure 9.11 indicates that interrupted indexing will be a more common occurrence
with larger files, since they take longer to index, especially on devices with slower
hard drives. Therefore, Dropbox will use network resources more efficiently when
dealing with files on the order of megabytes in size. Similarly, the fixed overhead of
updating the index server is easier to amortize over large files.

9.3.3   Other Cloud Storage Services and Operating Systems

We now survey seven additional cloud storage services to see if they also exhibit the
traffic overuse problem. For this experiment, we re-run our 1 byte per second append
test on each cloud storage application. As before, the maximum size of the file is
1 KB. All of our measurements are conducted on the following two test machines:

a desktop with a dual-core Intel processor @3.0 GHz, 4 GB of RAM, and a 7200 RPM, 1 TB hard drive, and a MacBook Pro laptop with a dual-core Intel processor @2.5 GHz, 4 GB of RAM, and a 7200 RPM, 512 GB hard drive. The desktop dual boots Ubuntu 12.04 and Windows 7 SP1, while the laptop runs OS X Lion 10.7. We test each cloud storage application on all OSes it supports. Because 360 CloudDisk, Everbox, Kanbox, Kuaipan, and VDisk are Chinese services, we executed these tests in China. Dropbox, UbuntuOne, and IDriveSync were tested in the US.

Figure 9.12 displays the results of our experiments, from which there are two important takeaways. First, we observe that the traffic overuse problem is pervasive across different cloud storage applications. All of the tested applications generate megabytes of traffic when faced with frequent, short file updates, even though the actual size of the file in only 1KB. All applications perform equal to or worse than Dropbox. Secondly, we see that the traffic overuse problem exists whether the client is run on Windows, Linux, or OS X.

Summary. Below we briefly summarize our observations and insights got from the experimental results in this section.

- The Dropbox client only synchronizes data to the cloud after the local data has been indexed, and any prior synchronizations have been resolved. File updates that occur within 200–400 ms intervals are likely to be batched due to file indexing. Similarly, file updates that occur within a 4 s interval may be batched due to waiting for a previous cloud synchronization to finish.
- The traffic overuse problem occurs when there are numerous, small updates to files that occur at intervals on the order of several seconds. Under these conditions, cloud storage applications are unable to batch updates together, causing the amount of sync traffic to be several orders of magnitude larger than the actual size of the file.

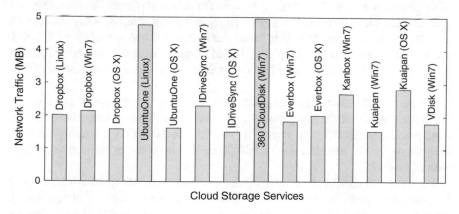

Fig. 9.12 Total network traffic for various cloud storage applications running on three OSes after appending 1 byte to a file 1024 times. (Reprinted with permission from [24].)

- Our tests reveal that the traffic overuse problem is pervasive across cloud storage applications. The traffic overuse problem occurs on different OSes, and is actually made worse by faster hard drive speeds.

9.4   The Traffic Overuse Problem in Practice

The results in the previous section demonstrate that under controlled conditions, cloud storage applications generate large amounts of network traffic that far exceed the size of users' actual data. In this section, we address a new question: are users actually affected by the traffic overuse problem? To answer this question, we measure the characteristics of Dropbox network traffic in real-world scenarios. First, we analyze data from a large-scale trace of Dropbox traffic to illustrate the pervasiveness of the traffic overuse problem in the real world. To confirm these findings, we use data from the trace to drive a simulation on our test machines. Second, we experiment with two practical Dropbox usage scenarios that may trigger the traffic overuse problem. The results of these tests reveal that the amount of network traffic generated by Dropbox is anywhere from 11 to 130 times the size of data on disk. This confirms that the traffic overuse problem can arise under real-world use cases.

9.4.1   Analysis of Real-World Dropbox Network Traces

To understand the pervasiveness of the traffic overuse problem, we analyze network-level traces from a recent, large-scale measurement study of Dropbox [5]. This trace is collected at the ISP level, and involves over 10,000 unique IP addresses and millions of data updates to/from Dropbox. To analyze the behavior of each Dropbox user, we assume all traffic generated from a given IP address corresponds to a single Dropbox user (unfortunately, we are unable to disambiguate multiple users behind a NAT). For each user, we calculate the percentage of Dropbox requests and traffic that can be attributed to frequent, short file updates *in a coarse-grained and conservative manner*.

As mentioned before, the exact parameters for frequent, short updates that trigger the traffic overuse problem vary from system to system. Thus, we adopt the following *conservative* metrics to locate a frequent, short update (U_i): (1) the inter-update time between updates U_i and U_{i-1} is <1 s, and (2) the size of (compressed) data associated with U_i is <1 KB.

Figures 9.13 and 9.14 plot the percentage of requests and network traffic caused by frequent, short updates, respectively. In both figures, users are sorted in descending order by percentage of short, frequent requests/traffic. Figure 9.13 reveals that for 11 % of users, $\geq$10 % of their Dropbox requests are caused by frequent, short updates. Figure 9.14 shows that for 8.5 % of users, $\geq$10 % of their traffic is due to frequent, short updates. These results demonstrate that a significant portion of the network

Fig. 9.13 Each user's percentage of frequent, short network requests, in descending order. (Reprinted with permission from [24].)

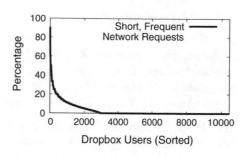

Fig. 9.14 Each user's percentage of frequent, short network traffic, in descending order. (Reprinted with permission from [24].)

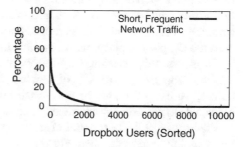

Fig. 9.15 Dropbox network traffic and log size corresponding to an active user's trace. (Reprinted with permission from [24].)

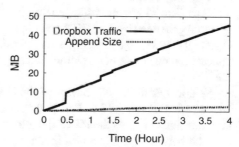

traffic from a particular population of Dropbox users is due to the traffic overuse problem.

Log Appending Experiment. To confirm that frequent, short updates are the cause of the traffic patterns observed in Figs. 9.13 and 9.14, we chose one trace from an active user and recreated her/his traffic on our test machine (i.e., the same Ubuntu laptop used in Sect. 9.3). Specifically, we play back the user's trace by writing the events to an empty log in the Dropbox Sync folder. We use the event timestamps from the trace to ensure that updates are written to the log at precisely the same rate that they actually occurred. The user chosen for this experiment uses Dropbox for 4 h, with an average inter-update time of 2.6 s. Figure 9.15 shows the amount of network traffic generated by Dropbox as well as the true size of the log file over time. By the end of the test, Dropbox generates 21 times as much traffic as the size of data on disk. This result confirms that an active real-world Dropbox user can trigger the traffic overuse problem.

9.4.2 Examining Practical Dropbox Usage Scenarios

In the previous section, we showed that real-world users are impacted by the traffic overuse problem. However, the traces do not tell us what high-level user behavior generates the observed frequent, short updates. In this section, we analyze two practical use cases for Dropbox that involve frequent, short updates.

HTTP File Download. One of the primary use cases for Dropbox is sharing files with friends and colleagues. In some cases, it may be expedient for users to download files from the Web directly into the Dropbox Sync folder to share them with others. In this case, the browser writes chunks of the file to disk as pieces arrive via HTTP from the web. This manifests as repeated appends to the file at the disk-level. How does the Dropbox application react to this file writing pattern?

To answer this question, we used wget to download a compressed, 5 MB file into the Dropbox Sync folder. All network traffic was captured using Wireshark. As before, we use a compressed file for the test because this prevents Dropbox from being able to perform any additional compression while uploading data to the cloud.

Figure 9.16 plots the amount of traffic from the incoming HTTP download and the outgoing Dropbox upload. For this test, we fixed the download rate of wget at 80 Kbps. The 75 MB of traffic generated by Dropbox is far greater than the 5.5 MB of traffic generated by the HTTP download (5 MB file plus HTTP header overhead). Figures 9.4 and 9.16 demonstrate very similar results: in both cases, Dropbox transmits at least one order of magnitude more data to the cloud than the data in the actual file.

We now examine the behavior of the Dropbox software as the HTTP download rate is varied. Figure 9.17 examines the ratio of network traffic to actual file size for Dropbox and HTTP as the HTTP download rate is varied. For the HTTP download, the ratio between the amount of incoming network traffic and the actual file size (5 MB) is constantly 1.1. The slight amount of overhead comes from the HTTP headers. For Dropbox, the ratio between outgoing traffic and file size varies between 30 and 1.1. The best case occurs when the HTTP download rate is high.

To explain why the network overhead for Dropbox is lowest when the HTTP download rate is high, we examine the interactions between wget and the hard drive. Figure 9.18 shows the time between hard drive writes by wget, as well as the size

Fig. 9.16 Dropbox upload traffic as a 5 MB file is downloaded into the Sync folder via HTTP. (Reprinted with permission from [24].)

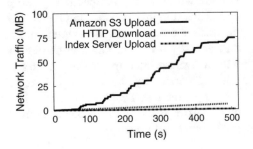

Fig. 9.17 Ratio of network traffic to real file size for Dropbox upload and HTTP download. (Reprinted with permission from [24].)

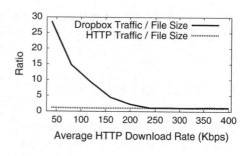

Fig. 9.18 Average inter-update time and data update length as HTTP download rate varies. (Reprinted with permission from [24].)

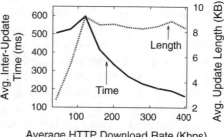

of writes, as the HTTP download rate is varied. The left hand axis and solid line correspond to the inter-update time, while the right hand axis and dashed line depict the size of writes. The network overhead for Dropbox is lowest when the HTTP download rate is ≥ 200 Kbps. This corresponds to the scenario where file updates are written to disk every 300 ms, and the sizes of the updates are maximal (≈ 9 KB per update). Under these conditions, the Dropbox software is able to batch many updates together. Conversely, when the HTTP download rate is low, the inter-update time between hard disk writes is longer, and the size per write is smaller. Thus, Dropbox has fewer opportunities to batch updates, which triggers the traffic overuse problem.

In addition to our tests with wget, we have run identical experiments using Chrome and Firefox. The results for these browsers are similar to our results for wget: Dropbox generates large amounts of network traffic when HTTP download rates are low.

Collaborative Document Editing. In this experiment, we simulate the situation where multiple users are collaboratively editing a document stored in the Dropbox Sync folder. Specifically, we place a 1 MB file full of random ASCII characters in the Dropbox Sync folder and share the file with a second Dropbox user. Each user edits the document by modifying or appending l random bytes at location x every t seconds, where l is a random integer between 1 and 10, and t is a random float between 0 and 10. Each user performs modifying and appending operations with the same probability ($= 0.5$). If a user appends to the file, x is set to the end of the file.

We ran the collaborative document editing experiment for a single hour. During this period of time, we measured the amount of network traffic generated by Dropbox.

By the end of the experiment, Dropbox had generated close to 130 MB of network traffic: two orders of magnitude more data than the size of the file (1 MB).

9.5 The UDS Middleware

In Sect. 9.3, we demonstrate that the design of cloud storage applications gives rise to situations where they can send orders-of-magnitude more traffic than would be reasonably expected. We follow this up in Sect. 9.4 by showing that this pathological application behavior can actually be triggered in real-world situations.

To overcome the traffic overuse problem, we implement an application-level mechanism that dramatically reduces the network utilization of cloud storage applications. We call this mechanism *update-batched delayed synchronization* (UDS). The high-level operation of UDS is shown in Fig. 9.1. Intuitively, UDS is implemented as a replacement for the normal cloud sync folder (e.g., the Dropbox Sync folder). UDS proactively detects and batches frequent, short updates to files in its "SavingBox" folder. These batched updates are then merged into the true cloud sync folder, so they can be transferred to the cloud. Thus, UDS acts as a middleware that protects the cloud storage application from file update patterns that would otherwise trigger the traffic overuse problem.

In this section, we discuss the implementation details of UDS, and present benchmarks of the system. In keeping with the methodology in previous sections, we pair UDS with Dropbox when conducting experiments. Our benchmarks reveal that UDS effectively eliminates the traffic overuse problem, while only adding a few seconds of additional delay to Dropbox's cloud synchronization.

9.5.1 UDS Implementation

At a high level the design of UDS is driven by two goals. First, the mechanism should fix the traffic overuse problem by forcing the cloud storage application to batch file updates. Second, the mechanism should be compatible with multiple cloud storage services. This second goal rules out directly modifying an existing application (e.g., the Dropbox application) or writing a custom client for a specific cloud storage service.

To satisfy these goals, we implement UDS as a middleware layer that sits between the user and an existing cloud storage application. From the user's perspective, UDS acts just like any existing cloud storage service. UDS creates a "SavingBox" folder on the user's hard drive, and monitors the files and folders placed in the SavingBox. When the user adds new files to the SavingBox, UDS automatically computes a compressed version of the data. Similarly, when a file in the SavingBox folder is modified, UDS calculates a compressed, binary diff of the file versus the original. If a time period t elapses after the last file update, or the total size of file updates surpasses a threshold c, then UDS pushes the updates over to the true cloud sync folder (e.g., the Dropbox Sync folder). At this point, the user's cloud storage application (e.g., Dropbox) syncs the new/modified files to the cloud normally. In the event that files in the true cloud sync folder are modified (e.g., by a remote user acting on a shared file), UDS will copy the updated files to the SavingBox. Thus, the contents of the SavingBox are always consistent with content in the true cloud synchronization folder.

As a proof of concept, we implement a version of UDS for Linux. We tested our implementation by pairing it with the Linux Dropbox client. However, we stress that it would be trivial to reconfigure UDS to work with other cloud storage software as well (e.g., Google Drive, SkyDrive, and UbuntuOne). Similarly, there is nothing fundamental about our implementation that prevents it from being ported to Windows, OS X, or Linux derivatives such as Android.

Implementation Details. Our UDS implementation uses the Linux inotify APIs to monitor changes to the SavingBox folder. Specifically, UDS calls inotify_add_ watch() to set up a callback that is invoked by the kernel whenever files or folders of interest are modified by the user. Once the callback is invoked, UDS writes information such as the type of event (e.g., file created, file modified, etc.) and the file path to an event log. If the target file is new, UDS computes the compressed size of the file using gzip. However, if the target file has been modified then UDS uses the standard rsync tool to compute a binary diff between the updated file and the original version in the cloud synchronization folder. UDS then computes the compressed size of the binary diff.

Periodically, UDS pushes new/modified files from the SavingBox to the true cloud sync folder. In the case of new files, UDS copies them entirely to the cloud sync folder. Alternatively, in the case of modified files, the binary diff previously computed by UDS is applied to the copy of the file in the cloud sync folder.

Internally, UDS maintains two variables that determine how often new/modified files are pushed to the true cloud sync folder. Intuitively, these two variables control the frequency of batched updates to the cloud. The first variable is a timer: whenever a file is created/modified, the timer gets reset to zero. If the timer reaches a threshold value t, then all new/modified files in the SavingBox are pushed to the true cloud sync folder.

The second variable is a byte counter that ensures frequent, small updates to files are batched together into chunks of at least some minimum size before they get pushed to the cloud. Specifically, UDS records the total size of all compressed data that has not been pushed to cloud storage. If this counter exceeds a threshold c, then all new/modified files in the SavingBox are pushed to the true cloud synchronization folder. Note that all cloud storage software may not use gzip for file compression: thus, UDS's byte counter is an estimate of the amount of data the cloud storage software will send on the network. Although UDS's estimate may not perfectly reflect the behavior of the cloud storage application, we show in the next section that this does not impact UDS's performance.

As a fail-safe mechanism, UDS includes a second timer that pushes updates to the cloud on a coarse timeframe. This fail-safe is necessary because pathological file update patterns could otherwise block UDS's synchronization mechanisms. For example, consider the case where bytes are appended to a file. If c is large, then it may take some time before the threshold is breached. Similarly, if the appends occur at intervals $< t$, the first timer will always be reset before the threshold is reached. In this practically unlikely but possible scenario, the fail-safe timer ensures that the append operations cannot perpetually block cloud synchronization. In our UDS implementation, the fail-safe timer automatically causes UDS to push updates to the cloud every 30 s.

9.5.2   Configuring and Benchmarking UDS

In this section, we investigate two aspects of UDS. First, we establish values for the UDS variables c and t that offer a good tradeoff between reduced network traffic and low synchronization delay. Second, we compare the performance of UDS to the stock Dropbox application by re-running our earlier benchmarks. In this section, all experiments are conducted on a laptop with a dual-core Intel processor @2.26 GHz, 2 GB of RAM, and a 5400 RPM, 250 GB hard drive. Our results show that when properly configured, UDS eliminates the traffic overuse problem.

Choosing Threshold Values. Before we can benchmark the performance of UDS, the values of the time threshold t and byte counter threshold c must be established. Intuitively, these variables represent a tradeoff between network traffic and timeliness of updates to the cloud. On one hand, a short time interval and a small byte counter would cause UDS to push updates to the cloud very quickly. This reduces the delay between file modifications on disk and syncing those updates to the cloud, at the expense of increased traffic. Conversely, a long timer and large byte counter causes many file updates to be batched together, reducing traffic at the expense of increased sync delay.

What we want is to locate a good tradeoff between network traffic and delay. To locate this point, we conduct an experiment: we append random bytes to an empty file in the SavingBox folder until its size reaches 5 MB while recording how much network traffic is generated by UDS (by forwarding updates to Dropbox) and the resulting sync delay. We run this experiment several times, varying the size of the byte counter threshold c to observe its impact on network traffic and sync delay.

Figures 9.19 and 9.20 show the results of this experiment. As expected, UDS generates a greater amount of network traffic but incurs shorter sync delay when c is small because there is less batching of file updates. The interesting feature of Fig. 9.19 is that the amount of network traffic quickly declines and then levels off. The ideal tradeoff between network traffic and delay occurs when $c = 250$ KB; any smaller and network traffic quickly rises, any larger and there are diminishing returns in terms of enhanced network performance. On the other hand, Fig. 9.20

Fig. 9.19 Network traffic corresponding to various thresholds of the UDS byte counter c. (Reprinted with permission from [24].)

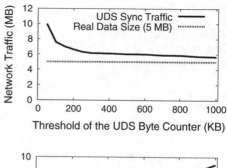

Fig. 9.20 Sync delay corresponding to various thresholds of the UDS byte counter c. (Reprinted with permission from [24].)

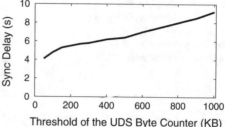

illustrates an approximately linear relationship between UDS's batching threshold and the resulting sync delay, so there is no especially "good" threshold c in terms of the sync delay. Therefore, we use $c = 250$ KB for the remainder of our experiments.

We configure the timer threshold t to be 5 s. This value is chosen as a qualitative tradeoff between network performance and user perception. Longer times allow for more batching of updates, however long delays also negatively impact the perceived performance of cloud storage systems (i.e., the time between file updates and availability of that data in the cloud). We manually evaluated our UDS prototype, and determined that a 5 s delay does not negatively impact the end-user experience of cloud storage systems, but is long enough to mitigate the traffic overuse problem.

Although the values for c and t presented here were calculated on a specific machine configuration, we have conducted the same battery of tests on other, faster machines as well. Even when the speed of the hard drive is increased, $c = 250$ KB and $t = 5$ s are adequate to prevent the traffic overuse problem.

UDS's Performance versus Dropbox. Having configured UDS's threshold values, we can now compare its performance to a stock instance of Dropbox. To this end, we re-run (1) the wget experiment and (2) the active user's log file experiment from Sect. 9.4. Figure 9.21 plots the total traffic generated by a stock instance of Dropbox, UDS (which batches updates before pushing them to Dropbox), and the amount of real data downloaded over time by wget. The results for Dropbox are identical to those presented in Fig. 9.16, and the traffic overuse problem is clearly visible. In contrast, the amount of traffic generated by UDS is only slightly more than the real data traffic. By the end of the HTTP download, UDS has generated 6.2 MB of traffic, compared to the true file size of 5 MB.

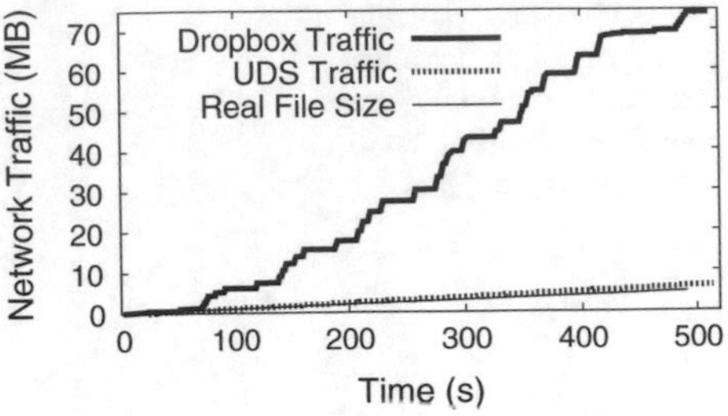

Fig. 9.21 Dropbox and
UDS traffic as a 5 MB file is
downloaded into the Sync
folder. (Reprinted with
permission from [24].)

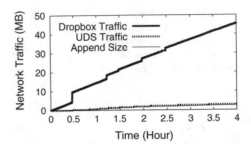

Fig. 9.22 Dropbox and
UDS traffic corresponding to
an active user's log file
backup process. (Reprinted
with permission from [24].)

Figure 9.22 plots the results of the log file append test. As in the previous experiment, the network traffic of UDS is only slightly more than the true size of the log file, and much less than that of Dropbox. These results clearly demonstrate that UDS's batching mechanism is able to eliminate the traffic overuse problem.

9.6   UDS+: Reducing CPU Utilization

In the previous section, we demonstrate how our UDS middleware successfully reduces the network usage of cloud storage applications. In this section, we take our evaluation and our system design to the next level by analyzing its CPU usage. First, we analyze the CPU usage of Dropbox and find that it uses significant resources to index files (up to one full CPU core for megabyte sized files). In contrast, our UDS software significantly reduces the CPU overhead of cloud storage. Next, we extend the kernel level APIs of Linux in order to further improve the CPU performance of UDS. We call this modified system UDS+. We show that by extending Linux's existing APIs, the CPU overhead of UDS (and by extension, all cloud storage software) can be further reduced.

9.6.1 CPU Usage of Dropbox and UDS

We begin by evaluating the CPU usage characteristics of the Dropbox cloud storage application by itself (i.e., without the use of UDS). As in Sect. 9.3, our test setup is a generic laptop with a dual-core Intel processor @2.26 GHz, 2 GB of RAM, and a 5400 RPM, 250 GB hard drive. On this platform, we conduct a benchmark where 2 K random bytes are appended to an initially empty file in the Dropbox Sync folder every 200 ms for 1000 s. Thus, the final size of the file is 10 MB. During this process, we record the CPU utilization of the Dropbox process.

Figure 9.23 shows the percentage of CPU resources being used by the Dropbox application over the course of the benchmark. The Dropbox application is single threaded, thus it only uses resources on one of the laptop's two CPUs. There are two main findings visible in Fig. 9.23. First, the Dropbox application exhibits two large jumps in CPU utilization that occur around 400 s (4 MB file size) and 800 s (8 MB). These jumps occur because the Dropbox application segments files into 4 MB chunks [26]. Second, the average CPU utilization of Dropbox is 54 % during the benchmark, which is quite high. There are even periods when Dropbox uses 100 % of the CPU.

CPU usage of UDS. Next, we evaluate the CPU usage of our UDS middleware when paired with Dropbox. We conduct the same benchmark as before, except in this case the target file is placed in UDS's SavingBox folder. Figure 9.24 shows the results of the benchmark (note that the scale of the y-axis has changed from Fig. 9.23). Immediately, it is clear that the combination of UDS and Dropbox uses much less CPU than Dropbox alone: on average, CPU utilization is just 12 % during

Fig. 9.23 Original CPU utilization of Dropbox. (Reprinted with permission from [24].)

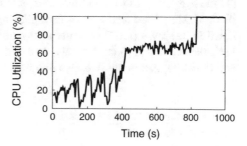

Fig. 9.24 CPU utilization of UDS and Dropbox. (Reprinted with permission from [24].)

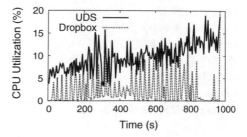

the UDS/Dropbox benchmark. Between 6 and 20 % of CPU resources are used by UDS (specifically, by rsync), while the Dropbox application averages 2 % CPU utilization. The large reduction in overall CPU utilization is due to UDS's batching of file updates, which reduces the frequency and amount of work done by the Dropbox application. The CPU usage of UDS does increase over time as the size of the target file grows.

9.6.2 Reducing the CPU Utilization of UDS

Although UDS significantly reduces the CPU overhead of using cloud storage software, we pose the question: can the system still be further improved? In particular, while developing UDS, we noticed a shortcoming in the Linux inotify API: the callback that reports file modification events includes parameters stating which file was changed, but not *where* the modification occurred within the file or *how much* data was written. These two pieces of information are very important to all cloud storage applications, since they capture the byte range of the diff from the previous version of the file. Currently, cloud storage applications must calculate this information independently, e.g., using rsync.

Our key insight is that these two pieces of meta-information are available inside the kernel; they just are not exposed by the existing Linux inotify API. Thus, having the kernel report where and how much a file is modified imposes no additional overhead on the kernel, but it would save cloud storage applications the trouble of calculating this information independently.

To implement this idea, we changed the inotify API of the Linux kernel to report: (1) the byte offset of file modifications, and (2) the number of bytes that were modified. Making these changes requires altering the inotify and fsnotify [7] functions listed in Table 9.2 (fsnotify is the subsystem that inotify is built on). Two integer variables are added to the fsnotify_event and inotify_event structures to store the additional file meta-data. We also updated kernel functions that rely directly on the

Table 9.2 Modified kernel functions

fsnotify_create_event()
fsnotify_modify()
fsnotify_access()
inotify_add_watch()
copy_event_to_user()
vfs_write()
nfsd_vfs_write()
compat_do_readv_writev()

Reprinted with permission from [24]

Fig. 9.25 CPU utilization of
UDS+ and Dropbox.
(Reprinted with permission
from [24].)

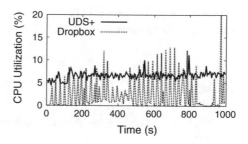

inotify and fsnotify APIs. In total, we changed around 160 lines of code in the kernel, spread over eight functions.

UDS+. Having updated the kernel inotify API, we created an updated version of UDS, called UDS+, that leverages the new API. The implementation of UDS+ is significantly simpler than that of UDS, since it no longer needs to use rsync to compute binary diffs. Instead, UDS+ simply leverages the "where" and "how much" information provided by the new inotify APIs. Based on this information, UDS+ can read the fresh data from the disk, compress it using gzip, and update the byte counter.

To evaluate the performance improvement of UDS+, we re-run the earlier benchmark scenario using UDS+ paired with Dropbox, and present the results in Fig. 9.25. UDS+ performs even better than UDS: the average CPU utilization during the UDS+ test is only 7%, compared to 12% for UDS UDS+ exhibits more even and predictable CPU utilization than UDS. Furthermore, the CPU usage of UDS+ increases much more slowly over time, since it no longer relies on rsync.

9.7   Conclusion

In this chapter, we identify a pathological issue that causes cloud storage applications to upload large amount of traffic to the cloud: many times more data than the actual content of the user's files. We call this issue the traffic overuse problem.

We measure the traffic overuse problem under synthetic and real-world conditions to understand the underlying causes that trigger this problem. Guided by this knowledge, we develop UDS: a middleware layer that sits between the user and the cloud storage application, to batch file updates in the background before handing them off to the true cloud storage software. UDS significantly reduces the traffic overhead of cloud storage applications, while only adding several seconds of delay to file transfers to the cloud. Importantly, UDS is compatible with any cloud storage application, and can easily be ported to different OSes.

Finally, by making proof-of-concept modifications to the Linux kernel that can be leveraged by cloud storage services to increase their performance, we implement an enhanced version of our middleware, called UDS+. UDS+ leverages these kernel enhancements to further reduce the CPU usage of cloud storage applications.

References

1. Dropbox-as-a-Database, the Tutorial. http://blog.opalang.org/2012/11/dropbox-as-database-tutorial.html
2. Dropbox CLI (Command Line Interface). http://www.dropboxwiki.com/Using_Dropbox_CLI
3. Dropbox Client (Ubuntu Linux Version). http://linux.dropbox.com/packages/ubuntu/nautilus-dropbox_0.7.1_i386.deb
4. Dropbox is now the Data Fabric Tying Together Devices for 100M Registered Users Who Save 1B Files a Day. http://techcrunch.com/2012/11/13/dropbox-100-million
5. Dropbox Traces. http://traces.simpleweb.org/wiki/Dropbox_Traces
6. DropboxTeams. http://dropbox.com/teams
7. fsnotify git hub. http://github.com/howeyc/fsnotify
8. inotify man page. http://linux.die.net/man/7/inotify
9. rsync web site. http://www.samba.org/rsync
10. Wireshark web site. http://www.wireshark.org
11. Bergen, A., Coady, Y., McGeer, R.: Client bandwidth: the forgotten metric of online storage providers. In: Proceedings of the 2011 IEEE Pacific Rim Conference on Communications, Computers and Signal Processing (PacRim), pp. 543–548 (2011)
12. Bessani, A., Correia, M., Quaresma, B., André, F., Sousa, P.: DepSky: dependable and secure storage in a cloud-of-clouds. ACM Trans. Storage (TOS) 9(4), 12 (2013)
13. Buyya, R., Yeo, C.S., Venugopal, S.: Market-oriented cloud computing: vision, hype, and reality for delivering IT services as computing utilities. In: Proceedings of the 10th IEEE International Conference on High Performance Computing and Communications (HPCC), pp. 5–13 (2008)
14. Calder, B., Wang, J., Ogus, A., Nilakantan, N., Skjolsvold, A., McKelvie, S., Xu, Y., Srivastav, S., Wu, J., Simitci, H., et al.: Windows azure storage: a highly available cloud storage service with strong consistency. In: Proceedings of the 23rd ACM Symposium on Operating Systems Principles (SOSP), pp. 143–157 (2011)
15. Chen, Y., Srinivasan, K., Goodson, G., Katz, R.: Design implications for enterprise storage systems via multi-dimensional trace analysis. In: Proceedings of the 23rd ACM Symposium on Operating Systems Principles (SOSP), pp. 43–56 (2011)
16. Drago, I., Bocchi, E., Mellia, M., Slatman, H., Pras, A.: Benchmarking personal cloud storage. In: Proceedings of the 13th ACM Internet Measurement Conference (IMC), pp. 205–212 (2013)
17. Drago, I., Mellia, M., Munafò, M., Sperotto, A., Sadre, R., Pras, A.: Inside Dropbox: understanding personal cloud storage services. In: Proceedings of the 12th ACM Internet Measurement Conference (IMC), pp. 481–494 (2012)
18. Halevi, S., Harnik, D., Pinkas, B., Shulman-Peleg, A.: Proofs of ownership in remote storage systems. In: Proceedings of the 18th ACM Conference on Computer and Communications Security (CCS), pp. 491–500 (2011)
19. Harnik, D., Kat, R., Sotnikov, D., Traeger, A., Margalit, O.: To zip or not to zip: effective resource usage for real-time compression. In: Proceedings of the 11th USENIX Conference on File and Storage Technologies (FAST), pp. 229–242 (2013)
20. Harnik, D., Pinkas, B., Shulman-Peleg, A.: Side channels in cloud services: deduplication in cloud storage. IEEE Secur. Priv. 8(6), 40–47 (2010)
21. Hu, W., Yang, T., Matthews, J.: The good, the bad and the ugly of consumer cloud storage. ACM SIGOPS Oper. Syst. Rev. (OSR) 44(3), 110–115 (2010)
22. Jackson, K.R., Ramakrishnan, L., Muriki, K., Canon, S., Cholia, S., Shalf, J., Wasserman, H.J., Wright, N.J.: Performance analysis of high performance computing applications on the amazon web services cloud. In: Proceedings of the 2nd IEEE International Conference on Cloud Computing Technology and Science (CloudCom), pp. 159–168 (2010)

23. Li, A., Yang, X., Kandula, S., Zhang, M.: CloudCmp: comparing public cloud providers. In: Proceedings of the 10th ACM Internet Measurement Conference (IMC), pp. 1–14 (2010)
24. Li, Z., Wilson, C., Jiang, Z., Liu, Y., Zhao, B., Jin, C., Zhang, Z.L., Dai, Y.: Efficient batched synchronization in Dropbox-like cloud storage services. In: Proceedings of the 14th ACM/IFIP/USENIX International Middleware Conference (Middleware), pp. 307–327. Springer (2013)
25. Mahajan, P., et al.: Depot: cloud storage with minimal trust. ACM Trans. Comput. Syst. (TOCS) 29(4), 12 (2011)
26. Mulazzani, M., Schrittwieser, S., Leithner, M., Huber, M., Weippl, E.: Dark clouds on the horizon: using cloud storage as attack vector and online slack space. In: Proceedings of the 20th USENIX Security Symposium, pp. 65–76 (2011)
27. Shilane, P., Huang, M., Wallace, G., Hsu, W.: WAN-optimized replication of backup datasets using stream-informed delta compression. ACM Trans. Storage (TOS) 8(4), 13 (2012)
28. Vrable, M., Savage, S., Voelker, G.: Cumulus: filesystem backup to the cloud. ACM Trans. Storage (TOS) 5(4), 14 (2009)
29. Vrable, M., Savage, S., Voelker, G.: Bluesky: a cloud-backed file system for the enterprise. In: Proceedings of the 10th USENIX Conference on File and Storage Technologies (FAST), p. 19 (2012)
30. Wallace, G., Douglis, F., Qian, H., Shilane, P., Smaldone, S., Chamness, M., Hsu, W.: Characteristics of backup workloads in production systems. In: Proceedings of the 10th USENIX Conference on File and Storage Technologies (FAST), p. 500 (2012)
31. Wang, H., Shea, R., Wang, F., Liu, J.: On the impact of virtualization on Dropbox-like cloud file storage/synchronization services. In: Proceedings of the 20th IEEE/ACM International Workshop on Quality of Service (IWQoS) (2012)

Part VI
Last Thoughts

Chapter 10
Research Summary and Future Work

Abstract This chapter summarizes Zhenhua Li's major research contributions during his Ph.D. and postdoc phases, advised by Yafei Dai, Guihai Chen, and Yunhao Liu. Also, it discusses the future work on Internet content distribution.

10.1 Research Summary

This book is a collection of Prof. Zhenhua Li's major research results during his Ph.D. and postdoc phases (from Sep. 2009 to Oct. 2015), advised by Prof. Yafei Dai (@ Peking University), Prof. Guihai Chen (@ Shanghai Jiao Tong University), and Prof. Yunhao Liu (@ Tsinghua University). The basic timeline of the involved researches is listed as follows:

1. In the first year of my Ph.D. study, I explored a number of frontier academic areas and state-of-the-art industrial systems in the Internet field, seeking for a promising and appropriate topic for my future Ph.D. thesis. During that period of time, I conducted two relatively theoretical researches on a traditional topic. The corresponding two papers [1, 2] appeared in my Ph.D. thesis, but not in this book.
2. When my first-year Ph.D. study came to an end, I spent the subsequent summer holiday at Tencent Research as a research intern. Specifically, I joined the QQXuanfeng team (http://xf.qq.com) to analyze the techniques and examine the performance of the system. To my great surprise, I found that this large-scale industrial content distribution system was subject to manifold performance bottlenecks which in fact could be effectively avoided or mitigated without much difficulty. Also, by digging its back-end system logs (i.e., "big data" of Internet content distribution) I observed several novel and interesting problems that can hardly be discovered or imagined in a small-scale or lab-scale system.
3. When I returned to the university lab after the summer holiday, I was quite clear that I would devote the remainder of my Ph.D. life to *system-style* research. Specifically, I determined to discover practical problems in real systems, solidly solve the problems under real environments, and achieve real performance enhancements. Meanwhile, I noticed that many people around me started to use iPhones

© Springer Science+Business Media Singapore 2016   227
Z. Li et al., *Content Distribution for Mobile Internet: A Cloud-based Approach*,
DOI 10.1007/978-981-10-1463-5_10

and Android smartphones rather than traditional Nokia/Motorola feature phones. And behind each smartphone, there seemed to be an invisible "cloud computing" platform that supports its "smartness." In a nutshell, I realized that human beings are entering a new era of mobile Internet and cloud computing.

4. For my second-year Ph.D. study, most time is cost in understanding the QQXu- anfeng system. As a matter of fact, this system is made up of two complementary subsystems: a cloud tracking (or Open-P2SP) system for quickly distributing popular files and a cloud downloading system (http://lixian.qq.com) for rapidly delivering unpopular files. The former is totally free for all Internet users, while the latter only serves the premium VIP users of Tencent due to its huge cloud-side infrastructure costs. Investigations into the two subsystems brought two papers published in the ACM-MM'11 conference, one being a long paper [3] and the other appearing in the doctoral symposium [4].

5. My third year of Ph.D. study was spent in the cold, peaceful, and beautiful Min- nesota of the US. Supported by the China's government, I visited the University of Minnesota, Twin Cities from September 2011 to September. 2012. My advisor there suggested I pay special attention to "cloud-based content distribution over the Internet." Hence, I made deeper investigations into cloud tracking and cloud downloading, which produced one paper on "cloud bandwidth scheduling" (pub- lished in IWQoS'12 [5]) and the other paper on "cloud transcoding" (published in NOSSDAV'12 [6]). In addition, I conducted a comprehensive study on the QQXuanfeng cloud tracking (or Open-P2SP) system, which eventually became a journal paper published in TPDS'13 [7].

6. In the final year of my Ph.D. study, I got interested in cloud storage services like Dropbox, Google Drive, and Microsoft OneDrive, since they represent a more advanced, fine-grained paradigm of Internet content distribution. Although Dropbox outperforms its competitors, I still felt that its performance is far from satisfactory oftentimes, especially in the presence of frequent, short data updates to user files. Therefore, we developed a middleware called UDS to optimize the performance of Dropbox on handling frequent, short data updates. Additionally, we extended UDS with a backwards compatible Linux kernel modification that further improves the performance of cloud storage applications by reducing the CPU usage. The resulting paper was then published in Middleware'13 [8].

7. After obtaining the Ph.D. degree, I joined the School of Software, Tsinghua Uni- versity as a postdoc Researcher. The first year of my postdoc life was mostly spent in two "generalization" researches. First, we generalized the network-efficiency optimization of Dropbox to other popular cloud storage services including Google Drive, Microsoft OneDrive, Box, Ubuntu One, and SugarSync. Second, we gen- eralized the study on cloud downloading to "offline downloading" by comparing the performance of Tencent Xuanfeng (http://lixian.qq.com) with that of smart home routers like HiWiFi, MiWiFi, and Newifi. The two generalizations led to two consecutive papers published in IMC'14 [9] and IMC'15 [10].

8. In the second, also the last year of my postdoc life, I collaborated with the Baidu Mobile Security Department to optimize the Baidu PhoneGuard system (http://shoujiweishi.baidu.com). Our first collaboration concerned TrafficGuard,

a cloud-based cellular traffic optimization system across heterogeneous Android applications. The resulting paper was published in NSDI'16 [11]. Our second collaboration aimed to detect and localize *fake base stations* in the wild. Different from legitimate base stations that constitute the basic content distribution infrastructure of cellular networks, fake base stations are largely utilized by criminal groups to send spam or fraud SMS messages to mobile users. Some preliminary results are available at http://shoujiweishi.baidu.com/static/map/pseudo.html.

10.2 Future Work

Internet content distribution is a research area that has long existed for decades and substantially influenced the life of human beings, e.g., online videos are substituting TV broadcasts, voice on IP is supplementing traditional phone calls, and cloud-based office is changing the way of routine work. Meanwhile, it is a novel research area that has constantly benefited from the innovations in other research areas, e.g., the invention of optical fibers, the upgrading of network switchers and routers, and the developing of quantum communications. In the near future, we believe that the promising topics worth to explore (at least) include:

- *Cloud-based CDN.* In the past decade, numerous Internet content providers have rented the CDN service to accelerate their content distribution. Some websites (e.g., Hulu and Netflix) even rent the services of multiple CDNs and utilize their own clouds to schedule the resources from multiple CDNs [12, 13]. On the contrary, in recent years we have noted that some CDNs start to rent cloud resources to provide better CDN services [14], which is referred to as cloud-based CDN. This is because CDN service providers also need the high scalability and resilience of cloud computing to help them adaptively adjust their infrastructure costs and quality of service.
- *Home router-based CDN.* Traditionally, CDN accelerates content distribution by strategically deploying a number of edge servers across the Internet. Recently in China, we have seen the idea and practice of home router-based CDN, which leverages smart home routers to construct or assist a CDN. Of course, the owners of participated home routers will get paid according to their contributed bandwidth and storage resources. Typical examples include the XY-CDN [15] based on Xunlei Red home routers [16], and the proprietary Youku CDN based on Youku home routers [17]. It is worth noting that home router-based CDN is distinct from P2P content distribution, since both its underlying protocols and distributed content are transparent to participated users.
- *Impact of operating systems on content distribution.* Generally speaking, the performance of content distribution relies on network conditions and protocols. Nevertheless, we have lately noticed that content distribution in some systems is also heavily determined by the operating system, particularly the file system. For

example, handling the same data updates with the same user device under the same network environment, Dropbox exhibits diverse performance when running on top of Linux, Windows, and Mac OS. The situation would become more complicated when mobile operating systems like iOS, Android, and Windows Phone are taken into consideration. Consequently, the impact of operating systems on Internet content distribution deserves further and deeper investigation.

- *CCN/NDN/SDN-driven content distribution.* In the past a few years, several new networking terms, CCN, NDN, and SDN, have quickly became eye-catching. Here CCN denotes content centric networking, NDN represents named data networking [18], and SDN means software-defined networking. Among them, the most promising seems to be the OpenFlow SDN project [19] initiated in Stanford University. Presently, Openflow has been adopted by large networking device manufacturers like Cisco, Huawei, and NEC.

As the underlying facilities of Internet content distribution, network switchers and routers have been regarded as hardware—once they are shipped by the manufacturers, their functions are generally fixed and the users can only make very simple configurations. The emergence of SDN renovated this situation by enabling network switchers and routers to support various software applications, like what personal computers and smartphones do. With SDN, programmers can run complex code on network hardware, realize advanced software functions, and eventually reshape the paradigm of Internet content distribution.

References

1. Li, Z., Cao, J., Chen, G., Liu, Y.: On the source switching problem of peer-to-peer streaming. J. Parallel Distrib. Comput. (JPDC) **70**(5), 537–546 (2010)
2. Li, Z., Wu, J., Xie, J., Zhang, T., Chen, G., Dai, Y.: Stability-optimal grouping strategy of peer-to-peer systems. IEEE Trans. Parallel Distrib. Syst. (TPDS) **22**(12), 2079–2087 (2011)
3. Huang, Y., Li, Z., Liu, G., Dai, Y.: Cloud download: using cloud utilities to achieve high-quality content distribution for unpopular videos. In: Proceedings of the 19th ACM International Conference on Multimedia (ACM-MM), pp. 213–222 (2011)
4. Li, Z., Huang, Y., Liu, G., Dai, Y.: CloudTracker: accelerating internet content distribution by bridging cloud servers and peer swarms. In: Proceedings of the 19th ACM International Conference on Multimedia (ACM-MM) Doctoral Symposium, vol. 46, p. 49 (2011)
5. Li, Z., Zhang, T., Huang, Y., Zhang, Z.L., Dai, Y.: Maximizing the bandwidth multiplier effect for hybrid cloud-P2P content distribution. In: Proceedings of the 20th IEEE/ACM International Workshop on Quality of Service (IWQoS), pp. 1–9 (2012)
6. Li, Z., Huang, Y., Liu, G., Wang, F., Zhang, Z.L., Dai, Y.: Cloud transcoder: bridging the format and resolution gap between internet videos and mobile devices. In: Proceedings of the 22nd SIGMM Workshop on Network and Operating Systems Support for Digital Audio and Video (NOSSDAV), pp. 33–38 (2012)
7. Li, Z., Huang, Y., Liu, G., Wang, F., Liu, Y., Zhang, Z.L., Dai, Y.: Challenges, designs and performances of large-scale open-P2SP content distribution. IEEE Trans. Parallel Distrib. Syst. (TPDS) **24**(11), 2181–2191 (2013)
8. Li, Z., Wilson, C., Jiang, Z., Liu, Y., Zhao, B., Jin, C., Zhang, Z.L., Dai, Y.: Efficient batched synchronization in dropbox-like cloud storage services. In: Proceedings of the

   14th ACM/IFIP/USENIX International Middleware Conference (Middleware), pp. 307–327. Springer (2013)
 9. Li, Z., Jin, C., Xu, T., Wilson, C., Liu, Y., Cheng, L., Liu, Y., Dai, Y., Zhang, Z.L.: Towards network-level efficiency for cloud storage services. In: Proceedings of the 14th ACM Internet Measurement Conference (IMC), pp. 115–128 (2014)
10. Li, Z., Wilson, C., Xu, T., Liu, Y., Lu, Z., Wang, Y.: Offline downloading in China: a comparative study. In: Proceedings of the 15th ACM Internet Measurement Conference (IMC), pp. 473–486 (2015)
11. Li, Z., Wang, W., Xu, T., Zhong, X., Li, X.Y., Wilson, C., Zhao, B.Y.: Exploring cross-application cellular traffic optimization with baidu trafficguard. In: Proceedings of the 13th USENIX Symposium on Networked Systems Design and Implementation (NSDI), pp. 61–76 (2016)
12. Adhikari, V., Guo, Y., Hao, F., Hilt, V., Zhang, Z.L.: A tale of three CDNs: an active measurement study of hulu and its CDNs. In: Proceedings of the 15th IEEE Global Internet Symposium, pp. 7–12 (2012)
13. Adhikari, V., Guo, Y., Hao, F., Varvello, M., Hilt, V., Steiner, M., Zhang, Z.L.: Unreeling Netflix: understanding and improving multi-CDN movie delivery. In: Proceedings of the 31st IEEE International Conference on Computer Communications (INFOCOM), pp. 1620–1628 (2012)
14. Yin, H., Liu, X., Min, G., Lin, C.: Content delivery networks: a bridge between emerging applications and future IP networks. IEEE Netw. 24(4), 52–56 (2010)
15. XY-CDN. http://xycdn.com
16. Xunlei Red home router. http://red.xunlei.com
17. Youku home router. http://yj.youku.com
18. Jacobson, V., Smetters, D.K., Thornton, J.D., Plass, M.F., Briggs, N.H., Braynard, R.L.: Networking named content. In: Proceedings of the 5th ACM International Conference on Emerging Networking EXperiments and Technologies (CoNEXT), pp. 1–12 (2009)
19. McKeown, N., Anderson, T., Balakrishnan, H., Parulkar, G., Peterson, L., Rexford, J., Shenker, S., Turner, J.: OpenFlow: enabling innovation in campus networks. ACM SIGCOMM Comput. Commun. Rev. (CCR) 38(2), 69–74 (2008)

Printed in the United States
By Bookmasters